Wireless Safety Certification

EC-Council | Press

This title maps to

Wireless | 5™

COURSE TECHNOLOGY
CENGAGE Learning™

Australia • Brazil • Japan • Korea • Mexico • Singapore • Spain • United Kingdom • United States

D1088132

COURSE TECHNOLOGY
CENGAGE Learning

Wireless Safety : EC-Council | Press

Course Technology/Cengage Learning Staff:

Vice President, Career and Professional Editorial: Dave Garza

Director of Learning Solutions: Matthew Kane

Executive Editor: Stephen Helba

Managing Editor: Marah Bellegarde

Editorial Assistant: Meghan Orvis

Vice President, Career and Professional Marketing: Jennifer Ann Baker

Marketing Director: Deborah Yarnell

Marketing Manager: Erin Coffin

Marketing Coordinator: Shanna Gibbs

Production Director: Carolyn Miller

Production Manager: Andrew Crouth

Content Project Manager: Brooke Greenhouse

Senior Art Director: Jack Pendleton

EC-Council:

President | EC-Council: Sanjay Bavisi

Sr. Director US | EC-Council: Steven Graham

For product information and technology assistance, contact us at
Cengage Learning Customer & Sales Support, 1-800-354-9706

For permission to use material from this text or product,
submit all requests online at **www.cengage.com/permissions**.
Further permissions questions can be e-mailed to
permissionrequest@cengage.com

Library of Congress Control Number: 2009935399

ISBN-13: 978-1-4354-8376-7

ISBN-10: 1-4354-8376-6

Cengage Learning
5 Maxwell Drive
Clifton Park, NY 12065-2919
USA

Cengage Learning is a leading provider of customized learning solutions with office locations around the globe, including Singapore, the United Kingdom, Australia, Mexico, Brazil, and Japan. Locate your local office at: **international.cengage.com/region**

Cengage Learning products are represented in Canada by Nelson Education, Ltd.

For more learning solutions, please visit our corporate website at **www.cengage.com**

Printed in the United States of America
1 2 3 4 5 6 7 12 11 10 09

Brief Table of Contents

Table of Contents

CHAPTER 8
Fundamentals of RFID. **8-1**

Hacking and electronic crimes sophistication has grown at an exponential rate in recent years. In fact, recent reports have indicated that cyber crime already surpasses the illegal drug trade! Unethical hackers, better known as *black hats,* are preying on information systems of government, corporate, public, and private networks and are constantly testing the security mechanisms of these organizations to the limit with the sole aim of exploiting them and profiting from the exercise. High-profile crimes have proven that the traditional approach to computer security is simply not sufficient, even with the strongest perimeter, properly configured defense mechanisms such as firewalls, intrusion detection, and prevention systems, strong end-to-end encryption standards, and anti-virus software. Hackers have proven their dedication and ability to systematically penetrate networks all over the world. In some cases, black hats may be able to execute attacks so flawlessly that they can compromise a system, steal everything of value, and completely erase their tracks in less than 20 minutes!

The EC-Council Press is dedicated to stopping hackers in their tracks.

About EC-Council

The International Council of Electronic Commerce Consultants, better known as EC-Council, was founded in late 2001 to address the need for well-educated and certified information security and e-business practitioners. EC-Council is a global, member-based organization comprised of industry and subject matter experts all working together to set the standards and raise the bar in information security certification and education.

EC-Council first developed the *Certified Ethical Hacker* (C|EH) program. The goal of this program is to teach the methodologies, tools, and techniques used by hackers. Leveraging the collective knowledge from hundreds of subject matter experts, the C|EH program has rapidly gained popularity around the globe and is now delivered in more than 70 countries by more than 450 authorized training centers with more than 60,000 information security practitioners trained.

C|EH is the benchmark for many government entities and major corporations around the world. Shortly after C|EH was launched, EC-Council developed the *Certified Security Analyst* (E|CSA). The goal of the E|CSA program is to teach groundbreaking analysis methods that must be applied while conducting advanced penetration testing. The E|CSA program leads to the *Licensed Penetration Tester* (L|PT) status. The *Computer Hacking Forensic Investigator* (C|HFI) was formed with the same design methodologies above and has become a global standard in certification for computer forensics. EC-Council, through its impervious network of professionals and huge industry following, has developed various other programs in information security and e-business. EC-Council certifications are viewed as the essential certifications needed when standard configuration and security policy courses fall short. Providing a true, hands-on, tactical approach to security, individuals armed with the knowledge disseminated by EC-Council programs are securing networks around the world and beating the hackers at their own game.

About the EC-Council | Press

The EC-Council | Press was formed in late 2008 as a result of a cutting-edge partnership between global information security certification leader, EC-Council and leading global academic publisher, Cengage Learning. This partnership marks a revolution in academic textbooks and courses of study in information security, computer forensics, disaster recovery, and end-user security. By identifying the essential topics and content of EC-Council professional certification programs, and repurposing this world-class content to fit academic programs, the EC-Council | Press was formed. The academic community is now able to incorporate this powerful cutting-edge content into new and existing information security programs. By closing the gap between academic study and professional certification, students and instructors are able to leverage the power of rigorous academic focus and high demand industry certification. The EC-Council | Press is set to revolutionize global information security programs and ultimately create a new breed of practitioners capable of combating the growing epidemic of cybercrime and the rising threat of cyber-war.

Wireless Safety

Wireless Safety introduces the learner to the basics of wireless technologies and their practical adaptation. *Wireless Safety* is tailored to cater to any individual's desire to learn more about wireless technology. It requires no pre-requisite knowledge and aims to educate the learner in simple applications of these technologies. Topics include wireless signal propagation, IEEE and ETSI wireless standards, WLANs and operation, wireless protocols and communication languages, wireless devices, and wireless security networks. The book also prepares readers to take and succeed on the Wireless|5 certification exam from EC-Council.

Chapter Contents

Chapter 1, *Introduction to Wireless Communications*, provides the fundamentals of wireless communication including history of, types of and uses for wireless communication. Chapter 2, *Wireless Signal Propagation*, discusses the creation, transmission and modulations of wireless signals. Chapter 3, *IEEE and ETSI Wireless Standards*, discusses IEEE and ETSI wireless communication standards. Chapter 4, *WLAN and Operations*, covers the advantages and disadvantages of WLAN and how to configure and troubleshoot a WLAN. Chapter 5, *Wireless Technologies*, discusses technologies used to connect computers, permit remote monitoring and data achievement and to provide access control and security. Chapter 6, *Wireless Protocols and Communication Languages*, familiarizes the reader with wireless protocols and programming languages used in wireless devices. Chapter 7, *Wireless Devices*, discusses the devices that make up a typical wireless infrastructure including antennas, access points, mobile stations, and more. Chapter 8, *Fundamentals of RFID*, discusses the components, applications and vulnerabilities of RFID technology. Chapter 9, *Wireless VoIP*, discusses the various types of VoIP available. Chapter 10, *Wireless Security*, introduces the types of wireless attacks, rogue access points, stream cipher, and more.

Chapter Features

Many features are included in each chapter and all are designed to enhance the learner's learning experience. Features include:

- *Objectives* begin each chapter and focus the learner on the most important concepts in the chapter.
- *Key Terms* are designed to familiarize the learner with terms that will be used within the chapter.
- *Chapter Summary*, at the end of each chapter, serves as a review of the key concepts covered in the chapter.
- *Review Questions* allow learners to test their comprehension of the chapter content.
- *Hands-On Projects* encourage learners to apply the knowledge they have gained after finishing the chapter.

Additional Instructor Resources

Free to all instructors who adopt the *Wireless Safety* product for their courses, a complete package of instructor resources is available. These resources are available from the Course Technology Web site, *www.cengage.com*, by going to the product page for this book in the online catalog, and choosing "Instructor Downloads." A username and password can be obtained from your Cengage Learning sales representative.

Resources include:

- *Instructor Manual*: This manual includes course objectives and additional information to help your instruction.
- *ExamView Testbank*: This Windows-based testing software helps instructors design and administer tests and pre-tests. In addition to generating tests that can be printed and administered, this full-featured program has an online testing component that allows students to take tests at the computer and have their exams automatically graded.
- *PowerPoint Presentations*: This book comes with a set of Microsoft PowerPoint slides for each chapter. These slides are meant to be used as teaching aids for classroom presentations, to be made available to students for chapter review, or to be printed for classroom distribution. Instructors are also at liberty to add their own slides.

- *Labs*: These are additional hands-on activities to provide more practice for your students.
- *Assessment Activities*: These are additional assessment opportunities including discussion questions, writing assignments, Internet research activities, and homework assignments along with a final cumulative project.
- *Final Exam*: This exam provides a comprehensive assessment of *Wireless Safety* content.

Information Security Community Site

This site was created for learners and instructors to find out about the latest in information security news and technology.

Visit *community.cengage.com/infosec* to:

- Learn what's new in information security through live news feeds, videos and podcasts;
- Connect with your peers and security experts through blogs and forums;
- Browse our online catalog.

How to Become Wireless|5 Certified

Wireless|5 certification seeks to break the myths of wireless computing. This certification provides the computer user with an understanding of security aspects of wireless computing and what can be done to secure access. As a knowledge worker, this certification will empower you with the knowledge to excel in your workspace. A student stands to gain a strong foundation to explore the technology further. As a professional in the communications field, this certification serves the path to career advancement.

Wireless|5 Certification exams are available through Prometric Prime. To finalize your certification after your training, you must:

1. Purchase an exam voucher from the EC-Council community site at Cengage: *www.cengage.com/community/eccouncil* if one was not purchased with your book.
2. **Speak with your instructor or professor about scheduling an exam session, or visit the EC-Council community site referenced above for more information.**
3. Take and pass the Wireless|5 certification examination with a score of 70% or better.

About Our Other EC-Council I Press Products

Network Security Administrator Series

The EC-Council I Press *Network Administrator* series, E|NSA, is intended for those studying to become system administrators, network administrators and anyone who is interested in network security technologies. This series is designed to educate learners, from a vendor neutral standpoint, how to defend the networks they manage. This series covers the fundamental skills in evaluating internal and external threats to network security, design, and how to enforce network level security policies, and ultimately protect an organization's information. Covering a broad range of topics from secure network fundamentals, protocols and analysis, standards and policy, hardening infrastructure, to configuring IPS, IDS and firewalls, bastion host and honeypots, among many other topics, learners completing this series will have a full understanding of defensive measures taken to secure their organizations information. The series, when used in its entirety, helps prepare readers to take and succeed on the E|NSA, Network Security Administrator certification exam from EC-Council.

Books in Series
- *Network Defense: Fundamentals and Protocols*/1435483553
- *Network Defense: Security Policy and Threats*/1435483561
- *Network Defense: Perimeter Defense Mechanisms*/143548357X
- *Network Defense: Securing and Troubleshooting Network Operating Systems*/1435483588
- *Network Defense: Security and Vulnerability Assessment*/1435483596

Ethical Hacking and Countermeasures Series

The EC-Council | Press *Ethical Hacking and Countermeasures* series is intended for those studying to become security officers, auditors, security professionals, site administrators, and anyone who is concerned about, or responsible for the integrity of the network infrastructure The series includes a broad base of topics in offensive network security, ethical hacking, as well as network defense and countermeasures. The content of this program is designed to immerse learners into an interactive environment where they will be shown how to scan, test, hack, and secure information systems. A wide variety of tools, virus', and malware is presented in this course providing a complete understanding of the tactics and tools used by hackers. By gaining a thorough understanding of how hackers operate, ethical hackers are able to set up strong countermeasures and defensive systems to protect the organizations critical infrastructure and information. The series, when used in its entirety, helps prepare readers to take and succeed on the C|EH certification exam from EC-Council.

Books in Series
- *Ethical Hacking and Countermeasures: Attack Phases*/143548360X
- *Ethical Hacking and Countermeasures: Threats and Defense Mechanisms*/1435483618
- *Ethical Hacking and Countermeasures: Web Applications and Data Servers*/1435483626
- *Ethical Hacking and Countermeasures: Linux, Macintosh and Mobile Systems*/1435483642
- *Ethical Hacking and Countermeasures: Secure Network Infrastructures*/1435483650

Security Analyst Series

The EC-Council | Press *Security Analyst* series is intended for those studying to become network server administrators, firewall administrators, security testers, system administrators and risk assessment professionals. This series covers a broad base of topics in advanced penetration testing and security analysis. The content of this program is designed to expose the learner to groundbreaking methodologies in conducting thorough security analysis, as well as advanced penetration testing techniques. Armed with the knowledge from the *Security Analyst* series, learners will be able to perform the intensive assessments required to effectively identify and mitigate risks to the security of the organizations infrastructure. The series, when used in its entirety, helps prepare readers to take and succeed on the E|CSA, Certified Security Analyst, and L|PT, License Penetration Tester certification exam from EC-Council.

Books in Series
- *Certified Security Analyst: Security Analysis and Advanced Tools*/1435483669
- *Certified Security Analyst: Customer Agreements and Reporting Procedures in Security Analysis*/1435483677
- *Certified Security Analyst: Penetration Testing Methodologies in Security Analysis*/1435483685
- *Certified Security Analyst: Network and Communication Testing Procedures in Security Analysis*/1435483693
- *Certified Security Analyst: Network Threat Testing Procedures in Security Analysis*/1435483707

Computer Forensics Series

The EC-Council | Press Computer Forensics Series is intended for those studying to become police investigators and other law enforcement personnel, defense and military personnel, e-business security professionals, systems administrators, legal professionals, banking, insurance and other professionals, government agencies, and IT managers. The content of this program is designed to expose the learner to the process of detecting attacks and collecting evidence in a forensically sound manner with the intent to report crime and prevent future attacks. Advanced techniques in computer investigation and analysis with interest in generating potential legal evidence are included. In full, this series prepares the learner to identify evidence in computer-related crime and abuse cases as well as track the intrusive hacker's path through client system. The series when used in its entirety helps prepare readers to take and succeed on the C|HFI, Certified Forensic Investigator certification exam from EC-Council.

Books in Series
- *Computer Forensics: Investigation Procedures and Response*/1435483499
- *Computer Forensics: Investigating Hard Disks, File and Operating Systems*/1435483502
- *Computer Forensics: Investigating Data and Image Files*/1435483510
- *Computer Forensics: Investigating Network Intrusions and Cybercrime*/1435483529
- *Computer Forensics: Investigating Wireless Networks and Devices*/1435483537

Cyber Safety/1435483715

Cyber Safety is designed for anyone who is interested in learning computer networking and security basics. This book gives individuals the basic security literacy skills that prepare them for high-end IT academic or training programs. *Cyber Safety* provides computer users with a solid base of knowledge to work towards Security|5 Certification or simply to better protect themselves and their information.

Network Safety/1435483774

Network Safety provides the basic core knowledge on how infrastructure enables a working environment. It is intended for those in office environments and home users who want to optimize resource utilization, share infrastructure, and make the best of technology and the convenience it offers. Topics include foundations of networks, networking components, wireless networks, basic hardware components, the networking environment and connectivity as well as troubleshooting. The book also prepares readers to take and succeed on the Network|5 certification exam from EC-Council.

Disaster Recovery Professional

The *Disaster Recovery Professional* series introduces the learner to the methods employed in identifying vulnerabilities and how to take the appropriate countermeasures to prevent and mitigate failure risks for an organization. It also provides a foundation in disaster recovery principles, including preparation of a disaster recovery plan, assessment of risks in the enterprise, development of policies, and procedures, and understanding of the roles and relationships of various members of an organization, implementation of the plan, and recovering from a disaster. Students will learn how to create a secure network by putting policies and procedures in place, and how to restore a network in the event of a disaster. The series, when used in its entirety, helps prepare readers to take and succeed on the E|DRP, Disaster Recovery Professional certification exam from EC-Council.

Books in Series
Disaster Recovery/1435488709
Business Continuity/1435488695

Acknowledgements

The publisher would like acknowledge Jean McKay, who served as the subject matter expert reviewer for this book. Jean McKay is the president of PuttyCove, Inc., a firm specializing in project management training/ consulting and IT technical instruction.

Jean holds numerous certifications issued by vendors in the IT industry including Microsoft, Cisco, Novell, EC-Council, and CompTIA, as well as the PMP, and PMP-RMP certifications sponsored by the Project Management Institute. A software developer, a manufacturing firm, and technical training companies formerly employed her as a senior trainer, LAN administrator, and project manager.

Planning and leading successful projects to completion, educating team members and other stakeholders in methods to improve their project management skills, and improving processes used on existing projects are among her work. With a focus on risk analysis, disaster recovery, and business continuity, she combines IT expertise with business objectives.

Chapter 1

Introduction to Wireless Networks

Objectives

After completing this chapter, you should be able to:

- Define key terms associated with wireless networks
- Recount the history of wireless communications
- Identify the types of wireless networks
- List the advantages and disadvantages of wireless communications
- Explain the limitations of wireless communications
- Describe the generations of wireless communications
- List the uses of wireless communications

Key Terms

Access point   a piece of wireless communications hardware that creates a central point of wireless connectivity; similar to a hub, the access point is a common connection point for devices in a wireless network

Antenna   a set of wires that transmit an electromagnetic field in response to EMF signals; antennas are used by several wireless communications devices, such as radios, broadcast television sets, radar, and cellular radio telephones. They are also called aerials.

Bluetooth   Bluetooth is preferred when communicating within short distances using voice and data communications; it offers robust functionality at low power and low cost

Circuit-based network   a fixed-channel, circuit-based communication network; a channel is established before users can communicate, and then all the users can access the resources

IrDA (Infrared Data Association)   defines physical specifications communications protocol standards that ensures there is no interference between two points of communication; it is for the short-range exchange of data over infrared light, for uses such as personal area networks (PANs), or in palmtop computers, mobile phones, and laptop computers

Packet-based network   a type of network in which the data is fragmented into packets that are transmitted from one point to the other; the packets are then reassembled at the other end. Packet-based networks are connectionless.

Radio waves   electromagnetic waves that have a wavelength of approximately 3 kilometers to 30 centimeters; compared to microwaves, infrared, x-rays, gamma-rays, and ultraviolet rays, radio waves are low-energy waves

Wireless   telecommunication in which electromagnetic waves carry a signal to transfer data over a distance without the use of electrical conductors or wires; examples include garage door openers, headsets, and GPS

Introduction to Wireless Networks

Wireless is a form of telecommunication in which electromagnetic waves carry a signal to transfer data over a distance without the use of electrical conductors or wires. The distances involved may be short (a few meters when utilized in a television remote control) or long (thousands or even millions of kilometers for radio communications). It encompasses various types of fixed, mobile, and portable two-way radios, cellular telephones, personal digital assistants (PDAs), and wireless networking. Other examples of wireless technology include GPS units; garage door openers; computer mice, keyboards and headsets; satellite television; and cordless telephones.

History of Wireless Communication

Many scientists have made contributions to the practical aspects of wireless radio broadcasting. For instance, in the 1860s the British scientist James Clerk Maxwell predicted the possibility of generating electromagnetic waves that would travel at the speed of light. Twenty years later the German physicist Heinrich Hertz did much to verify Maxwell's theories. In one experiment, Hertz discharged an induction coil with a rectangular loop of wire having a very small gap. When the coil discharged, a spark jumped across the gap. Hertz was able to prove that electromagnetic waves have many of the characteristics of light. Later experimenters managed to increase the distance across which Hertzian waves could be transmitted. Hertz's experiments ultimately led to the development of radio communication.

Radio waves are electromagnetic waves that have a wavelength of approximately 3 kilometers to 30 centimeters. Compared to mirowaves, infrared, x-rays, gamma-rays, and ultraviolet rays, they are low-energy waves.

Following are other important dates in the development of wireless communications:

- 1867: Maxwell predicted the existence of electromagnetic (EM) waves.

- 1887: The first spark transmitter generated a spark in a receiver that was several meters away from it. Hertz proved the existence of electromagnetic waves using this example.

- 1896: Guglielmo Marconi established the wireless telegraph for the British Post Office.

- 1897: "The birth of radio" took place, and Marconi Station was established at Needles Battery on the Isle of Wight.

- 1898: A wireless telegraphic connection was established between England and France.

- 1901: Marconi successfully transmitted a radio signal across the ocean.

- 1914: The first voice was transmitted over the radio.

- 1935: Armstrong established frequency modulation (FM).

- 1946: The birth of mobile telephony took place by the establishment of the interconnection of mobile users to the Public Switched Telephone Network (PSTN).

- 1960: Improved Mobile Telephone Service (IMTS) was developed, which allowed full-duplex, autodial, and autotrunking.

- 1979: NTT/Japan invented the first analog cellular communication system. The system carried 600 25-kHz FM duplex channels in two 25-MHz bands in the 800-MHz spectral range.

- 1983: In the U.S., the Advanced Mobile Phone System (AMPS) in 900-MHz bands, which supports the 666 duplex channels, was generated.

- 1993: In the U.S., the digital cellular system known as IS-95 Code-Division Multiple-Access (CDMA) was formed.

- 1994: The Global System for Mobile Communications (GSM) system was formed in the U.S.

Wired Networks	Wireless Networks
High bandwidth	Low bandwidth
Low bandwidth variation	High bandwidth variation
Low error rates (10-6)	High error rates (10-3)
More secure	Less secure
Less equipment dependent	More equipment dependent
Symmetric connectivity	Possible asymmetric connectivity
High power machines	Low power machines
High resource machines	Low resource machines
Low delay	Higher delay
Connected operation	Disconnected operation

Table 1-1   Comparison of wired and wireless networks

Wired Versus Wireless Networks

Table 1-1 compares wired networks to wireless networks. Wireless networks, while convenient, are less secure and generally slower than wired networks.

Types of Wireless Networks: Based on Connection

Wireless networks can be categorized based on the type of connection employed. The following section introduces these connections.

Peer-To-Peer Networks

In this type of network each wireless computer can communicate directly with all other computers in the wireless network without using an access point. A number of computers are present in this network; each is equipped with a wireless networking interface card. They can share files and printers, but they may not be able to access wired LAN sources, unless one of the computers acts as a bridge to the wired LAN using special software. Figure 1-1 illustrates a possible topology for a peer-to-peer network.

Extension to a Wired Network

An extension to a wired network can be obtained by placing *access points* between the wired network and the wireless devices (Figure 1-2). An access point is usually a piece of wireless communications hardware (which can be software based) that creates a central point of wireless connectivity. Similar to a hub, the access point is a common connection point for devices in a wireless network. Access points can be created using software or hardware:

- Software access points can be connected to the wired network, and run on a computer equipped with a wireless network interface card.

- Hardware access points (HAP) provide comprehensive support of most wireless features. With suitable networking software support, users on the wireless LAN can share files and printers situated on the wired LAN and vice versa.

A wireless network is also possible with the help of a base station. In this network, the access point acts as a hub, providing the connectivity for the wireless computers. It can connect the wireless LAN to a wired LAN, giving wireless computers access to LAN resources, such as file servers or existing Internet connectivity.

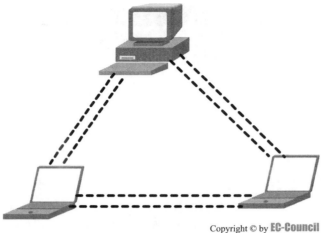

Figure 1-1   Peer-to-peer network.

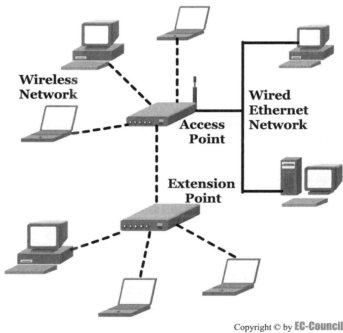

Figure 1-2   Extension to a wired network.

Multiple Access Points

If a single access point fails to cover a large area, then multiple access points can be used. Although an extension point has been developed by some manufacturers, it is not defined in the wireless standard (IEEE 802.11). When deploying multiple access points it is necessary to note that each wireless access point area should overlap its neighbors, thus providing users with seamless mobility. Extension points, which act as wireless relays, can be used to extend the range of a single access point. Multiple extension points can be used to give distant locations wireless access to the central access point. Figure 1-3 shows a network with multiple access points.

LAN-To-LAN Wireless Network

Access points provide wireless connectivity to local computers and computers on a different network. All hardware access points have the capability of directly interconnecting with another hardware access point. Interconnecting LANs over wireless connections is large and complex. Figure 1-4 illustrates a possible configuration for a LAN-to-LAN wireless network with multiple access points.

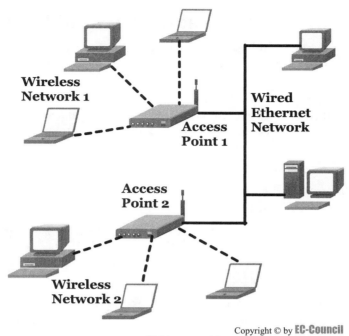

Figure 1-3   Network with multiple access points.

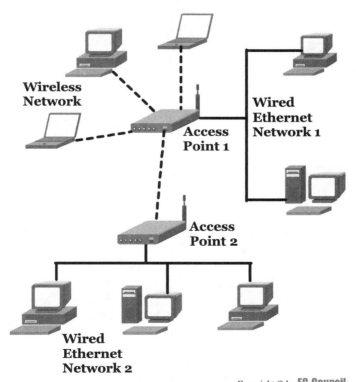

Figure 1-4   LAN-to-LAN network with multiple access points.

Types of Wireless Networks: Based on Geographical Area Covered

Wireless networks are also classified based on the area they cover geographically: WLAN, WWAN, WPAN, and WMAN, as outlined in this section.

WLAN (Wireless Local Area Network)

A WLAN (Wireless Local Area Network) connects users in a local area as a network. Figure 1-5 shows a possible WLAN configuration. The area may range from a single room to an entire campus. Other features of a WLAN are as follows:

- WLAN connects wireless users and the wired network.
- WLAN uses high-frequency radio waves.
- WLAN is also known as a LAWN (Local Area Wireless Network).
- In 1990, IEEE (Institute of Electrical and Electronic Engineers) formed a group to develop a standard for wireless equipment, resulting in the IEEE 802.11 standard.
- In the peer-to-peer mode, wireless devices within a range communicate directly with each other without using the central access points.
- While in infrastructure mode, the access point is wired to the Internet with wireless users. An access point functions as a mediator between the wired and the wireless networks.

The advantages and disadvantages of a WLAN are outlined following.

Advantages

- Flexible to install
- Easy to set up and use
- Are robust: If one base station is down, then users may be able to physically move their PCs to be in the range of another base station.
- Has a better chance of surviving a natural disaster

Disadvantage

- Data transfer speeds are not as high as in a wired network

Figure 1-5   Wireless Local Area Network.

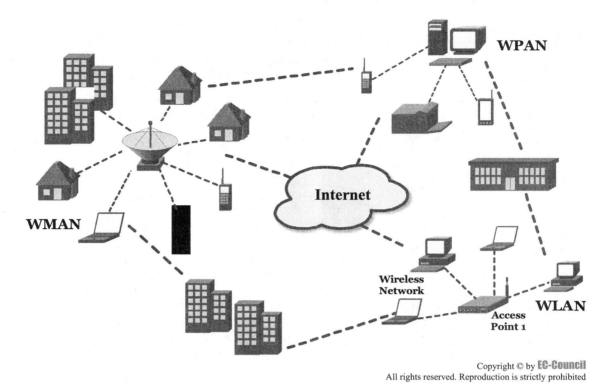

Figure 1-6   Wireless Wide Area Network.

WWAN (Wireless Wide Area Network)

The WWAN (Wireless Wide Area Network) can cover a larger area than the WLAN. Figure 1-6 illustrates the WWAN concept. Following are the features of a WWAN:

- WWAN handles cellular network technology such as CDMA, GSM, GPRS, and CDPD for transmission of data.

- This technology may cover a particular region, nation, or even the entire globe.

- The system has built-in cellular radio GSM/CDMA, which helps users send or receive data.

- In WWAN, the wireless data consists of fixed microwave links, digital dispatch networks, wireless LANs, data over cellular networks, wireless PANs, satellite links, one-way and two-way paging networks, laser-based communications, diffuse infrared, keyless car entry, the Global Positioning System, and more.

WPAN (Wireless Personal Area Network)

A Wireless Personal Area Network (WPAN) connects the devices positioned around an individual wirelessly. Figure 1-7 shows this type of network. The *IrDA* (Infrared Data Association) defines physical specifications communication protocol standards ensuring that there is no interference between two points of communication. They are the physical specifications communications protocol standards for the short-range exchange of data over infrared light, for uses such as personal area networks (PANs), or in palmtop computers, mobile phones, and laptop computers.

The IrDA-standards devices communicate through infrared LEDs. Bluetooth is the best example of a WPAN. *Bluetooth* is preferred when communicating within short distances using voice and data communications; it offers robust functionality at low power and low cost. These are some of the features of a WPAN:

- WPAN has a very short range. It can communicate within a range of 10 meters (33 feet).

- A WPAN connects the mobile network devices that people carry with them or keep at their desks.

- A main concept of WPAN technology is *plugging in*; that is, when any two WPAN-equipped devices come within close proximity of a central server, they can communicate as if connected by a cable.

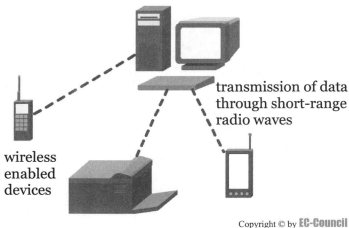

Figure 1-7   Wireless Personal Area Network.

- When any two WPAN operational devices come within range (a few meters) of the central server, they communicate with each other, like a wired network.
- WPAN has the ability to lock out other devices and prevent unusual interference.
- Every device in a WPAN can connect to any other device in the same WPAN, assuming they are in physical range of each other.
- Bluetooth specifications are the basis for the IEEE 802.15.1 standard for 1-Mbps WPANs.
- Channel conflict has become common and harsh with the increasing use of WPAN devices.

WMAN (Wireless Metropolitan Area Network)

WMAN is a wireless communication network that covers a metropolitan area, such as a city or suburb. Figure 1-8 illustrates the WMAN concept. These are its features:

- WMANs access a broadband area network by using an exterior *antenna*. (An antenna is a set of wires that transmit an electromagnetic field in response to EMF signals.)
- WMAN is a good option for a fixed line network. It is simple to build and is cost-effective.
- In the WMAN, the subscriber stations communicate with a base station that is connected to a central network or hub.
- WMAN uses wireless infrastructure or optical fiber connections to link its sites.
- The WMAN links WLANs. Distributed Queue Dual Bus (DQDB) is the MAN standard for data communications, specified by the IEEE 802.6 standards. With DQDB, a network over 30 miles long with speeds of 34 to 154 Mbps can be established.

Table 1-2 provides a comparison of the WLAN, WWAN, WPAN and WMAN technologies.

Advantages and Disadvantages of a Wireless Network

Wireless networks—no matter what form they take—do have distinct advantages and disadvantages.

Advantages of a Wireless Network

- It gives users the mobility to access their networks.
- It can be easily connected.
- The initial cost to set up the WLAN is low compared to manually cabling a new enterprise.
- Data can be transmitted in different ways through Cellular Networks, Mobitex, DataTAC, Cellular Digital Packet Data, etc.
- Sharing of data is easy between the wireless devices.

Figure 1-8   Wireless Metropolitan Area Network.

	Standards/ Technologies	Speed	Range	Applications
WLAN	802.11a, 11b, 11g and HiperLAN2	2–54+ Mbps	Medium	Enterprise networks
WWAN	GSM, GPRS, CDMA	10–384 Kbps	Long	PDAs, mobile phones, cellular access
WPAN	Bluetooth	<1 Mbps	Short	Peer-to-Peer, device-to-device
WMAN	802.11, LMDS, LMDS	22+ Mbps	Medium-long	Fixed, last-mile access

Table 1-2   Comparison of WLAN, WWAN, WPAN, and WMAN technologies

Disadvantages of a Wireless Network

- Mobility is the biggest disadvantage in a wireless network as there is no physical security to the wireless network.
- Risk of data sharing is high as the packets are sent through air, and an attacker can easily sniff the air using various wireless sniffing tools.
- Most wireless communication uses a wide spectrum frequency range, so it is simple to identify the signal, making it more susceptible to hackers.
- Cost of installing equipment for wireless is higher in comparison to wired networks.
- Wireless networks are less reliable than wired networks.
- Wireless systems perform less efficiently when compared to wired networks.
- Wireless systems are more vulnerable to security threats than wired networks.
- Wireless does not provide dedicated bandwidth for each computer.

Generations of Wireless Technology

This section discusses the important generations in wireless technology: 2G, 2.5G, 3G, and 4G.

2G (Second Generation)

2G stands for "second-generation" cellular technology; it began using digital signaling. It differed from its predecessor, 1G, which used analog radio signals. Depending upon the type of multiplexing used, 2G can be categorized into CDMA-based and TDMA-based standards.

The main 2G standards are:

- GSM (TDMA based)
- iDEN (TDMA based)
- PDC (TDMA based)
- IS-95(Interim Standard 95); brand name is cdmaOne (CDMA based)

With 2G, system capacity was increased using a digital signal. Digital data voice could be compressed or multiplexed more effectively using various CODECs, which helped to pack more calls into the same amount of radio bandwidth. A digital system, which emits less radio power from the handset, could place more cells in the same space. A CODEC, in this application, performs video and audio compression for transmission and then decodes for playback upon receipt. It is used in videoconferencing and streaming media applications.

The advantages of 2G were:

- The digital voice encoding aided in digital error checking, reducing noise and increasing the sound quality.
- Digital data services such as e-mail and SMS were introduced using the digital signals.
- 2G had low power emission, which addressed health concerns.

2.5G (Second and a Half Generation)

The 2.5 G stands for "second and a half generation." It falls between 2G and 3G technologies. In addition to the *circuit-based domain (network)*, 2.5 G also implements the *packet-based domain (network)*. The 2.5G system stands on High-Speed Circuit-Switched Data (HSCSD), General Packet Radio Service (GPRS), and Enhanced Data rates for Global Evolution (EDGE) technologies.

In packet-based networks, the data is fragmented into packets that are transmitted from one point to the other. The packets are reassembled at the other end. Packet-based networks are connectionless. Circuit-based networks are fixed-channel, circuit-based communication networks; a channel is established before users can communicate, and then all the users can access the resources.

In 2.5G, data communication speed increases up to 384 Kbit/s. 2.5G uses certain properties of 3G, such as the packet-switched properties, and certain 2G infrastructure in GSM and the CDMA network. (GSM and CDMA are competing network technologies used by various cellular carriers.) Time slots are bundled for circuit-switched data services (HSCSD), so it is not necessary to provide fast services. The GPRS is a 2.5G technology used by GSM operators. Some protocols like the EDGE for GSM and the CDMA2000 1X-RTT for CDMA have a data rate above 144 kbit/s. These qualify as 3G services but are considered 2.5G because they are several times slower than real 3G services.

3G (Third Generation)

3G is the third generation of wireless technology and offers high data transfer rates for handheld devices. It can transfer both voice data (e.g., telephone calls) and nonvoice data (e.g., downloading information and exchanging mails). 3G also provides some multimedia services that are a combination of both voice and data.

Data transfer rates for 3G are as follows:

- For a stationary device, the data transfer rate is 2.05 Mbit/s
- For slowly moving objects it is 384 kbit/s
- For fast moving objects, such as a handset in a moving vehicle, it is 128 kbit/s

The features of 3G are:

- Connectivity is always up because it uses IP connectivity, which is packet based.
- It supports multimedia services.
- It supports instant messaging with audio and video clips.
- It supports quick download of large files such as PowerPoint presentations and faxes.

Some of the 3G standards are:

- CDMA2000, WCDMA, and TD-SCDMA, based on CDMA
- FDMA/TDMA and TDMA-SC (EDGE), based on TDMA

Following are the advantages and disadvantages of 3G.

Advantages

- It provides both fixed and variable data rates.
- It provides security and reliability.
- 3G uses IP connectivity, which is packet based and not circuit based.
- In 3G, data rates are asymmetric.

Disadvantages

- The cost of upgrading base stations and cellular infrastructure to 3G is high.
- Power requirement is high, which requires larger handsets and larger batteries.

4G (Fourth Generation)

4G stands for "fourth generation." Initially Docomo (do communications over the mobile network, a Japanese mobile phone operator) had planned to introduce 4G around 2010, but moved it up to 2006. For 4G, the data transfer rates are intended to be up to 20 megabytes per second, which is 2,000 times faster than mobile rates established in 2001. 4G uses OFDM (Orthogonal Frequency Division Multiplexing) and OFDMA (Orthogonal Frequency Division Multiple Access) for better allocation of network resources to multiple users.

For making use of multiple channels simultaneously, 4G uses SDR (software-defined radio). 4G is based only on a packet-switching network, which helps in low-latency data transmission. 4G allows smooth video transmission with high quality and is 10–20 times faster than standard ADSL services, which are used for Internet connection over a copper cable. The ADSL services have developed a pervasive network in which the user can be connected to several wireless access technologies, such as Wi-Fi, UMTS, and EDGE, simultaneously. The advantages of 4G are:

- It uses SDR (software-defined radio).
- 4G allows smooth video transmission with high quality.
- It is based only on a packet-switching network, which helps in low-latency data transmission.

Uses of Wireless Technology

Wireless technology is mainly used in satellites, cellular phone networks, laptops, PDAs, smartphones, remote controls, and M-commerce.

Satellite

A satellite is an earth-orbiting communication device that is used for receiving and transmitting signals. Satellite communication uses electromagnetic waves to transfer data to the satellite from Earth and then back to Earth. The signals are transmitted from a dish-shaped station on Earth called an Earth or ground station. The satellite transponders receive the signal, amplify it, and then transmit it back to the Earth station. A satellite has a number of transponders called repeaters. Earth stations receive the signals transmitted by the satellite's transponders and transmit them to their final receiver through cables, phone lines, or microwaves. These satellites travel around Earth in a geostationary orbit, which is located 22,300 miles above the equator. The satellite rotates with the relative speed of the earth in a particular orbit, which helps to keep the antenna fixed on Earth.

Cellular (Mobile) Phone Network

A cellular phone network is a communication system in which the transmitter and receiver are connected through microwaves to a base transmitter and receiver system. In this network, the geographical area is separated into slightly overlapping regions called cells. Each cell contains a central base station and two assigned transmission frequencies. One frequency is used by the base station while the other is used by the mobile phone. To avoid radio interference, each cell has a different frequency. In each cell, the same frequency sets in other cells are used. Those cells are spaced miles apart to reduce interference, but allow a call to be handed off when a call leaves one cell and enters another. The base stations are connected to a telephone system.

Newer, advanced cellular phones have the ability to take photos and send them to another cellular phone, include alarm clocks and calendars, and have Internet capabilities.

Laptops

A laptop is a small, mobile personal computer, also called a notebook computer. Laptops usually have a liquid crystal display (LCD), and use a different memory module for RAM. In addition to a built-in keyboard, they may have a touch pad or a pointing stick for navigation. Some laptops use cache memory for fast access of data.

Memory types used in laptops are:

- Small Outline Dual Inline Memory Module (SODIMM)
- Dual Data Rate Synchronous RAM (DDR SDRAM)
- Single Data Rate Synchronous RAM (SDRAM)
- Proprietary memory modules

Laptop hard drives spin slower than desktop computer hard drives, which reduces both heat and power consumption. They either run on a single battery or from an AC/DC adaptor that charges the battery. The CPU of a laptop works at a lower voltage and clock speed, decreasing heat output and power consumption but slowing down the processor.

Some subcategories of laptop computers are:

- *Ultra-portable*: the screen size is less than 12 inches diagonally, and they weigh approximately 1.7 kg (~4 lbs) or less. They are expensive, and have excellent graphics rendering capabilities.
- *Thin and light*: the screen size is between 12 and 14 inches diagonally, and they weigh between 1.8 and 2.8 kg (~4–6 lbs).
- *Medium-sized*: the screen size is 15 to 15.4 inches diagonally, and they weigh between 3 and 3.5 kg (`6.5–8 lbs).

PDA (Personal Digital Assistant)

A PDA (Personal Digital Assistant) is a small mobile device with computing and information storage capability, including a calendar and address book. Most PDAs have a small keyboard, but some use an electronically sensitive pad on which handwriting is received as an input. PDAs can also be combined with paging and telephone systems.

Smartphones

Smartphones are mobile phones with advanced—often PC-like—capabilities. Two of the most popular brands of smartphones are Blackberry and iPhone. A smartphone allows the user to stay connected via e-mail, phone, and the Web. Other features include the following:

- Can access a high-speed wireless data network
- Is a completely integrated package that contains hardware, software, and provides a number of services
- Able to connect to multiple e-mail accounts
- Can add on applications that extend the capabilities of the device
- Can receive and place calls easily and quickly
- Has fast, wireless Internet capabilities
- Can be used to connect a laptop or a desktop computer to the Internet
- Sends and receives text messages via SMS (short message service)

- Has instant messenging and texting capabilities
- Runs Bluetooth wireless technology

Remote Control

A remote control is an electronic device used for remote operation of a machine. It is a small handheld device with buttons to adjust various settings such as changing television channels, adjusting volume settings or changing the screen color. The remote control communicates with other related equipment through infrared signal or radio signals. It is powered by small batteries.

Remote control technology is used in industry (e.g., to control the substations of pump storage power stations), in space travel (e.g., the Russian Lunokhod vehicles were controlled remotely from the ground), to play video games and to operate some toys.

M-Commerce

M-commerce is an electronic transaction, a business-to-consumer transaction, or an information interaction that is carried out through mobile devices. It enables the mobile user to purchase or receive services via mobile devices.

Some examples of M-commerce are:

- Booking airline or movie tickets
- Making reservations at hotels or restaurants
- Transferring money, downloading e-cash
- Making payments online
- Ordering goods for delivery

Some applications for M-commerce are:

- *UMCS (Universal Mobile Commerce System)*: The products are ordered using SMS.
- *PAYMOBIL*: Payment is made via mobile phones.

Chapter Summary

- *Wireless* is a term used to describe telecommunications in which electromagnetic waves (rather than some form of wire) carry the signal over part or the entire communication path.
- Types of wireless networks based on connections are peer-to-peer network, extension to a wired network, multiple access points, LAN-to-LAN wireless network.
- Types of wireless networks based on geographical area covered are WLAN, WWAN, WPAN, WMAN.
- Wireless does not provide dedicated bandwidth for each computer.
- Cellular phone technologies have evolved in several major phases, denoted by "Generations," or "G," for short.
- Wireless communications are used in satellites, laptops, PDAs, cellular phone networks, smartphones, remote controls, M-commerce.

Review Questions

1. Explain what is meant by the term *wireless* network.

_____

_____

_____

_____

2. List the advantages and disadvantages of wired and wireless networks.

_____

_____

_____

_____

3. _____ gave the first public demonstration of electromagnetic waves.

4. What are the types of wireless networks based on connection?

_____

_____

_____

_____

5. What are the types of wireless networks based on geographical area covered?

_____

_____

_____

_____

6. _____ generation includes HSCSD, GPRS, and EDGE technologies.

7. List the various 3G standards.

_____

_____

_____

_____

8. List five devices that use wireless technology.

_____

_____

_____

_____

9. What is M-commerce and how does wireless technology help it?

_____

_____

_____

_____

Hands-On Projects

Please attempt the following projects to reinforce what you have learned in this chapter. Write down your observations or process notes for later reference.

1. Identify the wireless network used in your classroom.

2. Determine the type of wireless network (based on connection) in your classroom.

3. Find out the data transfer speed of your classroom network.

4. Determine the network topology used in your wireless network.

5. Find out the geographical limit of your wireless network.

Chapter 2

Wireless Signal Propagation

Objectives

After completing this chapter, you should be able to:

- Explain the concepts involved in wireless signal propagation
- Define the terms associated with wireless signal propagation

Key Terms

Amplifier an electronic device that can be used for increasing the voltage, current, or power of the signal to be transmitted

Amplitude modulation (AM) a modulation technique in which the amplitude of the carrier wave is changed in direct proportion to the characteristics of the modulating signal while keeping the frequency and phase constant

Analog modulation a technique in which carrier analog signal parameters, such as amplitude, frequency, and phase, change according to the immediate values of the modulating analog signal

Analog signals uninterrupted electrical signals that vary with time and amplitude

Bandwidth the width of the range (or band) of frequencies that an electronic signal uses on a given transmission medium; bandwidth is expressed in terms of the difference between the highest-frequency signal component and the lowest-frequency signal component. Since the frequency of a signal is measured in hertz, a given bandwidth is the difference in hertz between the highest frequency the signal uses and the lowest frequency it uses.

Digital modulation also known as discrete modulation; a modified format of the carrier signal that can take only discrete values

Digital signals interrupted signals; they change in each step. Filters electronic circuits performing signal processing functions, often to remove unwanted or enhance desired frequency components.

Direct sequence spread spectrum (DSSS)   the best form of the spread spectrum technique; instead of sending one bit, numbers of bits are transmitted

Frequency   the number of cycles per second of a waveform; the standard unit of frequency is the hertz (Hz). If a current completes one cycle per second, then the frequency is 1 Hz; 60 cycles per second equals 60 Hz.

Frequency-hopping spread spectrum (FHSS)   instead of sending the signal on a single frequency, it is broadcast over a number of frequencies; the frequencies are changed during the transmission of the signal

Frequency modulation (FM)   the modulation technique in which amplitude and phase are kept constant and the frequency of the carrier wave gets changed according to a variation in the modulating signal

Full-duplex transmission   simultaneous data transmission in both directions

Half-duplex transmission   bidirectional, but not simultaneous, data transmission

Mixer   a nonlinear device used for frequency conversion

Modulation   the process of changing the carrier signal in such a way that it can be used for transmitting information

Phase modulation (PM)   sometimes used as an alternative to FM; in PM the amplitude and the frequency of the carrier signal remain constant, but as the amplitude of the modulating signal changes, the phase of the carrier wave is changed

Simplex transmission   unidirectional data transmission; in other words, data is transferred in one direction only

Spread spectrum   a form of wireless communication in which the frequency of the transmitted signal is deliberately varied; it uses a narrow signal, which it spreads over broad areas

Transmission speed   the rate at which data is moved across a communication channel

Ultra WideBand (UWB)   a short-range wireless technology; it is used for transmitting digital data on a large scale over a wide spectrum of frequency for a short distance

Introduction to Wireless Signal Propagation

Wireless operations permit services, such as long-range communications, that are impractical to implement with the use of wires. The term is commonly used in the telecommunications industry and refers to telecommunications systems that use some form of energy (radio frequency [RF], infrared light, etc.) to transfer information without the use of wires. The term wireless is a generic word used to describe communications in which electromagnetic waves or RF carry a signal over a part of or the entire communication path. The term *wireless* should not be confused with the term *cordless*, which describes devices that operate from a portable power source or battery pack.

Figure 2-1 illustrates the electromagnetic spectrum, the range of all possible electromagnetic radiation frequencies. *Frequency* is the number of cycles per second of a waveform; the standard unit of frequency is the hertz (Hz). If a current completes one cycle per second, then the frequency is 1 Hz; 60 cycles per second equals 60 Hz.

This chapter explores wireless signal propagation, which includes the creation, transmission, and modulations of the signal.

Analog and Digital Signals

Analog signals are uninterrupted electrical signals that vary with time and amplitude (Figure 2-2). These signals are easy to create and transfer from one place to another. However, if the pattern is changed due to unwanted noise or distortion, the output is then not the same as the input; thus, the data that is sent will not be received correctly—it will be distorted. For example, an old-fashioned, rotary dial telephone uses analog signals.

Digital signals are interrupted signals; they change in each step (Figure 2-3). They contain a pattern of bits of information: pulses with discrete levels or digits with values. The value of pulse is constant and the value of digit changes rapidly. Digital signals have two amplitude levels known as nodes. The value of each node varies between 1 and 0 for on and off, true and false, high and low. The sequence of 0s or 1s is the representation of the data (test or sound, etc.).

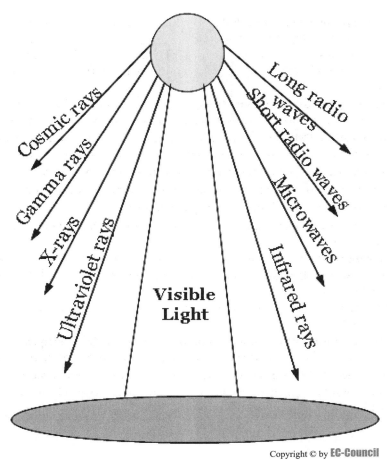

Figure 2-1   Electromagnetic spectrum.

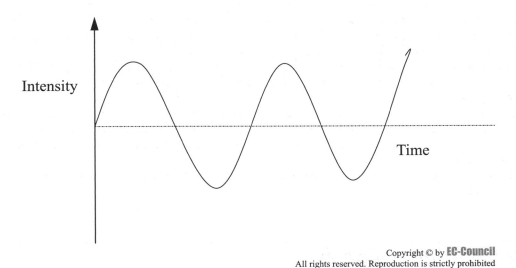

Figure 2-2   Analog signal.

Radio Waves

Radio waves are a type of electromagnetic radiation. The wavelength of radio waves is the longest in the electromagnetic spectrum, and they can be generated easily. Due to the electromagnetic nature of typical home building materials, radio waves can penetrate them. However, large office buildings may be built with metal, which can refract the waves around and degenerate the signal. These waves can travel long distances—up to approximately 1000 km (~620 miles).

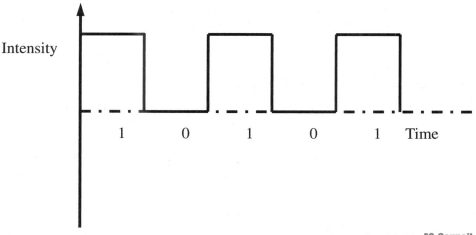

Figure 2-3   Digital signal.

Radio waves can transmit information in all directions, making it unnecessary for the transmitter and the receiver to be in a direct line of sight. Radio waves used for communication are modulated in two ways (modulation will be discussed in more detail later in the chapter):

- Amplitude modulation (AM—waves vary according to wavelength amplitude)
- Frequency modulation (FM—waves vary according to wavelength frequency)

Radio waves are used in both cellular phones and televisions.

Infrared Light

Infrared light is another type of electromagnetic radiation with a wavelength larger than visible light but smaller than radio waves. The wavelength of infrared light lies between 700 nanometers and 1 millimeter. The wavelength of "near infrared" light is closest to the wavelength of visible light, while the wavelength of "far infrared" light is closest to the microwave region of the electromagnetic spectrum (refer to Figure 2-1).

Far infrared waves are thermal; that is, they generate heat. The sun and fire are sources of far infrared waves. On the other hand, we cannot feel the near infrared waves as they are not hot. Remote controls use near infrared waves.

Here are some applications of infrared light:

- *Night-vision equipment*: Infrared light is used when there is insufficient visible light available to see.
- *Thermography*: The temperature of an object is calculated by measuring its infrared radiation.
- *Heating*: Infrared radiation can be used to generate heat; it is used for deicing the wings of aircraft.
- *Communication*: Infrared radiation is used in short range communication devices such as PDAs and computer devices.
- *Spectroscopy*: Infrared radiation is used to calculate the percentage of organic compound in a given sample.

Transmission Speed

The rate at which data is moved across a communication channel is called the *transmission speed*. Transmission speed is measured in kilobits (kbps), thousands of bits per second, or megabits (Mbps), millions of bits per second. The bits per second (bps) and baud rate are used to express the transmission rate.

Bits per second (bps, also called bit rate) is the number of bits of data traversed per second through a transmission media. Here, a bit refers to either 0 or 1. The baud rate is a measure of changes in the signal state during its transmission in a channel. The signal state can change with respect to its strength, frequency, voltage, or phase angle. A measure of one baud implies a change in signal one time. Therefore, 200 baud indicates that the signal has been changed 200 times in a second.

Components of a Radio System

The components that allow communication through radio frequency (RF) are filters, mixers, and amplifiers.

Filter

Filters are electronic circuits performing signal processing functions, often to remove unwanted or enhance desired frequency components. It removes the unwanted signals, and either passes or rejects the frequencies above or below the cutoff frequency. Filters can be classified as follows:

- *Passive*: Not dependent on an external power supply. RC, RL, LC, RLC all are passive filters.
- *Active*: Designed by using amplifying components. Generally, an operational amplifier is used for the design of an active filter.
- *Digital*: Performs the digital math operation on the signals.
- *SAW (Surface Acoustic Wave)*: An electromechanical device used for radio frequency purposes.

Filters come in three types:

1. *Low-pass*: Passes the low frequencies but rejects frequencies above the cutoff frequency.
2. *High-pass*: Passes the high frequencies but rejects frequencies below the cutoff frequency.
3. *Bandpass*: Combination of high-pass and low-pass filters; passes the frequencies between certain ranges and rejects the frequencies outside of that range.

Mixer

A *mixer* is a nonlinear device used for frequency conversion (Figure 2-4). It combines two or more input frequencies to produce a single output. It changes the RF power at one frequency to RF power at another frequency in order to make signal processing simple and low cost. This frequency conversion allocates amplification of the received signal at a frequency other than RF or audio frequency. The new signal may be in a different band than the input signals were.

Amplifier

An *amplifier* is an electronic device that can be used for increasing the voltage, current, or power of the signal to be transmitted (Figure 2-5). It improves the quality of the input signal and transmits it to the receiver. The transfer function used is the ratio of input to output.

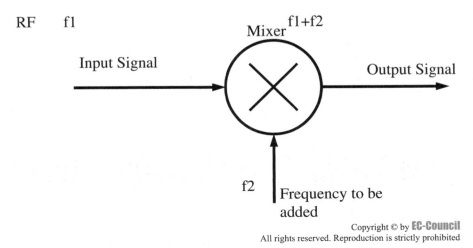

Figure 2-4 Two input signals are added to form a single output.

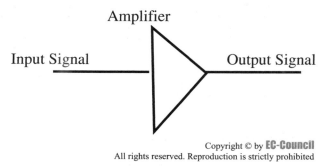

Figure 2-5 Amplifier.

Amplifiers have these characteristics:

- *Gain*: How much the level of the input signal is to be increased; it is measured in decibels (dB).
- *Output dynamic range*: The range between lowest useful output and highest useful output.
- *Bandwidth and rise time*: The difference between the upper and lower half-power points (the half-power point is the frequency at which the output power has dropped to half of its mid-band level).
- *Slew rate*: The maximum rate of change of the output signal.
- *Noise*: An unwanted distortion created during the amplification process.
- *Efficiency*: The amount of input power required compared to the amplifier's output.

Amplifiers are generally classified as follows:

- *Class A*: Efficiency is not a consideration; it amplifies all parts of the input signal.
- *Class B*: Each output device conducts only a half wave of input signal.
- *Class AB*: Transmits between 180 and 360 degrees.
- *Class C*: Amplifies less than 180 degrees of input signal; its efficiency is greater than A, AB, or B, but has poor linearity.
- *Class D*: Depends mainly on Pulse Width Modulation (PWM); it has high efficiency.

Some examples of amplifiers are:

- Vacuum tube amplifiers
- Transistor amplifiers
- Operational amplifiers
- Video amplifiers
- Microwave amplifiers

Transmission Direction

Data can be transferred from one point to another. Data transmission can be categorized into three types depending on the direction of the flow of data: simplex, half-duplex, or full-duplex.

Simplex Transmission

In *simplex transmission*, data transmission is unidirectional; in other words, data is transferred in one direction only. Simplex transmission is used in a smaller range of applications because it is not possible to send a reply to the transmitter end. For example, a television's signals are sent from a transmitter, but the TV cannot send a reply (Figure 2-6).

Half-Duplex Transmission

In *half-duplex transmission*, data transmission is bidirectional but not simultaneous. That is, data is transferred in both directions but not at the same time (Figure 2-7). In this type of transmission, if one end transmits the

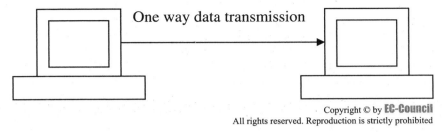

Figure 2-6   Simplex transmission.

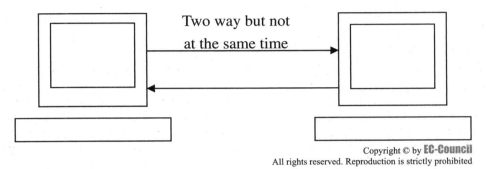

Figure 2-7   Half-duplex transmission.

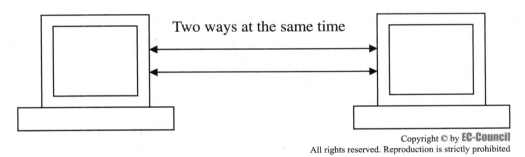

Figure 2-8   Full-duplex transmission.

data, then the other end only receives it and vice versa. In half-duplex transmission, it is possible to detect errors, and send a reply to the transmitter for retransmitting the data. For example, only one person can talk at a time on a police radio. When one person completes his speech and wants the other to speak, he has to say "over."

Full-Duplex Transmission

In *full-duplex transmission*, data transmission takes place in both directions simultaneously. Data is transmitted and received at the same time by both ends of the transmission (Figure 2-8). For example, a telephone uses full-duplex transmission.

Switching

Switching involves moving the signal from one frequency to another. Two types of signal switching are possible:

- *Packet-based networks*: In a packet-based network, the data is fragmented into packets that are transmitted from one point to another. The packets are reassembled at the other end. All the data packets follow the same path to reach the destination network. The packet-based networks are connectionless.

- *Circuit-based networks*: The communication channel is fixed and is a dedicated end-to-end connection in circuit-based networks (most commonly used for voice circuits).

Signal Strength

The strength of a signal is measured from a distance (called the reference point) where the signal is actually transmitted. The signal strength can be measured in terms of its voltage. It determines the strength at which the signal is transmitted, received, or predicted. The units for signal strength are: V/m^2, mV/m^2, $dB\mu V/m^2$, based on the intensity of the signal. Electromagnetic interference, or "noise," is a major factor that affects radio signal strength. The dynamic range is the amount by which the signal's maximum intensity exceeds its minimum detectable level. The measure of signal strength relative to background noise is the signal-to-noise ratio (SNR):

$$\text{SNR: } (P_{Signal}/P_{Noise}) = (A_{Signal}/A_{Noise})^2$$

Where P is the power of the signal and A is the amplitude of the signal

Ultra WideBand (UWB)

Ultra WideBand (UWB) is a short-range wireless technology. It is used for transmitting digital data on a large scale over a wide spectrum of frequency for a short distance. Because UWB requires lower power than normal or background noise, there is no chance of interference at any frequency band that is in use. UWB transmits digital signals that are timed correctly on a carrier signal across a broad spectrum at the same time. UWB is a technology for transmitting information spread over a large bandwidth (>500 MHz). *Bandwidth* is the width of the range (or band) of frequencies that an electronic signal uses on a given transmission medium. It is expressed in terms of the difference between the highest-frequency signal component and the lowest-frequency signal component. Since the frequency of a signal is measured in hertz, a given bandwidth is the difference in hertz between the highest frequency the signal uses and the lowest frequency it uses.

Features of Ultra WideBand are as follows:

- It can transmit large amounts of data over a short distance—up to 230 feet.

- It requires very low power—up to 0.5 milliwatts.

- It has the capacity to transmit signals through doors and other barriers, which would reflect a radio signal, with more bandwidth and high power.

Here are some applications of UWB:

- It is used in radar, in which the signal goes through nearby surfaces but reflects off surfaces that are farther away, allowing objects to be detected.

- It enables transfer of data from digital camcorders, wireless printing of digital pictures from a camera without the use of a personal computer, and the transfer of files between handheld devices like personal digital audio and video players.

Modulation

Modulation is the process of changing the carrier signal in such a way that allows it to be used for transmitting information. In modulation, the information can be added to the carrier signal by varying the amplitude, frequency, and phase to get the modulated signal. A device that performs the modulation is called a modulator, and the device that performs demodulation is called a demodulator. The device that performs both the operations is a modem.

There are two main types of modulation:

1. Analog modulation
2. Digital modulation

Analog Modulation

Analog modulation is a technique in which carrier analog signal parameters, such as amplitude, frequency, and phase, change according to the immediate values of the modulating analog signal. In this modulation, the contents of the data are not changed. Instead, the modulating signal mixes with the carrier signal of higher frequency and the modulated output signal defines the bandwidth as the same as the carrier signal. In digital data communication, analog modulation changes the analog data to digital before transmission of the modulated signal.

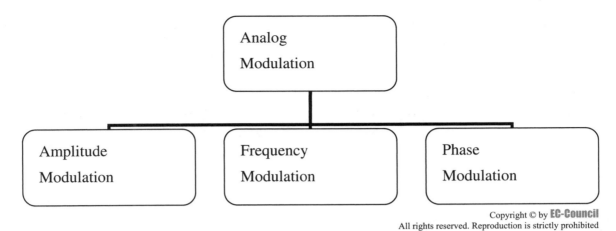

Figure 2-9   Analog modulation.

The actual scheme used to perform modulation depends on:

- Carrier waveform (sinusoidal or pulse)
- Type of transmission (analog or digital)
- Types of modulation (depends on change of amplitude, frequency, and phase of modulating signal)

Analog modulation is divided into

- Analog modulation for analog signal
- Analog modulation for digital signal

Analog modulation for analog signals is categorized by (Figure 2-9):

- Amplitude modulation
- Frequency modulation
- Phase modulation

Amplitude Modulation (AM)

Amplitude modulation (AM) is a modulation technique in which the amplitude of the carrier wave is changed in direct proportion to the characteristics of the modulating signal while keeping the frequency and phase constant. In Figure 2-10, the slow curve line may be an audio signal; the other is the carrier signal. The bottom picture shows the combination in which the audio signal is combined with the carrier to perform transmission. The varying height of the line represents amplitude.

AM is used in radio frequencies, and it was the first method to be used for broadcasting commercial radio. AM generates a modulated signal that has double the bandwidth of the modulating signal. It is generated by multiplying the sinusoidal data signal by a constant factor of the carrier signal. The result generates three sinusoidal components: carrier, lower sideband, and upper sideband, all of which have the same bandwidth as the modulating signal.

The simple sine wave of a carrier signal is given by

$$c(t) = C \sin(\omega_c t)$$

where,

ω_c: *frequency of carrier signal*
C: *amplitude of carrier signal*

The equation for the simple sine wave of frequency ω_m is

$$m(t) = M \sin(\omega_m t + \varphi),$$

where,

φ: phase offset relative to $c(t)$.
ω_m: frequency of modulating signal
M: amplitude of modulating signal

Amplitude modulation is performed simply by adding $m(t)$ to C. The amplitude-modulated signal is then

$$y(t) = (C + M \sin(\omega_m t + \varphi)) \sin(\omega_c t)$$

The formula for $y(t)$ above is:

$$y(t) = C \sin(\omega_c t) + M \frac{\cos(\emptyset - (\omega_m - \omega_c)t)}{2} - M \frac{\cos(\emptyset + (\omega_m + \omega_c)t)}{2}$$

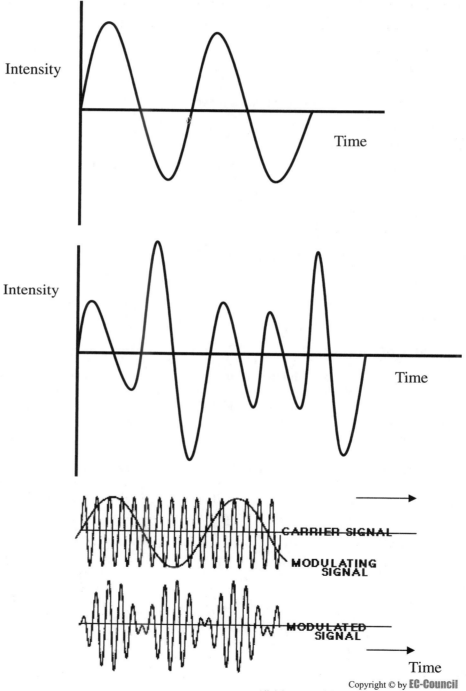

Figure 2-10 Amplitude modulation.

Frequency Modulation (FM)

Frequency modulation (FM) is the modulation technique in which amplitude and phase are kept constant and the frequency of the carrier wave gets changed according to a variation in the modulating signal. The second part of Figure 2-11 shows the modified frequency with constant amplitude. The height of the line is the same but it is not spaced evenly, representing frequency.

FM is a technique of impressing data onto the AC wave by changing the frequency of the wave immediately. In analog FM, the frequency of the carrier wave gets changed in proportion to the amplitude of the carrier signal. In digital modulation the frequency gets shifted.

Some advantages of FM over AM are:

- Improved signal-to-noise ratio with respect to man-made interference (up to 25dB)
- Smaller geographical interference between neighboring stations
- Less radiated power
- Well-defined service areas for given transmitter power

FM does have some disadvantages:

- Requires more bandwidth
- Receiver and transmitter are more complicated

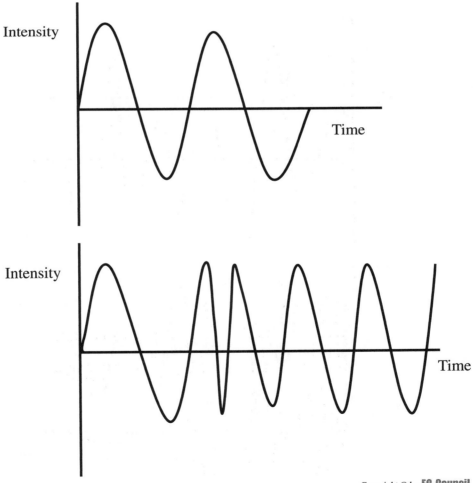

Figure 2-11 Frequency modulation.

Phase Modulation (PM)

Phase modulation (PM) is sometimes used as an alternative to FM. In PM the amplitude and the frequency of the carrier signal remain constant. However, as the amplitude of the modulating signal changes, the phase of the carrier wave is changed. The second part of Figure 2-12 shows the modified wave as the line shifts back and forth at each change of phase. This phase changes the starting point of the cycle, but the change can occur only when the bits getting transmitted change from a sequence or instance of 1s to 0s or vice versa.

PM is a technique of impressing the data onto an alternating current (AC) waveform by changing the phase of the wave. In analog PM, the frequency of the carrier wave is changed in proportion to the amplitude of the carrier signal. In digital modulation the frequency is shifted. PM is not often used because it needs a more complex hardware receiver.

Digital Modulation

Digital modulation is also known as discrete modulation. In this modulation, a modified format of the carrier signal can take only discrete values. The analog signal gets converted into number format for transmission purposes. The modulated digital signal can be transmitted through cable, satellite, or microwave. Digital modulation has the capacity to transmit a larger amount of data than analog.

Some advantages of digital modulation over analog modulation are as follows:

- Makes better use of bandwidth
- Requires less power for transmission purpose

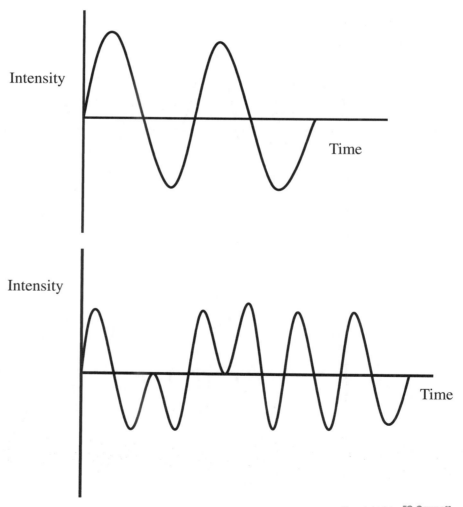

Figure 2-12   Phase modulation.

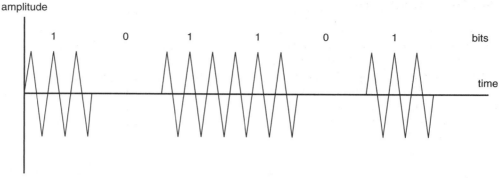

Figure 2-13 Amplitude Shift Keying (ASK).

- Handles signal interference better
- Error correcting techniques are friendlier with other digital systems

The various digital modulation techniques are:

- Amplitude Shift Keying (ASK)
- Frequency Shift Keying (FSK)
- Phase Shift Keying (PSK)

Amplitude Shift Keying (ASK)

Amplitude Shift Keying (ASK) is a binary modulation technique that is the same as amplitude modulation (Figure 2-13). In this modulation, by keeping the frequency and phase constant, the amplitude of the carrier signal is changed with the discrete values of the modulating signal. The peak amplitude of the signal during each bit is always constant and the value depends on the bit (0 or 1). In this modulation, NRZ (non-return-to-zero) coding is used. The 1 bit has a carrier signal, while the 0 bit is represented by no signal, which represents ON/OFF Keying (OOK). Like AM, it is affected by noise and distortion; however, both modulation and demodulation techniques are low cost.

Advantages of ASK are:

- It is used for transmitting digital data through fiber.
- Less energy is needed to transmit the information.

A disadvantage of ASK is:

- It requires extra bandwidth, which wastes power.

Frequency Shift Keying (FSK)

Frequency Shift Keying (FSK) is a modulation technique that is the same as FM (Figure 2-14). In this modulation, amplitude and phase remain constant. The value of the frequency is changed according to the discrete values of the modulating signal. Different frequencies are used for denoting bit 0 and bit 1, so the frequencies are transmitted in opposite directions, thus avoiding the overlapping of frequencies. It avoids most of the problems from noise, making it less susceptible to noise than ASK.

The advantages of FSK are:

- It is suitable for full-duplex transmission and is denoted by Digital FM (DFM).
- It is used in radio broadcasting transmission.
- Less bandwidth is required, so FSK supports 1200 bps or more bit rate.
- It is used in low-speed asynchronous application of data transmission.
- It is used in LANs by using broadcast-based networks.

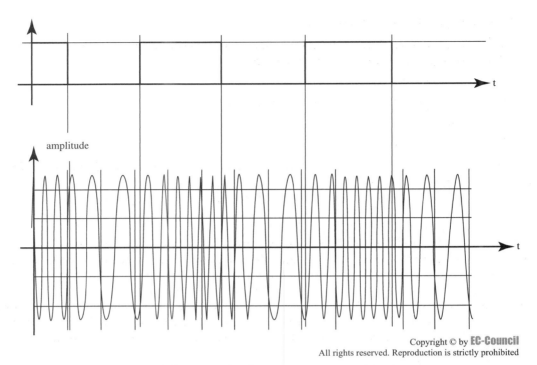

Figure 2-14   Frequency Shift Keying (FSK).

Phase Shift Keying (PSK)

Phase Shift Keying (PSK) is a binary modulation technique that is the same as PM. In this technique, both the peak amplitude and frequency remain constant while the phase gets changed according to the value 0 or 1. In this modulation, the current phase is compared with the phase of the previous state. The minimum bandwidth required for PSK transmission is the same as for ASK. It is used in WLAN.

Various PSK techniques are as follows:

- Binary Phase Shift Keying (BPSK) is a simple form of PSK. In this PSK, two phases (0 and 180) are used, which is why it is known as 2-PSK or binary PSK (BPSK). In BPSK, alternative sine waves are used for encoding the bits. The bandwidth is the same as the bandwidth of ASK. In BPSK, the signaling rate is equal to the bit rate. BPSK is more robust compared to other PSKs. It is generally used in satellite communication.

- Differential Phase Shift Keying (DPSK) is a simple form of coding. In this PSK, the modulating signal is not the binary code, but this code determines the variations in the binary code. Here, the two phases of successive symbols are compared to determine the data rather than doing demodulation. The demodulator is necessary to determine the changes in the incoming signal.

  The PSK signal is changed to a DPSK signal by the following rules:

  - A 1 in the PSK signal is indicated by no change in the DPSK signal
  - A 0 in the PSK signal is indicated by a change in the DPSK signal

- Quadrature Phase Shift Keying (QPSK) is also known as 4PSK. QPSK has 4 phases (0, 90, 135, and 180 degrees). QPSK uses four points and encodes two bits of information. It is a multilevel modulation technique. The bandwidth of QPSK is half the bandwidth of PSK.

Spread Spectrum

Spread spectrum is a form of wireless communication in which the frequency of the transmitted signal is deliberately varied; it uses a narrow signal, which it spreads over broad areas. This spectrum makes jamming and interception harder because interference affects only a small part of the signal rather than the entire signal.

The advantages of spread spectrum are:

- The signal gets spread over a broad frequency band, meaning less power spectral density is required and thus ensuring it does not affect other communication systems.
- It is resistant to interference.
- Users can set their transmission at any random time.
- Reduction of multipath effects.
- It has good antijam performance.

Spread spectrum uses two different methods: Frequency-Hopping Spread Spectrum (FHSS) and Direct Sequence Spread Spectrum (DSSS).

Frequency-Hopping Spread Spectrum (FHSS)

In *frequency-hopping spread spectrum (FHSS)*, instead of sending the signal on a single frequency, it is broadcast over a number of frequencies. The frequencies are changed during the transmission of the signal. In FHSS, transmission is done in bursts; a small burst is transmitted on one frequency, and then another burst is transmitted on another frequency. This process is continued until the end of transmission.

In FHSS, the receiver must know the hopping code to receive the transmitted signal correctly. During the transmission, if interference occurs on a given frequency, then that burst is transmitted over the next frequency. The FHSS signal gets affected by the interfering signal when both are transmitted at the same time and same frequency.

The advantages of FHSS are:

- Eavesdroppers hear only meaningless blips because FHSS appears for a very short duration.
- If any frequency gets jammed, only that part of the frequency gets affected, rather than the whole signal.
- The affected part of the signal can be retransmitted on another frequency.

Direct Sequence Spread Spectrum (DSSS)

Direct sequence spread spectrum (DSSS) is the best form of the spread spectrum technique. In this technique, instead of sending one bit, numbers of bits are transmitted. For a signal bit, DSSS uses the spreading code; in other words, it uses a different sequence of bits. That code is known as the chipping code.

This chipping code spreads the signal across a large frequency band in direct proportion to the number of bits used. For a single bit, ten bits of spreading code are used and the bandwidth of the signal is 10 times larger than the single bit.

Here is one DSSS method:

- Use the spreading code for each bit; combine that spreading code with the input bit by using the X-OR operation.
- If the input bit is 1, then it inverts the spreading code; if it is 0, then it does not make any change to the spreading code.
- The bits that are to be obtained are transmitted as a signal to the receiver.
- The data rate is equal to the original spreading code.

The advantages of DSSS are:

- If interference occurs while sending the chipping code rather than a single bit, then a statistical technique on the receiver side recovers the original data and does not require retransmission.
- If a third user receives the signal, then it appears as noise and is rejected.
- It is more secure to send chipping code than a single bit.
- WLANs use DSSS.

Chapter Summary

- Wireless is a generic word used to describe communications in which electromagnetic waves or radio frequency carry a signal over a part of or the entire communication path.

- Analog signals are continuous electrical signals that vary in both time and amplitude. Digital signals are noncontinuous, quantized signals that consist of patterns of bits of information.

- Radio waves are easy to generate, can travel long distances, and penetrate buildings.

- Infrared light lies between the visible and microwave portions of the electromagnetic spectrum.

- The components that allow communication through RF are filters, mixers, and amplifiers.

- Based on the direction of flow of data, the transmission of data can be classified into simplex transmission, half-duplex transmission, and full-duplex transmission.

- Switching involves moving the signal from one frequency to another.

- Ultra WideBand is a wireless technology for transmitting large amounts of digital data over a wide spectrum of frequency bands with low power for a short distance.

- Modulation is the process of changing the carrier signal in such a way that allows it to be used for transmitting information.

- Spread spectrum is a form of wireless communication in which the frequency of the transmitted signal is deliberately varied.

Review Questions

1. Define bandwidth.

_____

_____

_____

_____

2. Explain the difference between analog and digital signals.

_____

_____

_____

_____

3. What are the different components of a radio transmission system?

_____

_____

_____

_____

4. _____ can be used in night-vision equipment.

5. What are the different types of switching?

_____

_____

_____

_____

6. What is the equation for signal-to-noise ratio?

   _____

   _____

   _____

   _____

7. Define analog and digital modulation.

   _____

   _____

   _____

   _____

8. What is UWB?

   _____

   _____

   _____

   _____

9. Explain how the transmission signal state changes with respect to strength, frequency, voltage, and phase angle.

   _____

   _____

   _____

   _____

10. What is spread spectrum?

   _____

   _____

   _____

   _____

Hands-On Projects

Please attempt the following exercises to reinforce what you have learned in this chapter. Keep a copy of your notes for future reference.

1. Identify the modes of signal transmission in your network.

2. Determine which type of filter and amplifier are used in your radio transmission system.

3. Identify the type of transmission your network supports: simplex, half-duplex, or full-duplex.

4. Determine the signal strength at various points within your wireless network.

5. Identify the types of modulations used for signal transmission in your network.

Chapter 3

Wireless Communication Standards

Objectives

After completing this chapter, you should be able to:

- Discuss the institutions that produce wireless communication standards
- List and discuss the IEEE standards:
  - 802.1x
  - 802.11 (Wi-Fi standard)
  - 802.15
  - 802.16
- List and discuss the ETSI standards:
  - HiperLAN
  - HiperMAN

Key Terms

ATM (Asynchronous Transfer Mode)   a cell relay network protocol that encodes data traffic into small, fixed-sized cells instead of variable-sized packets, as is done in packet-switched networks

MIMO (Multiple In/Multiple Out)   allows a wireless device to make more efficient use of data transmissions indoors

OFDM (Orthogonal Frequency-Division Multiplexing)   transmission technique based on the idea of frequency-division multiplexing (FDM), where multiple signals are sent out at different frequencies

QoS (Quality of Service)   capability of a network to provide better service to select network traffic over various technologies, including Frame Relay, ATM, and Ethernet

Introduction to Institutes Offering Wireless Communication Standards

Following are the institutes that offer wireless communication standards, along with a brief description of each.

Wi-Fi Alliance

According to the Wi-Fi Alliance Web site (About the Alliance), "Wi-Fi Alliance is a global, nonprofit organization with the goal of driving the adoption of a single, worldwide accepted standard for high-speed wireless local area networking. . . . As Wi-Fi networks continue to expand through businesses, homes, and now public hotspots that provide wireless access locations for people on the go, compatibility is critical. The Wi-Fi Alliance develops rigorous tests and conducts Wi-Fi certification of wireless devices that implement the universal IEEE 802.11 specifications. The end result leads to the confidence that both home and enterprise users need to continue to embrace Wi-Fi."[1]

WLANA (Wireless LAN Association)

According to the WLANA Web site (About WLANA), "The Wireless LAN Association is a nonprofit educational trade association, comprised of the thought leaders and technology innovators in the local area wireless technology industry. Through the vast knowledge and experience of Sponsor and Affiliate members, WLANA provides a clearinghouse of information about wireless local area applications, issues, and trends, and serves as a resource to customers and prospects of wireless local area products and wireless personal area products and to industry press and analysts."[2]

IETF (Internet Engineering Task Force)

According to the IETF Web site (Overview of the IETF), "The Internet Engineering Task Force (IETF) is a large open international community of network designers, operators, vendors, and researchers concerned with the evolution of the Internet architecture and the smooth operation of the Internet. It is open to any interested individual. The IETF Mission Statement is documented in RFC 3935.

The actual technical work of the IETF is done in its working groups, which are organized by topic into several areas (e.g., routing, transport, security, etc.). . . . The Internet Assigned Numbers Authority (IANA) is the central coordinator for the assignment of unique parameter values for Internet protocols."[3]

ISO (International Organization for Standardization)

According to the ISO Web site (About ISO), "ISO (International Organization for Standardization) is the world's largest developer of standards. Although ISO's principal activity is the development of technical standards, ISO standards also have important economic and social repercussions. The International Standards which ISO develops are useful to industrial and business organizations of all types, to governments and other regulatory bodies, to trade officials, to conformity assessment professionals, to suppliers and customers of products and services in both public and private sectors, and, ultimately, to people in general in their roles as consumers and end users."[4]

ITU (International Telecommunication Union)

According to the ITU Web site, "The ITU, headquartered in Geneva, Switzerland, is an international organization within the United Nations System where governments and the private sector coordinate global telecom networks and services. The major purpose of ITU is to maintain and extend international cooperation between all its Member States for the improvement and rational use of telecommunications of all kinds. It promotes and enhances participation of entities and organizations in the activities of the Union, and to foster fruitful cooperation and partnership between them and Member States for the fulfillment of the overall objectives embodied in the purposes of the Union."[5]

ANSI (American National Standards Institute)

According to the ANSI Web site (About ANSI), "The American National Standards Institute (ANSI) coordinates the development and use of voluntary consensus standards in the United States and represents the needs and views of U.S. stakeholders in standardization forums around the globe. The Institute oversees the creation, promulgation, and use of thousands of norms and guidelines that directly impact businesses in nearly every sector: from acoustical devices to construction equipment, from dairy and livestock production to energy distribution, and many more. ANSI is also actively engaged in accrediting programs that assess conformance to standards—including globally recognized cross-sector programs such as the ISO 9000 (quality) and ISO 14000 (environmental) management systems."[6]

FCC (Federal Communications Commission)

According to the FCC Web site (About the FCC), "The Federal Communications Commission (FCC) is an independent United States government agency, directly responsible to Congress. The FCC was established by the Communications Act of 1934 and is charged with regulating interstate and international communications by radio, television, wire, satellite, and cable. The FCC's jurisdiction covers the 50 states, the District of Columbia, and U.S. possessions. It oversees cellular and PCS phones, pagers, and two-way radios. This bureau also regulates the use of radio spectrum to fulfill the communications needs of businesses, local and state governments, public-safety service providers, aircraft and ship operators, and individuals."[7]

UL (Underwriters Laboratories Inc.)

According to the UL Web site (About UL), "Underwriters Laboratories Inc. (UL) is an independent, not-for-profit, product-safety testing and certification organization. They have tested products for public safety for more than a century. UL is becoming one of the most recognized, reputable conformity assessment providers in the world. Today, their services extend to helping companies achieve global acceptance, whether for an electrical device, a programmable system, or an organization's quality process."[8]

IEEE (Institute of Electrical and Electronics Engineers):

According to the IEEE Web site (About IEEE), "The IEEE, a nonprofit organization, is the world's leading professional association for the advancement of technology. The IEEE is a leading developer of standards that underpin many of today's technologies. Their standards are developed in a unique environment that builds consensus in an open process based on input from all interested parties. With nearly 1,300 standards either completed or under development, they are a central source of standardization in both traditional and emerging fields, particularly telecommunications, information technology, and power generation."[9]

ETSI (European Telecommunications Standards Institute):

According to the ETSI Web site (About ETSI), "The European Telecommunications Standards Institute (ETSI) is an independent, nonprofit organization, whose mission is to produce telecommunications standards for today and for the future. Based in Sophia Antipolis (France), the European Telecommunications Standards Institute (ETSI) is officially responsible for standardization of Information and Communication Technologies (ICT) within Europe. These technologies include telecommunications, broadcasting, and related areas such as intelligent transportation and medical electronics."[10]

IEEE

This section focuses on the IEEE standards that cover wireless communication.

"IEEE standards encompass a striking range of industries. They address significant topics in high-impact technologies, whether for existing infrastructures basic to our society or disciplines that promise to change the nature of our world. Some of the fields our standards cover are:

- Information technology
- Power and energy
- Instrumentation and measurement
- Internet best practices
- Mobile and stationary batteries
- Nanotechnology
- Organic electronics

- Telecommunications, especially wired and wireless networking for personal, local, and metropolitan area networks
- Transportation safety, especially highway communications and rail safety

Benefits of Standards

Access to and participation in standards provides:

- Market growth for new and emerging technologies
- Reduced development time and cost
- Sound engineering practices
- Decreased trading costs and lowered trade barriers
- Increased product quality and safety
- Reduced market risks
- Protection against obsolescence"[11]

IEEE Standards

The (IEEE) Institute of Electrical and Electronics Engineering includes the following standards for wireless communication:

- 802.1x: An IEEE standard that attaches EAP (Extensible Authentication Protocol) over wired or wireless Ethernet, and provides several authentication techniques like token cards, Kerberos, certificates, and public key authentication.
- 802.11: A working group for WLAN. It denotes an "over the air" interface between a wireless client and a base station or access point.
  - 802.11a: Has a data transfer rate up to 26.4 Mbps, and it works at 40 MHz, in the 5-GHz range.
  - 802.11b: Works at 20 MHz, in the 2.4-GHz range, and it has *theoretical* speeds of up to 11 Mbps.
  - 802.11e: Provides quality-of-service (QoS) support for LAN applications. *Quality of service (QoS)* is the capability of a network to provide better service to select network traffic over various technologies, including Frame Relay, ATM, and Ethernet. *ATM (Asynchronous Transfer Mode)* is a cell relay network protocol that encodes data traffic into small, fixed-sized cells instead of variable-sized packets, as is done in packet-switched networks.
  - 802.11g: Works at the same frequency range as 802.11b; it has theoretical throughput of 54 Mbps.
  - 802.11h: Supplementary standard for the MAC layer to comply with European regulations for 5-GHz WLANs.
  - 802.11i: A standard for WLAN that provides better encryption for networks that use the popular 802.11a, 802.11b, and 802.11g standards.
  - 802.11j: An amendment of IEEE 802.11 to enable it to adopt new frequencies, different channel widths, operating parameters, and various applications.
  - 802.11k: A proposed standard specifically for radio resource management.
  - 802.11m: A proposal that started as a part of the 802.11 working group that is sometimes referred to as 802.11 housekeeping or 802.11 cleanup proposal.
  - 802.11n: Based on multiple in/multiple out (MIMO) technology; *MIMO (Multiple In/Multiple Out)* allows a wireless device to make more efficient use of data transmissions indoors.
- 802.15: Supplies standards for low-complexity and low-power-consumption wireless connectivity
- 802.16: A broadband wireless access group that provides standards for WMAN.
- P1451.5: A working group for a wireless standard that provides wireless communication methods and data formats for transducers (sensors and actuators).

Figure 3-1 illustrates the 802.x architecture.

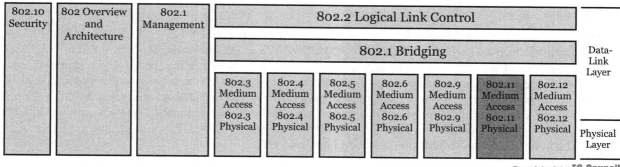

Figure 3-1   802.*x* architecture.

802.1*x*

802.1*x* is an IEEE standard that attaches EAP (Extendable Authentication Protocol) over wired or wireless Ethernet, and provides several authentication techniques like token cards, Kerberos, certificates, and public key authentication. 802.1*x* provides an authenticating and authorizing device to attach with LAN ports for the purpose of requesting and giving the authentication.

802.1*x* describes three different roles for communication:

1. *Supplicant*: The user or the client requesting the authentication.

2. *Authentication server*: The server that provides the authentication. It already has the data; if it matches the supplicant request, it then gives the authentication.

3. *Authenticator*: The device that accesses the request from the supplicant and gives it to the server. If the data provided by the supplicant matches the data in the server, the server then authenticates the supplicant and sends the response.

802.1*x* requires less power on the part of authenticator, so it is better for the wireless LAN application. The 802.11i RSN (Robust Security Network) makes the use of 802.1*x* for the purpose of authenticating wireless devices to the network.

802.11 (Wi-Fi Standard)

"The IEEE is developing an international WLAN standard identified as IEEE 802.11. This project was initiated in 1990, and several draft standards have been published for review. The scope of the standard is 'to develop a media access control (MAC) and physical layer (PHY) specification for wireless connectivity for fixed, portable, and moving stations within a local area.' The purpose of the standard is twofold:

- To provide wireless connectivity to automatic machinery, equipment, or stations that require rapid deployment, which may be portable, or handheld, or which may be mounted on moving vehicles within a local area.

- To offer a standard for use by regulatory bodies to standardize access to one or more frequency bands for the purpose of local area communication.

The IEEE 802.11 draft standard describes mandatory support for a 1-Mbps WLAN with optional support for a 2-Mbps data transmission rate. Mandatory support for asynchronous data transfer is specified as well as optional support for distributed time-bounded services (DTBS). Asynchronous data transfer refers to traffic that is relatively insensitive to time delay. Examples of asynchronous data are available bit rate traffic like electronic mail and file transfers. Time-bounded traffic, on the other hand, is traffic that is bounded by specified time delays to achieve an acceptable quality of service (QoS) (e.g., packetized voice and video)."[12]

802.11 Architecture

"The basic service set (BSS) is the fundamental building block of the IEEE 802.11 architecture. A BSS is defined as a group of stations that are under the direct control of a single coordination function (i.e., a DCF or PCF). The geographical area covered by the BSS is known as the basic service area (BSA), which is analogous to a cell in a cellular communications network. Conceptually, all stations in a BSS can communicate directly with all other stations in a BSS. However, transmission medium degradations due to multipath fading, or interference from nearby BSSs reusing the same physical-layer characteristics (e.g., frequency and spreading code, or hopping pattern), can cause some stations to appear 'hidden' from other stations."[13]

802.11 Architecture includes the following components:

- *STA (Station)*: The wireless station includes an adapter card, PC Card, or an embedded device that gives wireless connectivity.
- *AP (Wireless Access Point)*: The wireless AP works as a bridge between the wireless STAs and the existing network backbone for network access. APs are usually connected with wires. The AP gives connectivity to the wired LAN and supports the bridging functionality when one STA starts communicating with another STA or a node on the DS.
- *IBSS (Independent Basic Service Set)*: A wireless network consisting of a minimum of two stations. It is also known as an ad hoc wireless network, meaning no access point.
- *BSS (Basic Service Set)*: A wireless network consisting of a single AP. It supports one or many wireless clients. It is also known as infrastructure wireless network. STAs in a BSS communicate through the AP.
- *DS (Distribution System)*: The APs of different BSSs are connected by a DS. The DS is the component that interconnects the BSS. The DS offers services that allow the roaming of STAs between BSSs.
- *ESS (Extended Service Set)*: An ESS is a set in which two or more wireless APs are connected to the same wired network that defines a single logical network segment bounded by a router (known as a subnet).

Figure 3-2 illustrates ESS and IBSS architecture.

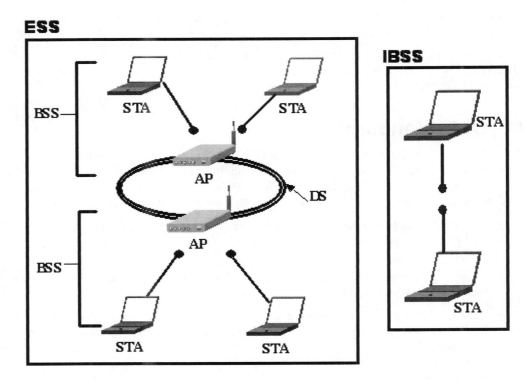

Figure 3-2   ESS and IBSS architecture.

Standard	802.11a	802.11b	802.11g
Speed	54 Mbps	11 Mbps	54 Mbps
Frequency	5 GHz	2.4 GHz	2.4 GHz
Non-overlapping channels	4	3	3
Range	10–60 m	50–90 m	20–90 m
Security standards	WEP, WPA	WEP, WPA	WPA 802.11i

Table 3-1   Specifications for 802.11a, 802.11b, and 802.11g

802.11 Standards

Table 3-1 summarizes the specifications for standards 802.11a, 802.11b, and 802.11g.

802.11a

802.11a is an amendment to 802.11 specifications for wireless LANs. Following are the basic features of the 802.11a standard:

- Works at 40 MHz, in the 5-GHz range
- Theoretical transfer rates of up to 54 Mbps
- Actual transfer rates of approximately 26.4 Mbps
- Use is limited as it is almost a line-of-sight transmittal that requires multiple WAPs (wireless access points)
- Uses a modulation technique called coded orthogonal frequency-division multiplexing (COFDM)
- Cannot operate in the same range as 802.11b/g
- Absorbed more easily than other wireless signals
- Overcomes the challenge of indoor radio frequency; that is, it is not affected by devices such as microwave ovens and cordless phones.
- It uses a single-carrier, delay-spread system

802.11b

802.11b is an amendment to 802.11. Following are the basic features of the 802.11b standard:

- Operates at 20 MHz, in the 2.4-GHz range
- Most widely used and accepted form of wireless networking
- Theoretical speeds of up to 11 Mbps
- Actual speeds depend on implementation:
  - 5.9 Mbps when TCP (Transmission Control Protocol) is used
    - error checking
  - 7.1 Mbps when UDP (User Datagram Protocol) is used
    - no error checking
- Can transmit up to 8 kilometers in the city
- Not as easily absorbed as 802.11a signal
- Can cause or receive interference from:
  - Microwave ovens (microwaves in general)
  - Wireless telephones
  - Other wireless appliances operating in the same frequency

802.11e

Qos Support Mechanisms of 802.11e "To support QoS, there are priority schemes currently under discussion. IEEE 802.11 Task Group E currently defines enhancements to the 802.11 MAC, called 802.11e, which introduces EDCF (Enhanced Distributed Coordination Function) and HCF (Hybrid Coordination Function). Stations, which operate under 802.11e, are called enhanced stations, and an enhanced station, which may optionally work as the centralized controller for all other stations within the same QBSS, is called the Hybrid Coordinator (HC). A QBSS is a BSS (Basic Service Set), which includes an 802.11e-compliant HC and stations. The HC will typically reside within an 802.11e AP. In the following, we mean 802.11e-compliant enhanced stations by stations.

With 802.11e, there may still be the two phases of operation within the superframes, i.e., a CP (Contention Period) and a CFP (Contention-Free Period), which alternate over time continuously. The EDCF is used in the CP only, while the HCF is used in both phases, which makes this new coordination function hybrid.

Enhanced Distributed Coordination Function The EDCF in 802.11e is the basis for the HCF. The QoS support is realized with the introduction of Traffic Categories (TCs). MSDUs are now delivered through multiple backoff instances within one station, each backoff instance parameterized with TC-specific parameters. In the CP, each TC within the stations contends for a TXOP (Transmission Opportunity) and independently starts a backoff after detecting the channel being idle for an Arbitration Interframe Space (AIFS); the AIFS is at least DIFS, and can be enlarged individually for each TC. After waiting for AIFS, each backoff sets a counter to a random number drawn from the interval [*1,CW+1*]. The minimum size (*CWmin[TC]*) of the CW is another parameter dependent on the TC. Priority over legacy stations is provided by setting *CWmin[TC]<15* (in case of 802.11a PHY) and *AIFS=DIFS*. As in legacy DCF, when the medium is determined busy before the counter reaches zero, the backoff has to wait for the medium being idle for AIFS again, before continuing to count down the counter. A big difference from the legacy DCF is that when the medium is determined as being idle for the period of AIFS, the backoff counter is reduced by one beginning the last slot interval of the AIFS period.

One crucial feature of 802.11e MAC is the Transmission Opportunity (TXOP). A TXOP is defined as an interval of time when a station has the right to initiate transmissions, defined by a starting time and a maximum duration. TXOPs are allocated via contention (EDCF-TXOP) or granted through HCF (polled-TXOP). The duration of an EDCF-TXOP is limited by a QBSS-wide TXOP limit distributed in beacon frames, while the duration of a polled TXOP is specified by the duration field inside the poll frame. However, although the poll frame is a new frame as part of the upcoming 802.11e, also the legacy stations set their NAVs upon receiving this frame."[14]

802.11g

"In June 2003, a third modulation standard was ratified: 802.11g. This flavor works in the 2.4-GHz band (like 802.11b) but operates at a maximum raw data rate of 54 Mbps, or about 24.7 Mbps net throughput like 802.11a. 802.11g hardware will work with 802.11b hardware. Details of making b and g work well together occupied much of the lingering technical process. In older networks, however, the presence of an 802.11b participant significantly reduces the speed of an 802.11g network. The modulation scheme used in 802.11g is orthogonal frequency-division multiplexing (OFDM) for the data rates of 6, 9, 12, 18, 24, 36, 48, and 54 Mbps, and reverts to (like the 802.11b standard) CCK for 5.5 and 11 Mbps and DBPSK/DQPSK+DSSS for 1 and 2 Mbps. Even though 802.11g operates in the same frequency band as 802.11b, it can achieve higher data rates because of its similarities to 802.11a. The maximum range of 802.11g devices is slightly greater than that of 802.11b devices, but the range in which a client can achieve full (54 Mbps) data rate speed is much shorter than that of 802.11b.

The 802.11g standard swept the consumer world of early adopters starting in January 2003, well before ratification. The corporate users held back and Cisco and other big equipment makers waited until ratification. By summer 2003, announcements were flourishing. Most of the dual-band 802.11a/b products became dual-band/tri-mode, supporting a, b, and g in a single mobile adaptor card or access point. Despite its major acceptance, 802.11g suffers from the same interference as 802.11b in the already crowded 2.4-GHz range. Devices operating in this range include microwave ovens, Bluetooth devices, and cordless telephones."[15]

Following are the basic features of the 802.11g standard:

- Operates at the same frequency range as 802.11b

- Theoretical throughput of 54 Mpbs

- Several factors are responsible for actual transmission rate, but averages 24.7 Mbps

- Logical improvement over 802.11b wireless networks is "backward compatibile"
- Suffers from same limitations as 802.11b network
- If network is not completely improved from 802.11b, then the systems may experience significant decrease in network speeds

802.11h

"The amendment, IEEE 802.11h™, 'Wireless LAN Medium Access Control (MAC) and Physical Layer (PHY) Specifications, Spectrum and Transmit Power Management Extensions in the 5-GHz Band in Europe,' allows WLANs to meet regulations initially adopted by European countries and then made a global requirement of the ITU Radio Regulations at World Radiocommunication Conference 03.

'IEEE 802.11h should help open the 5-GHz spectrum to WLANs in the many countries that have been concerned about the interference issues posed by wireless networks in this frequency band,' said Stuart J. Kerry, Chairman of the IEEE P802.11 Standards Committee. 'This amendment is part of the IEEE 802.11 Working Group's commitment to create standards for all aspects of wireless LAN operation worldwide.'

"ITU Radio Regulations call for WLANs and other devices to detect the presence of radars and EESS and SRS systems and then protect them from interference by selecting another operating channel or reducing transmit power. IEEE 802.11h creates a standard method to avoid interference so a manufacturer can create products that adhere to the ITU Radio Regulations and interoperate with similar products from other suppliers.

IEEE 802.11h amends the IEEE 802.11a PHY layer standard and the underlying IEEE 802.11 MAC layer standard to enhance network management and control extensions for spectrum and transmit power management in 5-GHz license-exempt bands. It improves channel energy measurement and reporting, channel coverage in many regulatory domains, and dynamic channel selection and transmit power control mechanisms."[16]

802.11i

802.11i is an IEEE WLAN standard that offers an enhanced encryption mechanism for wireless networks that utilize the popular 802.11a, 802.11b, and 802.11g standards. The 802.11i standard was officially ratified by the IEEE in June of 2004. Security is made up of three parts:

1. 802.1x for authentication (EAP and authentication server)
2. Robust security network (RSN) to keep track of associations
3. Countermode/CBC-MAC Protocol (CCMP) to provide confidentiality, integrity, and origin authentication

Table 3-2 summarizes the proposed Protocol Implementation Conformance Statement (PICS) for IEEE 802.11i. Proposed modifications to P802.11p PICs are as follows.

A.4.4.1 MAC Protocol Capabilities[17] Add the following, (where "X" in PCX is the next number for the protocol capabilities).

Item	Protocol Capability	References	Status	Support
	Are the following MAC protocol capabilities supported?			
PCX	Robust Security Network (RSN)		O	Yes o No o
PCX.1	RSN IE	7.3.2.17	PCX:M, FT1:M, FR1:M, FT2:M, FR2:M, FT3:M, FR3:M, FT4:M, FR4:M, FT6:M, FR6:M, FT7:M, FR7:M	Yes o No o
PCX.1.1	Group Key Cipher Suite	7.3.2.17	PCX.1:M	Yes o No o
PCX.1.2	Pairwise Key Cipher Suite List	7.3.2.17	PCX.1:M	Yes o No o
PCX.1.2.1	CCMP data privacy protocol	8.3.4	PCX:M	Yes o No o

Table 3-2 **Summary of the proposed Protocol Implementation Conformance Statement (PICS) for IEEE 802.11i** *(continues)*

Item	Protocol Capability	References	Status	Support
PCX.1.2.1.1	CCMP encapsulation procedure	8.3.4.1.1	PCX.1.2.1:M	Yes o No o
PCX.1.2.1.2	CCMP decapsulation procedure	8.3.4.1.2	PCX.1.2.1:M	Yes o No o
PCX.1.2.1.3	CCMP Security Serv. Mng.		M	Yes o No o
PCX.1.2.2	TKIP data privacy protocol	8.3.2	O	Yes o No o
PCX.1.2.2.1	TKIP encapsulation procedure	8.3.2.1.1	PCX.1.2.2:M	Yes o No o
PCX.1.2.2.2	TKIP decapsulation procedure	8.3.2.1.2	PCX.1.2.2:M	Yes o No o
PCX.1.2.2.3	TKIP counter measures	8.3.2.4.2	PCX.1.2.2:M	Yes o No o
PCX.1.2.2.4	TKIP Security Serv. Mng.		M	Yes o No o
PCX.1.2.3	WRAP data privacy protocol	8.3.3	O	Yes o No o
PCX.1.2.3.1	WRAP encapsulation procedure	8.3.3.1.1	PCX.1.2.3:M	Yes o No o
PCX.1.2.3.2	WRAP decapsulation procedure	8.3.3.1.2	PCX.1.2.3:M	Yes o No o
PCX.1.2.3.3	WRAP Security Serv. Mng.		M	Yes o No o
PCX.1.3	Auth. Key Mng. Suite List	7.3.2.17	PCX.1:M	Yes o No o
PCX.1.3.1	Unspec. EAP/802.11i Key Mng.	7.3.2.17	PCX.1:M	Yes o No o
PCX.1.3.2	Preshard key/802.11i Key Mng.	7.3.2.17	PCX.1:M	Yes o No o
PCX.1.3.3	802.11i Key Mng.	8.5	PCX.1:M	Yes o No o
PCX.1.3.3.1	Key Hierarchy	8.5	PCX.1:M	Yes o No o
PCX.1.3.3.1.1	Pairwise Key Hierarchy	8.5.1.2	PCX.1:M	Yes o No o
PCX.1.3.3.1.2	Group Key Hierarchy	8.5.1.3	PCX.1:M	Yes o No o
PCX.1.3.3.2	4-way handshake	8.5.3	PCX.1:M	Yes o No o
PCX.1.3.3.3	Group key handshake	8.5.4	PCX.1:M	Yes o No o
PCX.1.4	RSN Capabilities	7.3.2.17	PCX.1:M	Yes o No o

Table 3-2 Summary of the proposed Protocol Implementation Conformance Statement (PICS) for IEEE 802.11i *continued*

802.11j

IEEE 802.11j is an amendment to IEEE 802.11 that enables it to adopt new frequencies, different channel widths, operating parameters, and various applications. It presents international support and adaptability of IEEE standards.

This amendment is specifically made to work in Japan to maintain the new spectrum and their designated applications as new wireless bands for indoor, outdoor, and wireless have emerged there.

The foremost international experts produced this standard to permit WLAN devices to operate in new frequencies and operating modes. It is a wireless LAN media access control (MAC) and physical layer (PHY) specification. It operates in the range of 4.9–5 GHz in Japan.

The Japanese government has laid down new rules to employ 4.9- and 5-GHz bands in the following modes using wireless LAN technology:

- Hotspot (indoor)
- Fixed (outdoor)
- Nomadic (mobile)

802.11k

IEEE 802.11k is a proposed standard specifically for radio resource management. It is intended to improve the way traffic is distributed in a wireless network. 802.11k defines and describes radio and network information for maintaining the mobile and wireless LAN.

It is one of the key industry standards that give flawless Basic Service Set (BSS) transitions in the WLAN environment. The best available access points can be discovered using the information given by 802.11k.

It executes important portions of the IEEE standards and specifications. It is compatible with the IEEE 802.11 MAC.

802.11m

IEEE 802.11m is a proposal that has started as a part of the 802.11 working group and is sometimes called the 802.11 housekeeping or 802.11 cleanup proposal. It executes the following tasks related to documentation for 802.11 family specifications:

- Editorial maintenance
- Corrections
- Improvements
- Clarifications
- Interpretations

802.11n

802.11n is the next-generation Wi-Fi standard developed by Task Group N of IEEE. This standard merges the following to attain data rates up to 600 Mbps:

- Use of multiple antennas
- Cleverer encoding
- Optional doubling of spectrum

Following are the basic features of the 802.11n standard:

- It will be based on multiple in/multiple out (MIMO) technology and is expected to increase throughput to potentially well over 100 Mbps.
- It specifies improvements to the physical layer and media access control layer (PHY/MAC).
- 802.11n is supposed to have the following improvements over its predecessors:
  - Improved radio technology to increase physical data transfer
  - New methods to implement effective management of improved PHY performance modes
  - Improved data transfer efficiency to reduce the performance impacts of PHY headers and radio turn-around delays which adversely affect the physical transfer rate

802.11n: The Future of Wi-Fi "Today's Wi-Fi gear has limited range, is highly susceptible to interference from cordless phones and other wireless devices, and is much slower than old-fashioned Ethernet. All this is set to change with the advent of 802.11n. Products based on competing versions of 802.11n's powerful smart-antenna technology, called MIMO, are already on store shelves. MIMO stands for *multiple input multiple output* and allows a wireless device to make more efficient use of data transmissions in indoor environments. The new 802.11n will include some version of MIMO, and it promises to deliver faster throughput than Ethernet and double the range of today's Wi-Fi gear. We've already reviewed the first round of MIMO-enabled networking devices, including the Belkin Pre-N router, the Linksys WRT54GX, and the Netgear WPN824 RangeMax router, all of which offer clear performance gains over standard 802.11g gear."[18]

802.15

802.15 is a working group for Wireless Personal Area Network (WPAN). This IEEE 802.15 working group was formed in May 1999. It supplies standards for low-complexity and low-power-consumption wireless connectivity. Four active task groups of 802.15 are:

1. 802.15.1: This standard was published on June 14, 2002. It is an additional resource for Bluetooth devices and is a standard adaptation for Bluetooth specification. It specified a normative annex that provides a Protocol Implementation Conformance Statement (PICS).
2. 802.15.2: It was published in 2003. It provides coexistence of wireless personal area networks with other wireless devices operating in the unlicensed frequency band.
3. 802.15.3: It is a high-rate task group for WPANs. It provides a high rate up to 20 Mbps or greater. It also supports low power, and provides a low-cost solution for digital imaging and multimedia applications. It provides ad hoc peer-to-peer networking and strong security.

4. 802.15.4: It is working in an unlicensed, international frequency band. It has data rates of 250 Kbps, 40 Kbps, and 20 Kbps. It has two addressing modes: 16-bit short and 64-bit IEEE addressing. It supports critical latency devices, provides automatic network establishment by the coordinator, and supports power management to ensure low power consumption.

802.16

The IEEE 802.16 working group is a broadband wireless access group that provides standards for WMAN. It addresses the "first mile/last mile" connection in WMAN. It supports the use of bandwidth between 10 and 66 GHz, and describes a media access control (MAC) layer. It allows the interoperability between devices.

This standard supports the progress of fixed broadband wireless access systems to permit rapid worldwide operation of innovative, cost-effective, and interoperable multivendor broadband wireless access products. The 802.16 family of standards has been commercialized under the name WiMAX.

WiMAX

Created in April 2001, WiMAX is an acronym for Worldwide Interoperability for Microwave Access. It is a wireless technology that gives high-throughput broadband connection over large areas. It is planned in such a way that it performs like a wireless MAN. This technology allows the connection of all public wireless access points to each other and the Internet, enabling the delivery of last-mile wireless broadband access as an alternative to cable and DSL.

WiMax uses the point-to-multipoint transmission mode previously in a frequency range of 10 to 66 GHz, but new updated WiMAX provides a range up to 2 to 11 GHz. It also supports the connection of network endpoints without direct line of sight. It provides a linear service area range of up to 31 miles (45 km) and a data rate up to 75 Mbps.

Advantages of WiMAX are as follows:

- Used as a PMP broadband technology
- Provides users access to broadband data services
- Can connect Wi-Fi (802.11) hotspots with each other and the Internet
- Can be used as an alternative to cable and DSL ("last mile" broadband access)
- Allows services like VoIP (Voice over IP), video, and Internet access simultaneously
- Costs less and is easy to install

P1451.5

The IEEE P1451.5 working group is defining a wireless standard that provides wireless communication methods and data formats for transducers (sensors and actuators). It will improve the reception of wireless technology for transducers' connectivity. This standard defines Transducer Electronic Data Sheets (TEDS) that depend on the IEEE 1451 concept and protocols to access TEDS and transducer information.

It also accepts important wireless interfaces and protocols to make use of technically different, existing wireless technology easy. It never specifies the transducers' design, signal conditioning, or physical design of the wireless system.

ETSI Standards

ETSI (European Telecommunications Standards Institute) is an independent association that aims to provide telecommunication standards. ETSI generates the standards for ICT (Information and Communication Technologies) in Europe, which includes telecommunications, broadcasting, and related information about the communication world.

ETSI describes the following standards for wireless communication:

- *HiperLAN*: The best alternative to the IEEE 802.11 WLAN network used in the United States, it is a wireless LAN communication standards built by ETSI that includes:
  - *HiperLAN/1*: The first version of HiperLAN, it has the capacity to make communication up to 20 Mbps in the 5-GHz band.
  - *HiperLAN/2*: The second version of HiperLAN, it has the capacity to make communication up to 54 Mbps in the 5-GHz band.

- *HiperAccess*: Used for PMP communication.
- *Hyperlink*: Has a very high-speed interconnection of HiperLAN and HiperAccess.
- *HiperMAN*: It was developed by the ETSI BRAN group. It is an interoperable broadband fixed wireless communication access system. It operates at radio frequencies between the ranges of 2 and 11 GHz.

HiperLAN Family of Standards

Table 3-3 summarizes the HiperLAN family of standards.

HiperLAN/1

HiperLAN/1 operates at a bandwidth between 5.1 and 5.3 GHz, so it is not in conflict with microwaves. It is completely ad hoc, and does not require configuration and a central controller. Like 802.11, this standard contains the physical and MAC (media access control) part of the data-link layer. The new sublayer is known as the channel access and control sublayer (CAC). It compacts with the access request of the channel, depending on the usage of channel and the priority of request. From the CAC layer, hierarchical independence is obtained with the help of Elimination-Yield Non-Preemptive Multiple Access Mechanism (EY-NPMA).

Characteristics of HiperLAN/1 are as follows:

- Short range (up to 50 m)
- Mobility is low (up to 1.4 m/s)
- Supports both synchronous and asynchronous traffic
- Transmits sound at 32 Kbps, 10 ns latens
- Transmits video at 2 Mbps, 100 latens
- Transmits data at 10 Mbps; access is instantaneous

HiperLAN/2

HiperLAN/2 is an efficient, fast communication network design. It uses the 5-GHz band (5.4 to 5.7) and has a data rate up to 54 Mbps. It includes physical, data link control and a convergence layer. The convergence sublayer works on a physical layer to connect IP, ATM, and UMTS, making HiperLAN/2 suitable for wireless communication.

It supports high-speed access to various networks, such as:

- 3G mobile core network
- ATM network
- IP-based network
- WLAN system

Other features of HiperLAN/2 include:

- Supports high-speed data transmission
- Connections are either unidirectional, bidirectional, or multidirectional
- Allocates a particular quality of service in case of bandwidth, delay, bit error rate
- Supports automatic frequency allocation, which is already a built-in access point
- Provides authentication and encryption for security support

	HiperLAN/1	HiperLAN/2	HiperAccess	HiperLink
Application	Wireless Ethernet (LAN)	Wireless ATM	Wireless local loop	Wireless point-to-point
Frequency range	5 GHz	5 GHz	5 GHz	17 GHz
Data rate	23.5 Mbps	Approx. 20 Mbps	Approx. 20 Mbps	Approx. 155 Mbps

Table 3-3 HiperLAN family of standards

- Provides handover mobility support
- Is network and application independent
- Helps save power

Figure 3-3 shows a HiperLAN/2 radio network.

HiperAccess (High-Performance-Access Network Technology)

HiperAccess supports PMP networks. It is intended for high speed (up to 120 Mbps) and also supports high-QoS fixed wireless access. The HiperAccess standard supports a result for a frequency band above 11 GHz with high spectral efficiency under line of sight (LOS). It is an interoperable standard that supports a PMP system with base and terminal stations. It is used for these applications:

- Supports backhauling for a cellular network such as GSMTM and UMTSTM
- Provides broadband access for residential and business users in a wide variety of networks, such as UMTS core network, ATM network, and IP-based network

Here are some of the features of HiperAccess:

- Has efficient scheduling performance to support different services
- Provides full quality of service
- Provides efficient support of ATM and IP-based core networks
- Suitable for fast connection control management
- Provides strong security
- Supports fast adaptation of coding, modulation, and sends power to time-variant propagation and inter-ference conditions
- Supports robustness against loss of traffic and control information

HiperLink

HiperLink is a HiperLAN specification of HiperLAN built by TC (Technical Committee) BRAN (Broadband Radio Access Network). It supports the interconnection of HiperLANs and HiperAccess up to a short range but with very high speed (e.g., speed up to 155 Mbps over a distance of up to 150 m). The spectrum for HiperLink is accessible in the range of 17 GHz.

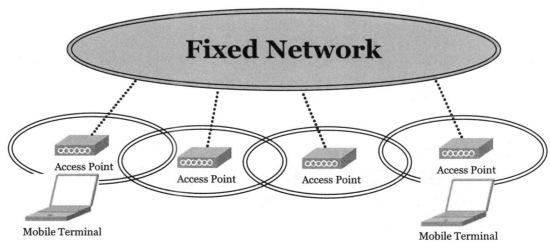

Figure 3-3 HiperLAN/2 radio network.

HiperMAN (High-Performance Radio Metropolitan Area Network)

HiperMAN is developed by the ETSI BRAN group. HiperMAN is an interoperable broadband fixed wireless communication access system. It operates at radio frequencies between the ranges of 2 GHz and 11 GHz, and supports data transmission using various broadband frequency ranges, which allows it to avoid interference with other wireless devices. HiperMAN is optimized for a packet-switched network.

Features of HiperMAN include:

- Permits PMP and flexible mesh pattern
- Provides frame-based transmission, where frame accepts variable length
- Provides full quality of services (QoS)
- Supports fast connection control management
- Provides strong security
- Can adapt coding fast
- Supports modulation and transmits the power to broadcast the condition

Chapter Summary

- The Institute of Electrical and Electronics Engineers is the world's leading professional association for the advancement of technology.
- 802.1x is an IEEE standard for EAP encapsulation over wired or wireless Ethernet.
- 802.11 is an IEEE standard for wireless local area networks (WLANs).
- 802.11e provides quality of service (QoS) support for LAN applications.
- 802.11g employs orthogonal frequency-division multiplexing (OFDM), the modulation scheme used in 802.11a, to obtain higher data speed.
- 802.11h is supplementary for the MAC layer to comply with European regulations for 5-GHz WLANs.
- 802.11i is a standard for wireless local area networks that provides improved encryption for networks that use the popular 802.11a, 802.11b, and 802.11g standards.
- The IEEE 802.16 or Broadband Wireless Access Working Group provides standards for WMANs.
- The European Telecommunications Standards Institute (ETSI) is an independent, nonprofit organization, whose mission is to produce telecommunications standards for today and for the future.
- HiperLAN is a set of WLAN communication standards, developed by the European Telecommunications Standards Institute.
- HiperLAN/2 is a flexible radio LAN standard that defines an efficient, high-speed wireless LAN technology that fully meets the requirements of Europe's spectrum regulation.
- HiperAccess is based on a point-to-multipoint (PMP) network architecture and is intended for high speed (up to 120 Mbps) and high-QoS fixed wireless access.
- The HiperLink specifications are being developed by TC (Technical Commitee) BRAN.

Review Questions

1. _____ is an IEEE standard for EAP encapsulation over wired or wireless Ethernet.

2. What are the components of 802.11 architecture?

_____

_____

_____

_____

3. Compare speed, frequency, number of nonoverlapping channels, range, and security standards supported by different 802.11 standards.

_____

_____

_____

_____

4. 802.11a operates at the frequency of _____.

5. What is WiMAX?

_____

_____

_____

_____

6. _____ is a cell relay network protocol that encodes data traffic into small, fixed-sized cells instead of variable-sized packets as in packet-switched networks.

7. Explain the role of ETSI standards in wireless communication.

_____

_____

_____

_____

8. How would you define orthogonal frequency-division multiplexing (OFDM)?

_____

_____

_____

_____

9. Define the term HiperLAN and give its versions.

_____

_____

_____

_____

10. Which of the following standards is developed by the Broadband Wireless Access Working Group of IEEE?

_____

_____

_____

_____

Hands-On Projects

Please complete the following projects to reinforce what you have learned in this chapter. Write down your observations or process notes for later reference.

1. Visit *http://www.ieee.org* and read all the wireless communication standards. Write a summary for all the standards.

2. Determine which IEEE standard your network supports.

3. Check whether your wireless network supports WiMAX technology.

4. Visit *http://www.etsi.org* and read all the wireless communication standards. Write a summary for all the standards.

5. Determine which ETSI standard your network supports.

Endnotes

[1] www.wi-fi.org (accessed June 2008).

[2] www.wlana.org (accessed June 2008).

[3] www.ietf.org (accessed June 2008).

[4] www.iso.org (accessed June 2008).

[5] www.itu.int (accessed June 2008).

[6] www.ansi.org (accessed June 2008).

[7] www.fcc.gov (accessed June 2008).

[8] www.ul.com (accessed June 2008).

[9] www.ieee.org (accessed June 2008).

[10] www.etsi.org

[11] http://www.ieee.org/web/standards/home/index.html (accessed June 2008).

[12] "An Abstract on IEEE 802.11 Wireless Local Area Networks," http://mia.ece.uic.edu/~papers/net/pdf00001 .pdf (accessed June 2008).

[13] http://mia.ece.uic.edu/~papers/net/pdf00001.pdf

[14] Mangold S., C. Sunghyun, P. May, O. Klein, G. Hiertz, and L. Stibor "IEEE 802.11e Wireless LAN for Quality of Service," ComNets RWTH, Aachen University of Technology (Aachen, Germany); Philips Research USA (Briarcliff Manor, New York, USA); Philips Research Germany (Aachen, Germany), http://www.mwnl .snu.ac.kr/~schoi/publication/Conferences/02-EW.pdf (accessed May 4, 2009).

[15] Wikipedia (accessed June 2008).

[16] IEEE. "Amendment to IEEE 802.11a™ Avoids Interference with Other 5 GHz-Band Devices," September 19, 2003. http://standards.ieee.org/announcements/pr_80211hwlan.html (accessed May 4, 2009).

[17] http://www.ieee802.org/11/Documents/DocumentHolder/2-647.zip (accessed June 2008).

[18] Fear, A. "Catch the New Wave in Wireless Networking: 802.11n," *CNET Reviews* September 26, 2005. http://reviews.cnet.com/4520-3243_7-5124418.html (accessed May 4, 2009).

Chapter 4

WLAN and Operations

Objectives

After completing this chapter, you should be able to:

- Define WLAN
- Explain the advantages of using a WLAN
- List the basic components of a WLAN
- Access a WLAN
- List the types of WLAN
- Explain WLAN management
- Set up a WLAN
- Configure a WLAN
- Configure a firewall on a WLAN
- Troubleshoot a WLAN

Key Terms

Ad hoc network   provide direct communication between the wireless devices; there is no need for an access point

Bridged network   configuration in which two or more networks are connected using a bridge, which forwards packets between them

Distributed coordination function (DCF)   MAC (media access control) technique that initiates the standard CSMA/CA (carrier sense multiple access with collision avoidance) access within Wi-Fi WLANs

Enhanced DCF (eDCF)   provides higher priority traffic first access to the WLAN media

Enterprise encryption gateway (EEG)   an encryption device allowing for strong authentication and encryption for data across the wireless media

Enterprise wireless gateway   a device placed between the wired network and the wireless AP to connect the two segments of an enterprise network; it is used to control network access from the WLAN into the wired network segment, providing enhanced security and management

Infrastructure network   clients are not directly connected; they are connected to an access point through which they connect to the network

Mesh networks   multihop systems in which devices or nodes help each other to transmit the data

Mobile ad hoc network (MANET)   an independent collection of mobile devices that communicate over bandwidth-constrained wireless links

Passphrase   a series of words or text that secures access to a computer system, program, or data

Proxy Mobile IP (PMIP)   an access point proxies the IP addresses of client mobile devices so there is no need to change a client device's IP address as it roams around various access points

Repeater networks   used for increasing the range of an existing WLAN instead of adding more access points; repeaters are physical-layer devices that function only at the physical layer of the OSI model

Roaming   extending connectivity service in a location that is different from the home location where the service was registered

Transmission opportunity (TXOP)   a bounded time interval during which a station can send as many frames as possible

Virtual AP   a logical unit that is present in a physical access point

Virtual LAN (VLAN)   network of computers that acts like a normal LAN, but the computers do not need to be physically connected to the same segment

WLAN array   consists of a WLAN switch and 16 802.11 WLAN (Wi-Fi) access points in a single device

WLAN management   helps companies have excellent performance with the strongest security from their WLANs and consists of three main functions: discovering, monitoring, and configuring the WLAN devices

Introduction to WLAN and Operations

A WLAN (wireless local area network) connects computers over a local network that exchanges data and other information without the use of cables. Connecting nodes must be placed within the range of access points (Figure 4-1). WLANs are usually implanted within small client-server architecture. The IEEE has specified 802.11 WLAN standards for comprehensive implementation and deployment of a wireless LAN. It operates at the data-link layer and the physical layer of the OSI Reference Model. WLAN has throughput of 2 Mbps, which is less than IEEE 802.3, the Ethernet standard. Later, IEEE issued 802.11b, a standard extension increasing the throughput to 11 Mbps. The 802.11b standard can be operated at a 2-Mbps data rate on the 2.4-GHz band. It has effectively raised high-speed data communications.

Its major advantage is user mobility within the range. It has sufficient bandwidth to assist a wide range of applications and services. It provides freedom and flexibility—compared to a wired network—high speed, simplicity of physical setup, and scalability. It enables security features like encryption, frequency hopping, and firewalls.

The disadvantages of WLAN are its high cost, limited range, and mutual interference (interference between two sensors when the signal from one sensor is unintentionally picked up by another sensor nearby). Additionally, because a WLAN does not offer a high level of security, it is not preferable for clients who require high security. It also has limited capacity to provide good quality support to multimedia applications.

Advantages of Using a WLAN

WLAN is efficient for home offices, small and medium businesses, and campus area networks. In addition, it provides the following advantages over a wired LAN:

- *Mobility*: Users can freely roam anywhere (within the WLAN range) and remain connected to the WLAN.
- *Scalability*: Users can be added without installing physical infrastructure, so the network can be expanded quickly.
- *Flexibility*: WLANs can be used in several setups that contain mobile clients in one building or across a number of metropolitan sites.
- *Installation*: WLAN is easy to install because it gives connectivity over sites separated by physical or geographical obstacles.

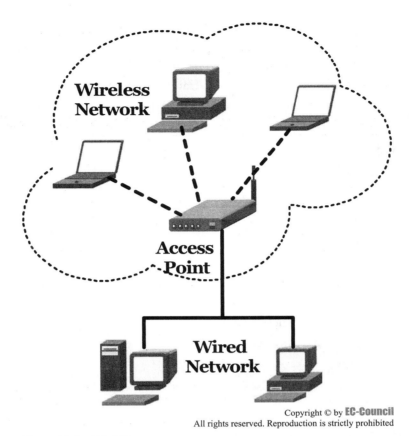

Figure 4-1   WLAN.

- *Reliability in harsh environment*: WLAN connections can be used in harsh environments (where the scope of a wired network is not possible), which may be critical to physical media. For example, a physical wire may not function in certain harsh environments, such as extreme cold, where a wireless setup would not be affected.

- *Reduced installation time and cost saving*: For installation, all you need to do is set the base station and wireless adapter, reducing the installation and implementation time and cost.

Basic Components of a WLAN

The major components of a WLAN are:

- *Wireless NIC (Network Interface Card) or Client Adapter*: Every wireless client needs a wireless NIC or client adapter. These can be PCMCIA and PCI cards, which give wireless connectivity to laptops and desktop stations.

- *Wireless Access Point*: A wireless LAN transceiver provides the connectivity between a wired and wireless network.

- *Wireless Bridge*: These bridges have high speed (11 Mbps), provide long-range connectivity— up to 25 miles—and also provide wireless connectivity between Ethernet networks.

- *Antennas*: These devices transmit and receive the wireless signal. There are various types of antennas available for different transmission patterns, gains, and ranges.

- *Cables and accessories*: Coaxial cables are used for connecting the antenna to RF equipment.

Accessing a WLAN

Follow these general steps to access a WLAN:

1. Use a laptop with a wireless NIC (WNIC).

2. Configure the NIC to automatically set up its IP address, gateway, and DNS servers.

3. Use the software that came with the NIC to automatically detect an available wireless network and go online.

4. To check if the system is online, run an intrusion detection system (IDS).

   • An IDS can send an alert to an administrator of a system when network traffic is recognized.

5. Another way to locate a wireless access point is by running software such as Wi-Fi Finder or NetStumbler.

Types of WLAN

The different kinds of WLAN are:

• Ad hoc network

• Mobile ad hoc network

• Infrastructure network

• Repeater networks

• Bridged networks

• Mesh networks

• Enterprise wireless gateway networks

• Enterprise encryption gateway networks

• Virtual AP networks

• WLAN array

Ad Hoc Networks

Ad hoc networks provide direct communication between the wireless devices (Figure 4-2). In this network, there is no need for an access point. Wireless devices that are in the range of each other communicate directly without the use of central access points.

Characteristics of an ad hoc network include the following:

• Connection is autonomous; that is, an ad hoc network is the connection of independent nodes or terminals that forms a decentralized multihop radio network.

• The topology used is dynamic, because connectivity between the nodes changes with time due to removal of some nodes and the arrival of new nodes.

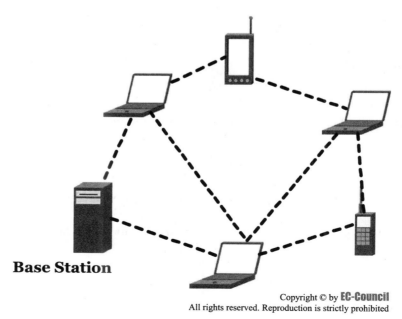

Base Station

Figure 4-2   Ad hoc network.

- Limited security is provided, because although security applications require a high degree of security, they are essentially weak to security attacks.

- A limited amount of power is required.

- Direct communication between the devices increases its performance.

Mobile Ad Hoc Networks (MANET)

A *mobile ad hoc network (MANET)* is an independent collection of mobile devices that communicate over bandwidth-constrained wireless links. This wireless topology is dynamic because the mobile routers move randomly, so the topology changes suddenly from time to time. The network is decentralized, so all the activities, like transferring messages or creating topologies, are executed by the nodes. The nodes themselves radiate low power as required and transfer as rarely as possible to reduce the probability of detection and interception.

Factors that affect the quality of a MANET are as follows:

- *Fading*: A change in the reduction of a communications channel

- *Power expended*: Lack of power affects the MANET

- *Topological changes*: The sudden change in topology affects the MANET

- *Propagation path loss*: Several losses during the transmission may occur

Infrastructure Networks

In *infrastructure networks*, clients are not directly connected; they are connected to an access point through which they connect to the network (Figure 4-3). An access point may be a hub or router that has an antenna to transmit and receive radio frequencies. An infrastructure network also contains bridges to connect the wireless

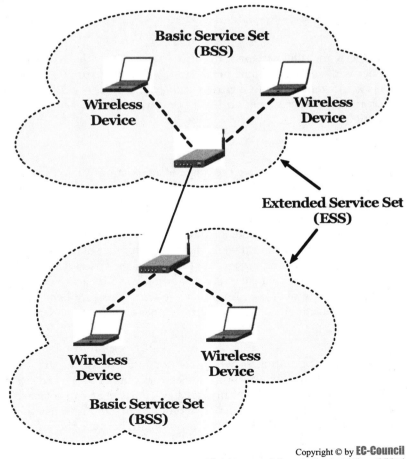

Figure 4-3   Infrastructure network.

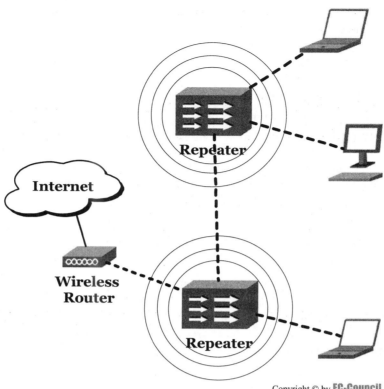

Figure 4-4   Repeater network.

network to a wired network. The network administrator arranges the access point through a Web interface or telnet. In a small network such as a home network, the infrastructure network is connected to a single access point, but large networks require a number of access points. Access points increase the communication range and consistency of an infrastructure network over that of an ad hoc network. It is not necessary for the users to be in the line of sight.

Repeater Networks

Repeater networks are used for increasing the range of an existing WLAN instead of adding more access points (Figure 4-4). Repeaters are physical-layer devices; they function only at the physical layer of the OSI model. They are never physically connected by wire to any part of the network. A repeater regenerates an electrical, wireless signal coming from user devices or from other repeaters, maintaining the signal integrity and expanding it to cover a large distance. Repeaters take a small amount of time to regenerate the signals, so it causes some propagation delay during communication when there are a number of repeaters available in a chain. Some access points contain the repeater mode and act as a repeater, e.g., the Cisco Aironet 350 series access points.

One problem with repeaters is that they receive and retransmit each frame, or data packet, on the same RF channel, which doubles the number of frames that are sent. This problem becomes complex as the number of frames increases, because each repeater doubles the frames that are to be sent.

Bridged Networks

A *bridged network* is a configuration in which two or more networks are connected using a bridge, which forwards packets between them (Figure 4-5). The networks may use the same or different data-link protocols. Bridges are protocol independent. WLAN bridges have ports that can forward traffic between two or more WLANs. It receives the packets from one network on one port and retransmits them to another network on a different port. Collision does not occur during transmission, because the bridge will not retransmit the packet until it receives the complete packet.

Wireless building-to-building bridges connect separate LANs at high speed. Access points can be used to connect multiple nodes in one WLAN to each other or to a wired LAN. On the other hand, bridges connect different networks. It offers high-speed Internet access and fast deployment at a lower cost.

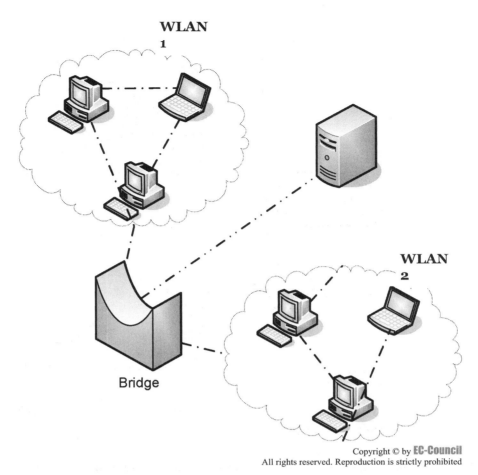

Figure 4-5   Bridged network.

A bridge plays two roles in a radio network:

- Determines functionality within the WLAN

- Determines which type of clients will be supported

Following are three types of WLAN bridges:

1. *Basic Ethernet-to-wireless*: This bridge provides direct connection to a device through an Ethernet port and then offers a wireless connection to an access point.

2. *Workgroup bridges*: These bridges are useful for connecting wireless networks to larger, wired Ethernet networks. They act as wireless nodes on WLAN and then connect to a wired network.

3. *Access points/wireless bridge combos*: This is an access point that can be configured as a bridge, but it cannot function as both at the same time. It can operate in point-to-point and point-to-multipoint bridge mode.

Mesh Network

Mesh networks are multihop systems in which devices or nodes help each other to transmit the data (Figure 4-6). In these networks, a node acts as a router; if a link fails, then it can receive and transfer the messages to its neighbor's node. Mesh networks reduce the distance between the nodes, which increases the link quality. They are self-organizing, because they never require manual configuration to define how a message gets transferred to its destination.

Mesh networks are self-healing, so there is no need for human interference in rerouting messages. They are more reliable and adjust to the environmental limitations; they are scalable and can handle thousands of nodes.

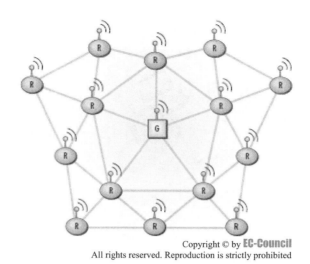

Figure 4-6   Mesh network.

Enterprise Wireless Gateway Networks

An *enterprise wireless gateway* is a device placed between the wired network and the wireless AP to connect the two segments of an enterprise network. It is used to control network access from the WLAN into the wired network segment, providing enhanced security and management. An enterprise wireless gateway network requires complex and careful study and evaluation. Following are some important considerations for design and deployment of an enterprise WLAN:

- *Policy and architecture*: Before starting the network design, users must frame their corporate policies. This policy should consist of many clauses like acceptable use of wireless, sources of authorized WLAN installation, use of wireless ID to identify the WLAN.

  - The enterprise WLAN needs WLAN architecture (how the wireless part is connected to the rest of the network), and the architecture must contain authentication and encryption techniques. There must also be physical security for access points and other infrastructure.

- *Configuration management*: Make a system configure for all changes in the access point.

- *Proper site survey should be performed prior to WLAN deployment*: A site survey is necessary to determine proper placement of access points for the required connectivity and throughput.

- *End-user training*: Users should be trained on the proper handling of the wireless devices. A company could make use of a Hotspot and personal wireless networks for training purposes before users are allowed to connect to the corporate wireless network.

- *Security of all WLAN clients*: Secure all the WLAN clients by installing antivirus software, and update it regularly; install firewalls.

- *Strong authentication and encryption is required on the WLAN*: Use the stronger authentication and encryption techniques. Use the AES encryption algorithm, use the mechanism that has centralized authentication, and avoid the use of broken authentication protocols.

- *Change default passwords*: Change the default password and configuration setting for security from the hackers.

Enterprise Encryption Gateway Networks

The *enterprise encryption gateway (EEG)* is new for the WLAN security. The EEG is an encryption device allowing for strong authentication and encryption for data across the wireless media. The client device has software that hits the encryption termination point, offloading encryption from the access point. It is different from other devices and justifies identification while discussing the segmentation devices. EEG functions as a gateway device because it segments the wireless network from the network's backbone. The EEG and access point are handled from the unencrypted part of the network.

Virtual AP Network

A *virtual access point* is a logical unit that is present in a physical access point. A single physical AP contains a number of virtual APs. Every virtual AP behaves like a station with a separate physical AP. A number of virtual APs can share the same SSID but have different capability sets.

As APs are used by a number of sources, virtual APs provide each source with different authentication and accounting data for their users. It allows a single provider to offer a number of services and also allows multiple providers to handle the same physical infrastructure.

Following are some of the advantages of a virtual AP:

- *Channel conservation*: If there is one channel and it is used by existing APs, then other APs interface with each other and decrease the performance. Thus, by using the single network for multiple goals, virtual APs protect the channel.

- *Capital expenditure reduction*: It is cheaper to build this infrastructure, which can be shared by multiple users.

- *Interoperability*: Every virtual AP uses its own BSSID (basic service set ID).

- *Capabilities advertisement*: Every virtual AP sends its capabilities (through beacon and probe responses); hence, it provides several rates and security mechanisms through a single network.

WLAN Array

A **WLAN array** consists of a WLAN switch and 16 802.11 WLAN (Wi-Fi) access points in a single device. This type of approach to a WLAN increases the available bandwidth and the range performance. It also increases the high gain, the performance, and the capacity of the WLAN.

A WLAN array has the following key benefits:

- It uses the 16 access points together, which delivers up to 864 Mbps of Wi-Fi capacity per WLAN array.

- It increases the coverage area up to four times greater than other solutions.

- It uses fewer devices for solving the arrangements, management, and support of the WLAN.

- It uses all 16 nonoverlapping channels, so it increases the use of the RF spectrum, which increases speed and performance.

Roaming

A WLAN network should be deployed in a way that *roaming* (extending connectivity service in a location that is different from the home location where the service was registered) between nodes will be easy. One of the major concerns related to WLAN roaming is the ability of users to roam between 3G and WLAN services. This capability is a key factor in providing seamless service among all the network service providers.

Two factors need to be considered when designing a WLAN with seamless roaming capabilities for devices that are powered on while moving from one point to another:

1. Coverage must be sufficient for the entire path.

2. A consistent IP address should be available throughout the entire path.

Clients will associate with an initial AP. If the strength of the initial AP's signal weakens, the client will immediately reassociate with the next AP for seamless roaming.

Steps for Association

The client access point association takes place as described following (Figure 4-7):

1. Client sends probe

2. AP sends probe response

3. Client evaluates AP response, selects best AP. Client sends authenticated request to selected AP (A)

4. AP (A) confirms authentication and registers client

5. Client sends association request to selected AP (A)

6. AP (A) confirms association and registers client

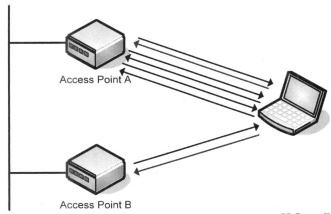

Figure 4-7 Association.

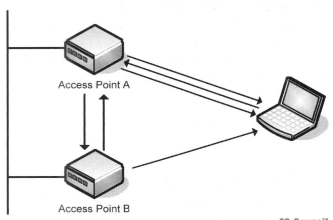

Figure 4-8 Reassociation.

Steps for Reassociation

The client needs to reassociate with different access points as it enters a new service provider's area. As the strength of the initial AP weakens, the client will reassociate with another AP as described following (Figure 4-8):

1. Adapter listens for beacons from APs
2. Adapter evaluates AP beacons, selects best AP
3. Adapter sends association request to selected AP (B)
4. AP (B) confirms association and registers adapter
5. AP (B) informs AP (A) of reassociation with AP (B)
6. AP (A) forwards buffered packets to AP (B) and deregisters adapter

Campus Topologies

Campus topologies are access systems that integrate complete mobility. They permit users to access information from unwired places outdoors, in dining halls, in informal study spaces, from classroom seats, and on the athletic fields. They are not replacements for wired LANs, but provide networking in hard-to-reach and temporary locations. They allow the users to work together in common areas while maintaining network access.

Virtual LAN (VLAN)

A *virtual LAN (VLAN)* is a network of computers that acts like a normal LAN, but the computers do not need to be physically connected to the same segment. The computers behave as if they are connected through the same wire in the same LAN.

The features of VLAN are:

- *Security*: It can separate the systems that have confidential data from the rest of the network.

- *Departments/job types*: VLANs can be set up for departments containing more network users or can be dedicated to specific types of employees depending on their jobs.

- *Broadcasts/traffic flow*: The computers that are not present in the VLAN cannot receive the broadcast traffic, so it automatically lowers the broadcasts.

- WLANs can now fit into the larger network as VLANs are enabled on the access points. Thus, it is possible for WLAN users to roam from AP to AP in different network providers while maintaining connectivity to the proper VLAN.

Distributed Coordination Function (DCF)

Distributed coordination function (DCF) is the MAC (media access control) technique that initiates the standard CSMA/CA (carrier sense multiple access with collision avoidance) access within Wi-Fi WLANs. It permits the node to listen to surrounding nodes to check their transmissions before transmitting themselves and thus controls the total transmission over a medium. It first determines whether the radio link is free before transmission and starts a random backoff to evade collision. Sometimes it uses RTS (request-to-send) and CTS (clear-to-send) to evade more collisions.

DCF is a default setting for Wi-Fi hardware.

Enhanced DCF (eDCF)

Enhanced DCF (eDCF) provides higher-priority traffic first access to the WLAN media. High-priority data packets will be immediately backed off instead of backing off for a random period of time to ensure QoS. The packets with higher priority pass through the AP faster than lower-priority traffic.

Transmission Opportunity (TXOP)

Transmission opportunity (TXOP) is a bounded time interval during which a station can send as many frames as possible. It was developed under IEEE's 802.11e specifications for environments that have a large amount of WLAN traffic. Data packets or frames that can be transmitted in a TXOP are only allowed to be transferred in a wireless network. If a data packet is too big to be transferred in a TXOP, it will be fragmented into smaller data packets that can be transferred in the TXOP.

TXOPs are designed to reduce the problems of low-rate stations gaining an inordinate amount of channel time in the legacy 802.11 DCF MAC. The TXOP technique guarantees priority packet handling, which means the data packets of higher priority will be sent first. If the traffic volume is too high, the high-priority packet will continue to be re-sent again and again. Transmission of data packets with equal priorities will go into a queue, but TXOP always reserves the first few seconds for high-priority packets to ensure that the high-priority data is sent first. All Wi-Fi multimedia (WMM)-certified APs must be enabled for EDCA (enhanced distributed channel access) and TXOP.

Proxy Mobile IP (PMIP)

In *Proxy Mobile IP (PMIP)*, an access point proxies the IP addresses of client mobile devices so that there is no need to change a client device's IP address as it roams around various access points. All mobile functions are continuous without any IP address switching interruptions. Seamless network connectivity is ensured while moving from one access point to another. Proxy Mobile IPs are helpful in a complex networked scenario with multiple access points.

When a mobile wireless device leaves an area covered by one access point and enters the next, the new access point queries the device for its home agent. The home agent is a router on a wireless network to which the mobile device belongs and is also known as the mobile device's home network. It maintains information about the device's current location as identified in its care-of address, which is a temporary IP address for a mobile device that enables message delivery when the device is being connected from somewhere other than its home network. After the home agent has been located, packet forwarding is established automatically between the new and old access points to ensure the device can exchange data transparently. This process does not require installation of any client-side software, but both the router and the access points of network must be configured to support Proxy Mobile IPs.

WLAN Management

WLAN management helps a company have excellent performance with the strongest security from their WLAN. WLAN management consists of three main functions:

1. *Discovering the WLAN devices*: WLAN management discovers the WLAN devices, but changes in each approach used affects efficiency. Some are based on the wired network information, which helps in finding high-end access points. They carry a low-security problem. To overcome this problem, several techniques like ICMP, SNMP, Telnet, CLI, AP Scan, RF Scan and CDP are used which disclose the security level. These techniques help with security by identifying rogue (unauthorized) access points.

2. *Monitoring the WLAN devices*: It is necessary to monitor the WLAN devices. Monitoring may be started with fault monitoring, performance monitoring, and service monitoring that tells the user when a device's performance degrades.

   There are many Wi-Fi manager tools that give complete monitoring functions, including:

   - *Trap reception*: As the WLAN device sends the trap (information sent as part of the SNMP protocol), Wi-Fi manager accepts it and informs the operator.

   - *Severity-based color-coded alarms*: Wi-Fi manager allocates the severity to each failure network and produces a color-coded alarm.

   - *E-mail-based notification*: When any fault occurs, Wi-Fi manager informs the operator through e-mail.

   - *Threshold monitoring*: Wi-Fi manager allocates the user some threshold value for the key parameters, and when those values are exceeded, the manager alerts the user.

   - *Service monitoring*: Wi-Fi manager checks the services running in the user's access point.

   - *Performance monitoring*: Wi-Fi managers check the WLAN devices for several parameters like utilization, data rate, and errors.

   In addition to monitoring the WLAN devices, WiFi manager provides the flexibility of delivering that information in various formats.

3. *Configuring the WLAN devices*: The largest value that WLAN management software provides is bulk configuration of access points. The operator is able to group the access points and use configuration with one click. The manager can solve it in two ways:

   - By supporting group-based configuration; and

   - Helping the template-based configuration. The operator takes the template, fills in the relevant values, and uses it to select the access point.

Setting Up a WLAN

The set of stations that communicate together within an 802.11 WLAN is called a Basic Service Set (BSS). The logical sector where several BSSs can work together is called an Extended Service Set (ESS). An SSID is an alphanumeric name of 1 to 32 bytes that is assigned to every ESS. It helps devices to establish and maintain wireless connectivity with an appropriate access point when multiple independent networks operate in the same physical area. SSIDs act as a single shared password between access points and clients. It is a unique identifier that identifies the wireless network.

For example, one organization operates its departmental WLAN, consisting of different APs and stations, using the same SSID. Another organization in the same building may operate its own departmental WLAN, composed of APs and stations, using a different SSID.

The access point and stations communicate as follows:

1. Every access point broadcasts beacon frames that have an SSID and promotes its presence. The stations operating in that WLAN can search the access point in two ways:

   - By inactively listening for beacon frames
   - By actively sending probe frames with the desired SSID

2. The station sends relative request frames having the desired SSID after searching the suitable access point.

3. The access point sends a relative response frame having the SSID as a reply.

Some frames can carry a zero-length, or null, SSID, also called a broadcast SSID. For example, if the station is sending a probe request with a broadcast SSID, then the access point must send a probe reply with an actual SSID. Some access points are set to send the beacon frames with a broadcast SSID rather than an actual SSID.

Configuring WLAN: Prerequisites

To set up a wireless network, perform the following tasks:

1. Have a USB flash drive with a minimum capacity of 2 megabytes (MB).

2. Have a wireless AP, and use the producer's documentation to connect to your network.

3. Verify which of the wireless devices support Windows Connect Now.

4. Select the encryption and authentication techniques that are suitable for the wireless network. There are two techniques for authentication and encryption that support Windows XP with SP2: WPA-PSK/TKIP and open system/WEP. Use either of them.

   - Read the documentation that accompanies the wireless AP and determine which authentication and encryption techniques it supports.
   - Determine the level of authentication and encryption technique which the other wireless devices (such as printers) also support.

   If all the wireless devices support WPA, select it because it is more reliable than open system/WEP.

5. If the wireless network has any external switches, then make sure that the switches are turned on (for example, a laptop computer's external switch).

6. Use Windows Update, so all the computers running Windows XP are updated to Windows XP with SP2.

7. Make sure that wireless client computers are configured for automatic addressing and that automatic wireless network configuration is enabled.

Configure Computers for Automatic Addressing

Perform the following steps to configure a computer for automatic addressing:

1. Go to Network Connections:

   - **Start -> Connect to -> Show all connections.**

2. Right-click **wireless network connection -> Properties.**

3. In the **General** tab:

   - Under **This connection uses the following items** -> select **Internet Protocol (TCP/IP) -> Properties.**

4. In the **Internet Protocol (TCP/IP) Properties** dialog box:

   - Select **General** tab -> click **Obtain an IP address automatically.**
   - Click **OK** twice, and then close Network Connections.

Enable Automatic Wireless Network Configuration

Perform the following steps to enable automatic wireless network configuration:

1. Go to Control Panel -> double-click **Network Connections.**
2. Right-click **Wireless Network Connection** -> **Properties.**
3. In **Wireless Networks** tab -> select **Use Windows to configure my wireless network settings** check box.

Run the Wireless Network Setup Wizard

Perform the following steps to run the wireless network setup wizard in Windows:

1. Click **Start** -> **My Network Places** -> **Network Tasks** -> **Set up a wireless network for a home or small office** to launch the wireless network setup wizard.
2. The **Welcome to the Wireless Network Setup Wizard** page (Figure 4-9) is displayed -> click **Next.**
3. If it is the first time the wireless network setup wizard has been launched on the computer:
   - The **Create a name for your wireless network** page will be displayed (Figure 4-10)
   - Type in a name in the **Network name (SSID)** box
   - Select **Automatically assign a network key**
   - Select the **wireless encryption** for your network
   - Click **Next**
4. If the wireless network setup wizard has been launched on the computer before:
   - The **What do you want to do?** page will be displayed
   - Select **Set up a new wireless network** -> click **Next**

Figure 4-9   Wireless Network Setup Wizard page.

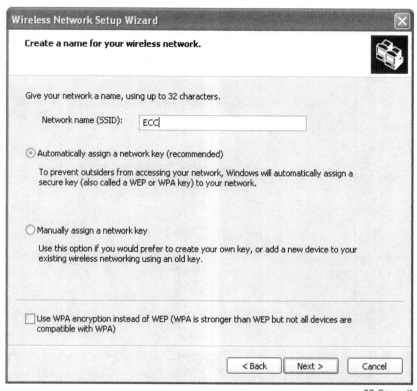

Figure 4-10   Create a name for your wireless network page.

5. On the **How do you want to set up your network?** page (Figure 4-11):
   - Select **Use a USB flash drive**
   - Click **Next**
6. On the **Save settings to your flash drive** page (Figure 4-12):
   - Insert your UFD
7. The wireless network setup wizard copies the wireless network settings to the UFD, and then displays the **Transfer your network settings to your other computers or devices** page (Figure 4-13).
8. Configure wireless AP and Windows Connect Now–capable wireless devices.
   - Plug the UFD into a Windows Connect Now capable wireless device.
   - After configuration, remove the UFD from the device.
9. Configure wireless computers.
   - Plug the UFD into the computer -> **Removable Disk** page will be displayed -> Select **Wireless Network Setup Wizard using the program provided on the device.**
   - When prompted to add the computer to the wireless network, click **OK.**
   - When the wizard displays the message You **have successfully added this computer to the wireless network,** click.
10. Plug the UFD back into the computer on which the wireless network setup wizard was initially launched.
11. On the **Transfer your network settings to your other computers or devices** page, click **Next.**
12. **The wizard completed successfully** page (Figure 4-14) lists the wireless computers and devices that have been configured.
13. Click **Finish.**

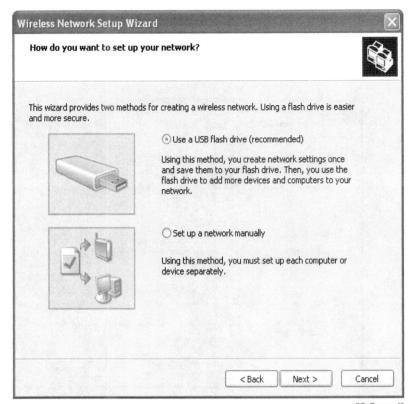

Figure 4-11 How do you want to set up your network? page.

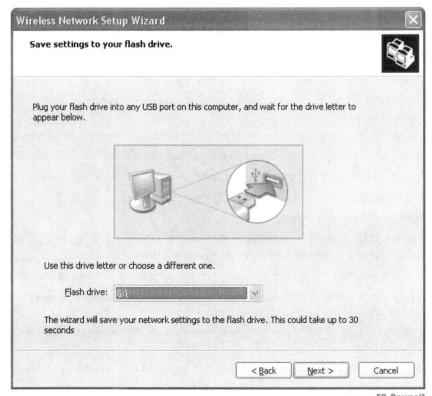

Figure 4-12 Save settings to your flash drive page.

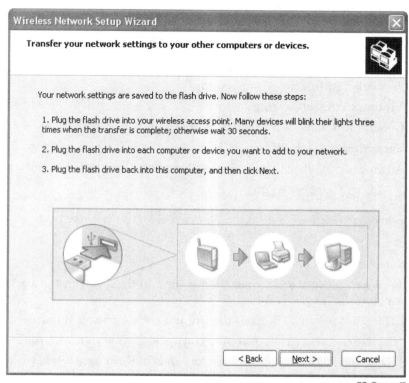

Figure 4-13   Transfer your network settings to your other computers or devices page.

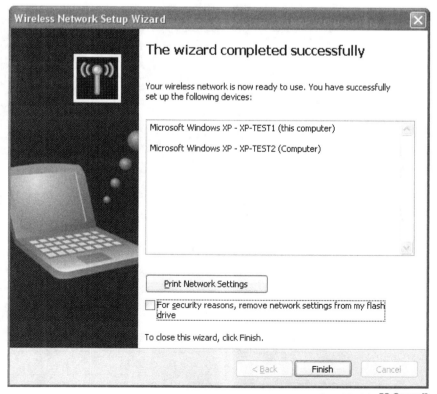

Figure 4-14   The wizard completed successfully page.

Configuring a Firewall on a WLAN

Perform the following steps to configure the firewall on WLAN:

1. Go to Control Panel.
2. Click **Network and Internet Connections.**
3. Click **Windows Firewall settings.**
4. In the **General** tab, make sure that the **On** option is selected (Figure 4-15).
5. In the **Exceptions** tab, check for the programs and services that are to be blocked (Figure 4-16).
6. In the **Advanced** tab, check that **Wireless Network Connection** is selected (Figure 4-17).

Connecting to an Available Wireless Network

Perform the following steps for connecting to an available wireless networks:

1. Go to Control Panel.
2. Click **Network Connections.**
3. Click the **Wireless Network Connection** icon, and then, under **Network Tasks, click View available wireless networks** (Figure 4-18).
4. Choose the wireless network from the list and click **Connect** (Figure 4-19).
5. Follow the instructions in the **Wireless Network Connection** wizard (Figure 4-20).
   - Type the network key in the **Network key** and **Confirm network key** boxes, and click **Connect.**
6. Connection is established with the available wireless network (Figure 4-21).

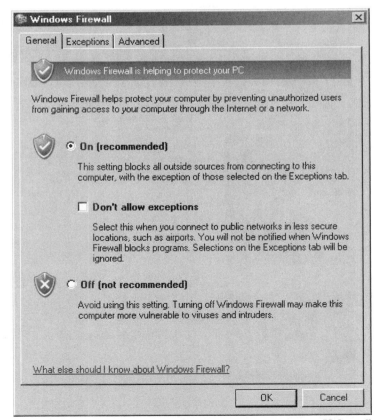

Figure 4-15   **On** option selected.

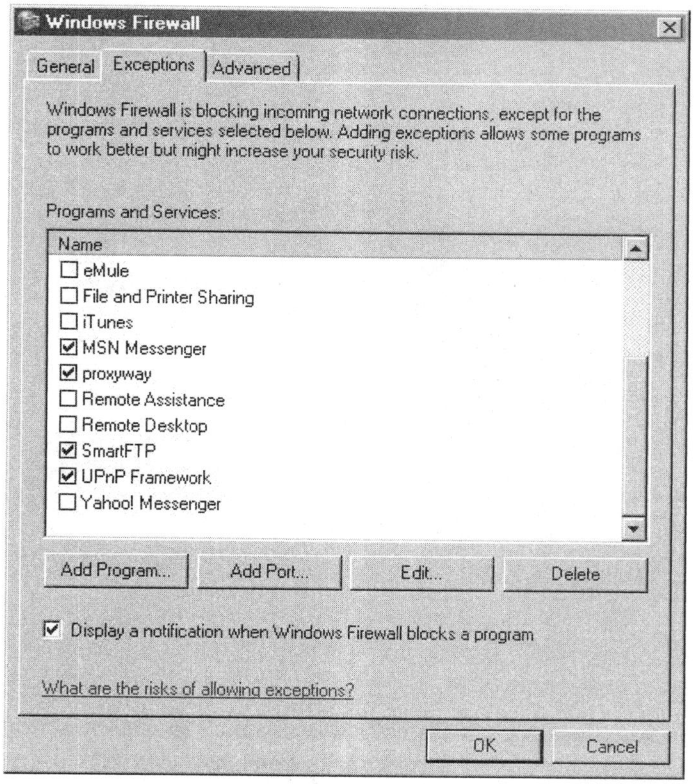

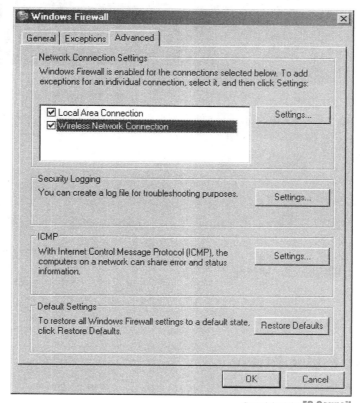

Figure 4-16   Exceptions tab.

Figure 4-17   Advanced tab.

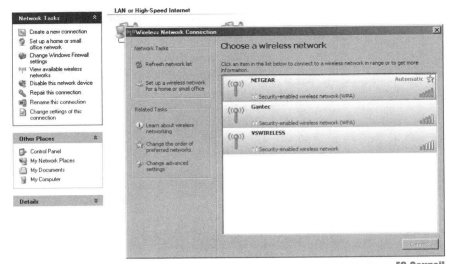

Figure 4-18 View available wireless networks.

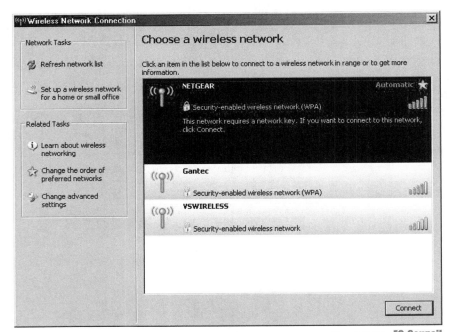

Figure 4-19 Click **Connect.**

WLAN Security: Passphrase

A *passphrase* is a series of words or text that secures access to a computer system, program, or data. It is the same as a password, but because it is longer than a typical password, it is more secure.

A password contains only six to eight characters, whereas a passphrase is a complete sentence that can use 20 to 30 characters. A sentence is harder to guess. A password is less safe because the word may be present in

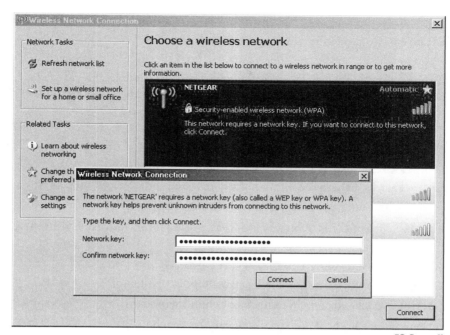

Figure 4-20   Wireless Network Connection wizard.

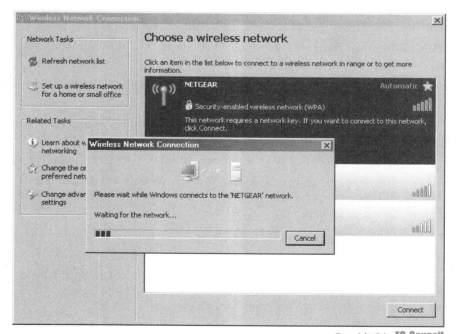

**Figure 4-21   Connection established.

a dictionary, which can lead to a dictionary attack. Passphrases are more easily remembered than passwords. A passphrase can be used to control access and operate cryptographic programs and systems. A passphrase is mainly applicable to systems that use it as an encryption key.

Following are some suggestions for choosing a passphrase:

- The sentence must be long enough that it is hard to guess by a program that might search from a list of famous phrases.

- It must not be a famous quotation from literature or holy books.

- It must be hard to guess even by someone who knows the user well.
- It must be easy to remember and type accurately.

One example for a passphrase is, "The quick brown fox jumps over the lazy dog," which becomes *tqbfjotld*. Include this phrase in "Now is the time for all good men to come to the aid of their party," which becomes the passphrase "Now is the time for all good tqbfjotld to come to the aid of their party."

Troubleshooting a WLAN

1. Recheck the physical connections at starting.
   - Ensure that all Ethernet cables are fully inserted into devices such as routers and modems.
2. Ensure that the wireless adapter is connected properly.
3. Ensure that the router's LAN port is active, noting its IP address and subnet, using the wireless router's admin interface.
4. Check the wireless adapter's IP address either by:
   - Using the Network Connection's **Status/Support** panel; or
   - Entering ipconfig from a Windows command window.
5. Ping the router's LAN IP address to verify its reachability.
   - If successful, then ping another host on the LAN.
   - If unsuccessful, go to next step.
   - If both attempts fail, go to step 7.
6. Disable the Windows Firewall. Now retry ping.
   - If successful, then reenable firewalls on both hosts, configuring each firewall to permit only the desired traffic to be exchanged between LAN hosts.
7. Check that the router and adapter use the same SSID, channel, wireless mode, and security settings.
   - Examine the router's log or Wireless status page for hints about what may be wrong.
8. To find and fix a wireless security parameter mismatch, temporarily disable security on both the adapter and router.
   - If the problem disappears, then reenter matching security parameters on both ends.
9. If RADIUS (the protocol that provides centralized authentication, authorization, and accounting) is flowing but access requests are being rejected, you may have an 802.1*x* EAP mismatch or credential problem.
   - Fixing this depends on the EAP used.

WLAN Diagnostic Tools

CommView and AirMagnet are just two of many WLAN diagnostic tools available. The following descriptions outline their capabilities.

CommView for WiFi PPC

According to the Web site, *http://www.tamos.com/products/commwifippcl*: CommView for WiFi PPC is the newest member of the TamoSoft's renowned CommView network monitoring product family. CommView for WiFi PPC transforms your PDA into a portable network analyzer.

CommView for WiFi PPC is a special lightweight edition of CommView for WiFi that runs on Pocket PC handheld computers. This product is a cost-effective WLAN diagnostic solution designed for express wireless site surveys, as well as for capturing and analyzing network packets on wireless 802.11b/g networks. CommView for WiFi PPC gathers information from the wireless adapter and decodes the analyzed data.

With CommView for WiFi PPC, you can scan the air for WiFi signals, select channels for monitoring, detect access points and wireless stations, capture packets, measure signal strength, view the list of network connections, and examine and filter individual packets. If the packets are WEP-protected, you can decrypt them on-the-fly by entering the correct WEP key.

Wireless network administrators can use this portable solution as a source of important information on network parameters, radio interference, security holes, or rogue access points, which is necessary for deployment and maintenance of WLANs. Although CommView for Wi-Fi PPC is a full-fledged packet monitor and analyzer, it is often feasible to use it in conjunction with the standard CommView for Wi-Fi edition for Windows 2000/XP for far more sophisticated network traffic analysis tools. The most efficient way to use CommView for Wi-Fi PPC is to perform express traffic monitoring and analysis, and then conduct in-depth research using CommView for Wi-Fi on your Windows 2000/XP notebook computer.

The following 802.11b/g wireless adapters are currently officially supported in CommView for Wi-Fi PPC:

- Linksys Wireless-G Compact Flash WCF54G
- Linksys WCF12 Wireless CompactFlash Card
- Belkin F5D6060 802.11b Wireless PDA Network Card
- NETGEAR MA701 802.11b 11Mbps Compact Flash Card
- TRENDnet TEW-222CF Wireless CompactFlash Network Adapter
- Pretec CompactWLAN CompactFlash Card
- D-Link DCF-650W CompactFlash Card

AirMagnet Handheld Analyzer

According to the AirMagnet Web site, *http://www.airmagnet.com/products/handheld.htm*: AirMagnet's Handheld Analyzer is a convenient, inexpensive way to solve serious problems in the enterprise wireless LAN. The Handheld Analyzer helps IT staff make sense of end-user complaints to quickly resolve performance problems, while automatically detecting hundreds of security threats and other network vulnerabilities.

Its features include:

- *Automatically Detect Vulnerabilities*: Handheld Analyzer performs a continuous vulnerability assessment of your Wi-Fi network to detect weaknesses that often go overlooked, enabling you to take corrective action before problems occur. Handheld Analyzer automatically identifies hundreds of vulnerabilities and performance problems, such as 11b/g conflicts, 802.11e problems, QoS, etc. Handheld Analyzer also alerts you on dozens of wireless intrusions and hacking strategies, including rogue devices, denial-of-service attacks, dictionary attacks, faked APs, RF jamming Stumbler tools, and many more.

- *Lockdown Security Policies*: The Handheld Analyzer enables you to set detailed security policies for all devices in your network. Designate your encryption and authentication methods then monitor your wireless LAN to check all devices for compliance with those policies. Also validate that the encryption methods themselves function correctly over the WLAN. Establish an even higher level of organized security by designating a list of approved APs for client access, and monitor for exposed wireless stations, ad-hoc devices, and other vulnerabilities.

- *Perform Live, Interactive Network Tests*: In addition to the issues that Handheld Analyzer automatically locates for you, a suite of active troubleshooting tools are available at your fingertips to help you quickly pinpoint network problems—RF interferences, traffic/infrastructure overloads, hardware failures, connectivity issues and more. Test connections with traditional tools such as DHCP, ping, and traceroute or use AirMagnet's Diagnostic Tool to view the step-by-step progress of a connection between a client and AP to pinpoint exactly where the process has broken down. Run AP performance tests to identify mismatched settings in the network, coverage, multipath interference, and Jitter and Roaming for Voice over Wi-Fi.

- *Track Down Rogues and Devices*: The Handheld Analyzer offers a zero-tolerance approach to rogue management enabling you to detect and block rogues wirelessly or at the wired port. The convenient Find Tool locks on to a particular AP or station and guides you to the physical location of a device, enabling you to quickly track down rogue APs and noncomplying devices. Also use the Find Tool to align signals between antennas to quickly optimize reception in line-of-sight bridging.

- *Detailed Packet and Frame Analysis*: Handheld Analyzer shows real-time packet flows for any Wi-Fi asset. Track data and management packets live, watch CRC errors, utilization, packet speed, media type and more. View a real-time decode page for detailed network analysis. Handheld Analyzer decodes the most popular protocols such as FTP, HTTP, SMTP, POP, and Telnet, with advanced filtering options that allow you to focus on particular conversations based on IP address or port number.

- *Access the AirWISE Expert*: AirWISE is your encyclopedia source for understanding the threats and performance issues at work in your Wi-Fi environment. All system alarms are explained for you in plain-English detail, including why they are important and what steps you should take to resolve issues.

- *GPS Support*: Handheld Analyzer provides GPS coordinates with your alarms to help you quickly pinpoint the location of security and performance issues in your outdoor 802.11b network.

- *Flexible Mobile Form Factor*: Handheld Analyzer is the most flexible troubleshooting solution for 802.11b networks on the market today. The Handheld Analyzer software works on any hardware platform that supports AirMagnet's Wireless Compact Flash Card (Mercury NL_2511 CF) or the Cisco Aironet 352 (AIR-LMC352 or AIR-PCM352).

Chapter Summary

- WLAN is a local area network that exchanges data or other information without the use of a physical medium.

- WLAN is efficient for home offices, small and medium businesses, and campus networks as it is mobile, scalable, and flexible.

- The basic components of a WLAN are a wireless client adapter, a wireless access point, a wireless bridge, antennas, cables, and accessories.

- The types of WLAN networks are ad hoc, mobile ad hoc (MANET), infrastructure, repeater, mesh, enterprise wireless gateway, enterprise encryption gateway, virtual AP, and WLAN array.

- WLAN management consists of three main functions: discovering, monitoring, and configuring the WLAN devices.

- When setting up a WLAN, the channel and service set identifier (SSID) must be configured.

Review Questions

1. What are the advantages of a wireless LAN?

_____

_____

_____

_____

2. List the various components of a WLAN.

_____

_____

_____

_____

3. Explain the methods used to access a WLAN.

_____

_____

_____

_____

4. What is a MANET?

_____

_____

_____

_____

5. _____ allow wireless devices to communicate directly with each other.
   a. Infrastructure networks
   b. Ad hoc networks
   c. Repeater networks
   d. Virtual AP networks

6. Define the term WLAN array.

_____

_____

_____

_____

7. What is a Proxy Mobile IP network?

_____

_____

_____

_____

8. Discuss various steps of association and reassociation of a mobile device with access points during roaming.

_____

_____

_____

_____

9. What are the prerequisites for configuring the WLAN?

_____

_____

_____

_____

10. Which three tasks are important for WLAN management?

_____

_____

_____

_____

Hands-On Projects

Please attempt the following projects to reinforce what you have learned in Chapter 4. Write down your observations or notes for later reference.

1. Write down the basic components used in your wireless LAN.

2. Determine the type of your WLAN.

3. Try to connect your Wi-Fi devices to an already available wireless network.

4. Try to configure a wireless LAN for your organization.

5. Configure the firewall on your wireless LAN.

Chapter 5

Wireless Technologies

Objective

After completing this chapter, you should be able to:

- Discuss the wireless technologies presented in this chapter

Key Terms

Broadband a form of telecommunication in which a wide band of frequencies are available for transmitting data; the data can be multiplexed and transmitted on varied frequencies or channels concurrently within the bands, which allows for transmission of more detail in a specified amount of time

CPE (Customer Premises Equipment) a device that connects a customer to an access circuit or a cable modem

Digital Sense Multiple Access with Collision Detection (DSMA-CD) protocol that transmits channel and decode status flags from a base station to a mobile unit to indicate the status of the associated reverse channel; these flags signify whether it is busy or idle and whether or not there were errors

DoCoMo the major mobile provider in Japan, it is a unique network that permits subscribers to access the Internet continuously via mobile technology; users can send and receive e-mails, exchange pictures, conduct e-business, shop, download ringtones and wallpapers, and browse various Web sites

Gaussian Minimum Shift Keying (GMSK) uninterrupted phase frequency shift keying; it is used in the Global System for Mobile Communication (GSM). The base band modulation generated initiates with a bit stream 0/1 and a bit clock with a time slice for each bit. It has high spectral efficiency. It requires a higher power level than other shift keying methods to reliably communicate an equal amount of data.

High-Q filter passes frequencies within a desired range

Intersymbol interference distortions that occur in digital transmission systems; this distortion is manifested in the temporary spreading of individual pulses. At a certain threshold, intersymbol interference compromises the integrity of received data. Intersymbol interference attributable to the statistical nature of quantum mechanisms sets the basic limit to receiver sensitivity. It is calculated by eye patterns.

Linear Predictive Coding (LPC)   used to process audio signals and speech; it is also used in place of the spectral envelope of the digitized signals of speech in compressed form. It is frequently used for encoding high-quality speech at a low bit rate in order to provide exact estimates of speech parameters.

Narrowband   a form of telecommunication system that carries voice in narrow bands of frequencies; it occupies a small space on the radio spectrum, as compared to broadband or wideband. It is also used in audio spectrum to depict sound that occupies a narrow range of frequencies. There is an assumption that the fading in narrowband is flat, but in reality no channel has flat fading.

Quadrature amplitude modulation (QAM)   a modulation scheme that conveys two digital bit-streams or two analog message signals by changing (*modulating*) the amplitudes of two carrier waves, using the amplitude-shift keying (ASK) digital modulation scheme or amplitude modulation (AM) analog modulation scheme

Introduction to Wireless Technologies

Wireless technology has revolutionized almost all areas of our day-to-day lives. Whether in a university, office, home, or shopping mall, wireless technology is a flexible and cost-effective solution for technology needs. The desire for uninterrupted access to networks has given rise to the ever-increasing demand for wireless technologies. This technology is used to connect computers, permit remote monitoring and data achievement, and to provide access control and security. This chapter will discuss several of these technologies.

IrDA

IrDA (Infrared Data Association) is an organization that defines "a standard for an interoperable universal two way cordless infrared light transmission data port." It is also defined as a data transfer through a short, line-of-sight distance. The following are examples of connections and their data transfer rates:

- Async serial-IR - 9,600–115 kb/s
- Sync Serial-IR - 1.152Mbs/s
- Sync 4PPM - 4Mb/s

The main design feature in the IrDA standard is a high-speed, short-range, point-to-point data transfer that is quite appropriate for handheld PCs and digital cameras. However, it does not support any kind of security measures.

Some other features of the IrDA standard are:

- Bidirectional communication is the foundation of all specifications
- It supports a maximum bandwidth of 16Mb
- Designed range 1 meter
- Designed to an infrared frequency
- Throughput—either 115.2 Kbps or 4 Mbps
- Data transmission from 9,600 b/s with basic speed/cost steps of 115 kb/s and maximum speed up to 4 Mb/s
- Data packets are confined using a CRC (CRC-16 for speeds up to 1.152Mb/s and CRC-32 at 4 Mb/s)

IrDA contains protocols that enable users to connect to all data transportation layers; it also supports network management, security, and some interoperability designs. The protocols include IrDA DATA for data delivery and IrDA CONTROL for controlling information. Some of the specifications in IrDA include IrPHY, IrLAP, IrCOMM, Tiny TP, IrOBEX, and IrLAN. IrDA technology is used in optical communication, palmtop computers, and mobile phones.

Bluetooth

Bluetooth technology is a specification for short-range radio links between mobile computers, mobile phones, digital cameras, and other portable devices. It enables a link with ad hoc and existing networks. It is a short-range communications technology designed to replace the cables connecting handheld devices. It allows the user to connect without wires.

Bluetooth technology has the capability to manage both data and voice transmission. This feature enables applications such as a hands-free headset for voice calls, printing and fax capabilities, and synchronizing PDA, laptop, and mobile phone applications.

Following are some of the features of Bluetooth:

- Operates in unlicensed ISM band 2.56 GHZ; ISM band is globally available. It restricts signals from hopping into other signals
- Uses FHSS
- Can support up to eight devices in a piconet
- Omnidirectional, non-line-of-sight transmission through walls
- 1-mW power
- Max bandwidth: 1Mb
- Range: 10 meters
- Frequency 2.40 GHz–2.483.5 Ghz (U.S. and Europe) or 2.472 Ghz–2.497 Ghz (Japan)
- Extended range with external power amplifier (100 meters)
- Supports stationary and mobile communications
- Fast acknowledgement and frequency hopping makes Bluetooth more robust, and less complex
- Consumes less power and is low cost
- Developed to function in a noisy frequency environment

Following are some of the applications of Bluetooth:

- Wireless control and information transfer between mobile devices such as cell phones and handsets
- Wireless communications with computer input devices such as keyboards and mice and output devices such as printers
- File transfers among devices through OBEX
- Replacement of traditional, wired serial communications in test equipment, GPS receivers, and medical equipment
- Sends small advertisements from Bluetooth-enabled advertising hoardings to other discoverable Bluetooth devices

Wibree

Wibree is a digital radio technology that consumes ultralow power, complementing other connectivity technologies. Wibree technology was introduced by Nokia. It provides cheaper implementations and can be integrated easily with Bluetooth solutions. It is intended to replace Bluetooth. Its specifications are:

- Frequency: 2.4-GHz ISM band
- Data Rate: Physical-layer bit rate of 1 Mbps
- Range: Link distance of 10 meters

It is the first open wireless technology that integrates the following features into one product:

- Low cost and small size for accessories and human-interface devices (HID)
- Very low peak-, average-, and idle-mode power consumption
- Global, intuitive, and secure multivendor interoperability
- Lower-cost and smaller-size addition to mobile phones and PCs

Wibree technology has two implementations:

- Dual mode:
  - In dual mode, Wibree technology is implemented inside the Bluetooth devices so that power consumption of the final product should be low.
  - Dual mode is implemented in devices such as mobile phones, multimedia computers, and PCs.
- Standalone mode:
  - Standalone mode is implemented to optimize power and cost.
  - It is implemented in sport, wellness, and HID product categories.

Wi-Fi

The term *Wi-Fi* stands for wireless fidelity. It is developed by the Wi-Fi Alliance, which certifies products based on IEEE 802.11. These products are labeled "Wi-Fi certified." Figure 5-1 illustrates a Wi-Fi WLAN.

Wi-Fi is a standard radio technology that defines wireless local area networks (WLANs). It only uses 802.11-family specifications. Wi-Fi is a standard designed by the Institute of Electrical and Electronic Engineers (IEEE). It includes many standards within various radio frequencies. For example, 802.11b is a standard for wireless LANs that operate in the 2.4-GHz spectrum with a maximum bandwidth of 11 Mbps. Wireless technology can be used across wide ranges and is now common in metropolitan areas. WLANs can be found in Internet cafés, airports, and hotels, in which the access connection must be configured; others work with your Wi-Fi radio to automatically log on. A WLAN is an alternative to a wired LAN.

Wi-Fi specifications are:

- Operating range: unlicensed 2.4- and 5-GHz radio bands
- Data transfer rate: 11 Mbps (802.11b) or 54 Mbps (802.11a)

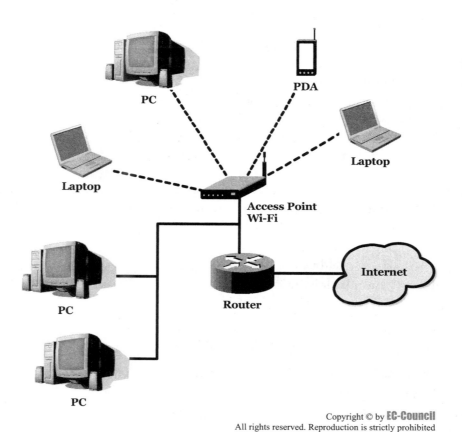

Figure 5-1   Wi-Fi.

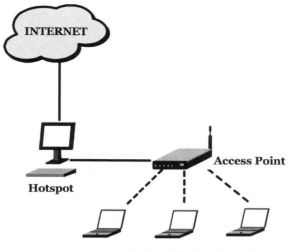

Figure 5-2   Hotspot.

The Wi-Fi network should be secured against illegitimate users with the Wired Equivalent Privacy (WEP) encryption standard, the more recent Wi-Fi Protected Access (WPA), Internet Protocol Security (IPSec), or a virtual private network (VPN).

Wi-Fi has the following advantages:

- Allows WLANs to be deployed
- Supports roaming
- Less expensive and easily available

Hotspot

A hotspot is a network area where public wireless access points are located (Figure 5-2). They are used for accessing Internet services by Wi-Fi laptops and other devices that support Wi-Fi. The user can connect to the Internet by utilizing these access points. It also provides a VPN from a particular location. Hotspots are offered in places such as hotels, coffee shops, airports, and railway stations.

WISP

WISP is an Internet service provider (ISP) that provides public wireless network services. It installs Wi-Fi hotspots in public places such as airports and hotels, and permits the users within the hotspot to connect to a server. A user would need to subscribe to the wireless (at no charge or for a fee) service to use the WISP.

WISPs provide broadband service. **Broadband** is a form of telecommunication in which a wide band of frequencies are available for transmitting data. The data can be multiplexed and transmitted on varied frequencies or channels concurrently within the bands, which allows for transmission of more detail in a specified amount of time. WISP permits the subscriber computers to access the Internet within the hotspot zone provided by the server antenna. Subscribers can access the Internet using any mobile network devices including handheld devices, laptops, and cell phones.

A subscriber should determine the following when choosing a WISP:

- Provider's equipment (bandwidth capacity and attainable speed)
- Software compatibility with their own device

WISP may be a basic service set having several stations and servers connected by wireless, or an extended service set having two or more BSSs connected at access points. T-Mobile is an example of a WISP. It offers Internet access to wireless laptop users in the 2,000-plus chain of Starbucks coffee houses.

GSM

The Global System for Mobile Communications (GSM) supports global roaming.
Its specifications are:

- *Frequency band*: 1,850 to 1,990 MHz (mobile station to base station)
- *Duplex distance*: 80 MHz
- *Channel separation*: 200 KHz
- *Modulation technique*: **Gaussian Minimum Shift Keying (GMSK)**, which is uninterrupted phase frequency shift keying, is used in the Global System for Mobile Communication (GSM). The base band modulation generated initiates with a bit stream 0/1 and a bit clock with a time slice for each bit. It has high spectral efficiency. It requires a higher power level to reliably communicate an equal amount of data.
- *Transmission rate*: Bit rate of 270 kbps
- *Access method*: Time Division Multiple Access (TDMA)
- *Speech coder*: **Linear Predictive Coding (LPC)**, which is used to process audio signals and speech. It is also used in place of the spectral envelope of the digitized signals of speech in compressed form. It is frequently used for encoding high-quality speech at a low bit rate to provide exact estimates of speech parameters.

The GSM network has three major systems (Figure 5-3):

- The base station system (BSS)
- The switching system (SS),
- The operation and support system (OSS)

The Switching System (SS)

The switching system (SS) is required for call processing and subscriber-related functions. The switching system includes:

- *Home Location Register (HLR)*: a database carrying data for storage and management of subscriptions. It contains data about the subscribers and their profiles.
- *Mobile Services Switching Center (MSC)*: facilitates the telephony switching functions of the system. It monitors calls to and from other telephone and data systems. It works as toll ticketing, network interfacing, common channel signaling, and other services.
- *Visitor Location Register (VLR)*: a database that holds the temporary information of the subscribers and is used to provide services to the subscribers.

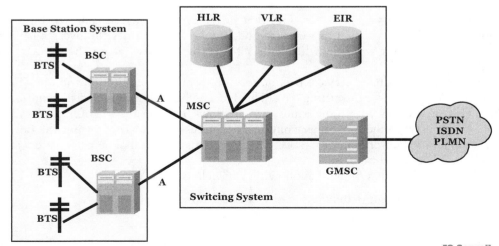

Figure 5-3   GSM network.

- *Authentication Center (AUC)*: facilitates authentication and encryption to check the user's identity and secures network operators from various deceptions.
- *Equipment Identity Register (EIR)*: a database that holds information about mobile equipment in case of theft or unauthorized use.

The Base Station System (BSS)

BSS contains radio-related functions. It is composed of base station controllers (BSCs) and the base transceiver stations (BTSs).

- BSC—offers all control parameters and physical links between the MSC and BTS. It is a high-capacity switch.
- BTS—monitors the radio interface to the mobile station.

The Operation and Support System

The operations and maintenance center (OMC) is linked to all devices in the switching system as well as the base station controller (BSC). Execution of OMC is known as the operation and support system (OSS). The OSS is the functional entity from which the network administrator manages and controls the system. The main function of OSS is to present the customer cost-effective support for centralized, regional, and local operational and maintenance activities needed for a GSM network. The function of the OSS is to maintain and configure network components, and manage faults and provision services.

GSM Subscriber Services

GSM offers the following subscriber services:

- Dual Tone Multi Frequency (DTMF)
- Short message services
- Cell broadcast
- Voice mail
- Fax mail
- Call forwarding
- Barring of outgoing calls
- Barring of incoming calls
- Call hold
- Call waiting
- Multiparty service

GPRS

General Packet Radio Service (GPRS) is a standard for wireless communications. Its data transfer speed supports a minimum of 115 kbps or a maximum of 171 kbps. The speed of data transfers depends on the cell/sector capacity, considering the time slots. In practical application, it only supports 20–50 Kbps. This packet-based technique adds packet-switching protocols and facilitates a shorter setup time for ISP (Internet service provider) connections.

GPRS architecture includes the following:

- *Gateway GPRS Support Node (GGSN)*: works as a gateway to other networks
- *Serving GPRS Support Node (SGSN)*: a serving node for data transfers

GPRS has the following features:

- Provides "always-on" capability
- Autonomous service is realized through the always-on capability
- Supports wide-range bandwidth that is required to send and receive data
- Provides tremendous infrastructure efficiency and service delivery improvements
- Allows the use of WAP (Wireless Application Protocol) on a per-transaction basis

These are the applications of GPRS:

- Sending multimedia messages
- Enables Internet applications from Web browsing to chat over the mobile network
- Accessing and controlling in-house appliances remotely
- Chat, images, audio, and video
- Textual and visual information
- Web browsing
- Document sharing/collaborative working
- Dispatch calling, which uses one channel to call several listeners
- Remote LAN access

EDGE

EDGE (Enhanced Data Rates for GSM Evolution) is an advanced technology of wireless communications and an extension of GPRS. It facilitates higher data transfers and data throughputs. It supports data rates of 384 kbps and more. It is defined as an evolution of GSM and GPRS. With the support of EDGE technology, GSM users can gain greater network coverage and unparalleled spectral efficiency. It enables customers to initiate revenue generating data services such as video streaming and enhances data penetration in emerging markets. EDGE is the first and best prospect for users to convert wireless networks into next-generation Wireless Data Networks. The high-performance data capability of the EGDE technology ensures greater service continuity among UMTS (Universal Mobile Telecommunications System) and GSM/GPRS/EDGE networks. This technology is based purely on packet core network without any changes.

The following are some of the EDGE specifications:

- Data rates: 384 kbps and above
- Channel coding:
  - Outer block coding
  - Inner convolutional coding
  - Interleaving scheme for error bursts
- Modulation
  - GMSK (Gaussian Minimum Shift Keying)
  - 8-PSK (Phase-Shift Keying)
- Multiple Access: Combination of TDMA and FDMA
- RF carrier spacing: 200 kHz
- Number of TDMA slots on each carrier: 8
- Channel allocation: 1 to 8 time slots per TDMA
- One time slot: (Physical channel) 0.577 ms
- Frame interval: 4.615 ms
- Asymmetric data traffic: Different time slots for Uplink and downlink
- Frequency hopping: 217 hops/s (slow)

FDMA

FDMA stands for Frequency Division Multiple Access (Figure 5-4, which shows the block being split by frequency). It defines the frequency allotted for a range of wireless cellular telephone communications into nearly 30 channels. Each channel includes a voice conversation or digital information in it. The block of available bandwidth is split up by frequency, with each call on a separate frequency. Think of it like your television access, which comes in through one cable but it is split by channel. You turn from one channel to another to watch one

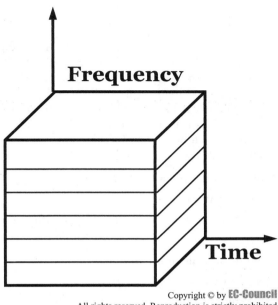

Figure 5-4   FDMA.

program or another. In TDMA, your access would be a slice of time you could use instead of a channel. Times are split up between all the conversations that need to be carried on—each taking its turn. This technology is used in analog standards like Advanced Mobile Services (AMPS) and Total Access Communication System (TACS). Each conversation has its unique channel. A single base station can serve multiple callers. FDMA is used in conjunction with TDMA or CDMA (discussed in the following sections).

Some advantages of FDMA are:

- Simple to design, and proven technology

- Reliable

- Narrowband (no intersymbol interference)
  Narrowband is a form of telecommunication that carries voice in narrow bands of frequencies. It occupies a small space on the radio spectrum, as compared to broadband or wideband. It is also used in audio spectrum to depict sound. This sound occupies a narrow range of frequencies. There is an assumption that the fading in narrowband is flat, but in reality no channel has flat fading.

  Intersymbol interference refers to distortions that occur in digital transmission systems. This distortion is manifested in the temporary spreading of individual pulses. At a certain threshold, intersymbol interference compromises the integrity of received data. Intersymbol interference attributable to the statistical nature of quantum mechanisms sets the basic limit to receiver sensitivity. It is calculated by eye patterns.

- Synchronization is easy

- No interference among users in a cell

Some disadvantages of FDMA are:

- Narrowband interference

- Lack of flexibility in case of reconfiguration

- Less throughput at large number of accesses

- Static spectrum allocation

- Frequency reuse is a problem

- High-Q analog filters or large guard band required

TDMA

TDMA (Time Division Multiple Access) is technology through which digital wireless transmission permits multiple users to distribute a single radio-frequency channel without interference, by assigning unique time slots to each user within the channel (see Figure 5-5, which shows the block split by time). TDMA depends on the way the audio signals are digitized; they are divided into milliseconds-long packets. It distributes a single frequency channel for a short time and then turns to another channel. It can also partition time, allowing the users to take turns using the channel. IS-54 (2G) is used for the same 30-KHz channels, but with three users sharing it (3 slots). Compare that to GSM, which has 8 slots/270 KHz.

The following are some of the advantages of TDMA:

- It is appropriate for digital communication
- Often gets higher capacity than FDMA
- Relaxes need for **high-Q filters**, which pass frequencies within a desired range
- No intermodulation effect
- Throughput remains high for large number of accesses
- All stations transmit and receive on the same frequency
- Provides the user with extended battery life and talk time
- Provides significant savings in base station equipment, space, and maintenance, an important factor as cell sizes grow ever smaller
- Cost-effective technology for upgrading a current analog system to digital
- Efficient utilization of hierarchical cell structures (HCSs), offering pico, micro, and macro cells

Disadvantages of TDMA are:

- Single time slot is not allotted to the user who is roaming from one cell to another
- Strict synchronization makes the system more complex
- Guard time needed
- Multipath distortion
- Still vulnerable to jamming, other-cell interference

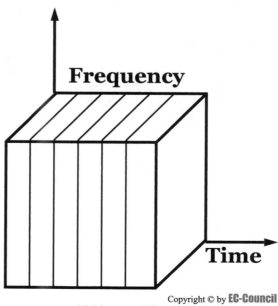

Figure 5-5   TDMA.

CDMA

Code Division Multiple Access (CDMA) is a "spread spectrum" technology; it does not distribute frequency or time, but both parameters can be involved simultaneously (see Figure 5-6, which shows the block not split by time or frequency alone). Thus, the data transfer is in codes in which multiple users can be allocated the same time and frequency within the given band/space. It offers better capability for voice and data communications than other commercial mobile technologies (see Figure 5-7). Unwanted signals entering with different codes, however, can spread more noise. It offers efficient voice and data communication. It allows many users by distributing the airwaves at the same time. Both 2G and 3G networks use the CDMA air interface. It is the basis for 3G services: the two dominant IMT-2000 standards, CDMA2000 and WCDMA, are based on CDMA.

These are the features of CDMA:

- Flexible network: The terminals are connected directly to the system
- Broad terminal integration: It can integrate the terminals of dissimilar speeds
- Compatibility
- Easy network access
- Line utilization
- Error-free transmission
- Cell frequency reuse: No frequency planning needed
- Soft handoff increases capacity
- Interference limited: Power control is required
- Narrowband message signal multiplied by wideband spreading signal
- Each user has his own pseudonoise (PN) code
- Wide bandwidth induces diversity: It uses rake receiver

Table 5-1 compares CDMA and TDMA.

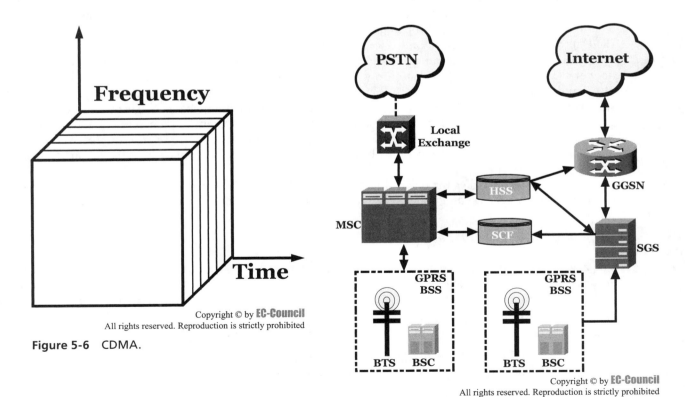

Figure 5-6   CDMA.

Figure 5-7   CDMA network.

CDMA	TDMA
Segment a single (1.25 MHz) channel into 64 multiple channels using a code to identify users	Segment a single (30 KHz) channel into (3 × 8kb/s) time slots, carrying specific user information
More immune to interference	Less immune to interference
Potentially supports more users	Potentially supports less users
Capacity dependent on coverage	Capacity dependent on number of available time slots
Spreads call over entire spectrum	Does not spread call over entire spectrum

Table 5-1   CDMA and TDMA compared

Quadrature Amplitude Modulation (QAM)

Quadrature amplitude modulation (QAM) is a modulation scheme that conveys two digital bit-streams or two analog message signals by changing (*modulating*) the amplitudes of two carrier waves, using the amplitude shift keying (ASK) digital modulation scheme or amplitude modulation (AM) analog modulation scheme. The modulated waves are summarized, and the resulting waveform is a combination of both phase-shift keying (PSK) and amplitude-shift keying (ASK), or in the analog case, of phase modulation (PM) and amplitude modulation (AM). In the digital case of QAM, a finite number of at least two phases and at least two amplitudes are used.

ZigBee

ZigBee is a specification for communication protocols based on the IEEE 802.15.4 standard. The ZigBee specification defines a stack protocol that allows the interoperability of wireless devices at a low cost with low power consumption for a low data-rate network. The ZigBee protocol handles more than 65,000 devices on a single network. A consumer can install the protocol and forget it, allowing the consumer to maintain the network easily.

ZigBee is established over the IEEE 802.15.4 standard, that describes the media access control (MAC) and physical (PHY) layers of the protocol. MAC and PHY layers describe RF and communications components of neighboring devices. The physical layer allows high levels of integration while maintaining the requirement for low cost. Direct sequence makes the analog circuitry simple and tolerant toward inexpensive implementation. The MAC layer allows multiple topologies without any complexity. MAC uses reduced functionality devices (RFDs) that do not require flash or a large amount of RAM or ROM.

Zigbee stack layers include a network layer, an application layer, and a Security Service Provider (SSP). The network layer allows the network to grow without the need for high-power transmitters. The network layer also handles a number of nodes with relatively low latencies. The ZigBee application layer consists of APS sublayer, ZDO (ZigBee Device Object), and manufacturer-defined application objects. The APS sublayer has the ability to match two devices together, depending on the requirement of their services and needs. ZDO defines the role of devices in the network that initiate and establish the secure relationship between the devices. The manufacturer-defined application objects implement the actual applications based on ZigBee-defined application descriptions.

ZigBee Profiles describes the environment of the application, devices that are used, and the clusters used to communicate between them. Public profiles assure the interoperability of various vendors for the same application space.

ZigBee Stack Architecture

The ZigBee stack architecture consists of an application layer, network layer, MAC layer, physical layer, and Security Service Provider (SSP) (Figure 5-8).

The application layer consists of the APS sublayer, ZDO (ZigBee Device Object), and manufacturer-defined application objects:

- APS sublayer:
  - Maintains the table for binding, which is capable of matching two devices together depending on their services and requirements, and forwards the messages between the bound devices
  - Also has the capability to find out which different devices are operating in the operating space of the particular device

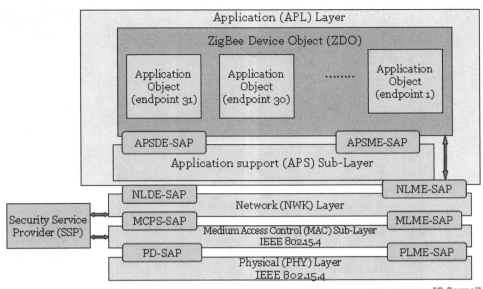

Figure 5-8 ZigBee stack architecture.

- ZDO:
  - Describes the role of different devices such as the ZigBee coordinator or the end device within the network
  - Initiates a binding request between the devices and establishes a secure relation between them
- Manufacturer-defined application objects:
  - Implements the actual applications based on ZigBee-defined application descriptions

The network layer has the following responsibilities:

- The capability to create a successful network
- The ability to join or leave the network
- Configures new devices for the operation, if required
- Capability of the ZigBee coordinator to assign addresses to every device that joins the network
- Synchronization with other devices within a network, through tracking beacons or by polling
- Applies security to the outgoing frames and removes the security from the frames that are terminating
- Ability to route the frames to their particular destination

When the network layer transmits or receives a frame with a particular security suite, it uses the Security Services Provider (SSP) that processes that particular frame. The SSP sees the destination or the source of the frame and takes out the key related to them. SSP gives primitives to the network layer for applying the security to the outgoing frames and removing the security from the incoming frames.

ZigBee Devices

Every ZigBee device includes a public or private profile. Profiles describe the environment of the application, the type of devices, and the clusters used for the communication.

The ZigBee standard defines three types of devices:

- Coordinator:
  - In every ZigBee network there should be only one coordinator
  - Main function is to start and configure the network
  - Supports the associations, holds the binding table for indirect addressing, and designs the trust center

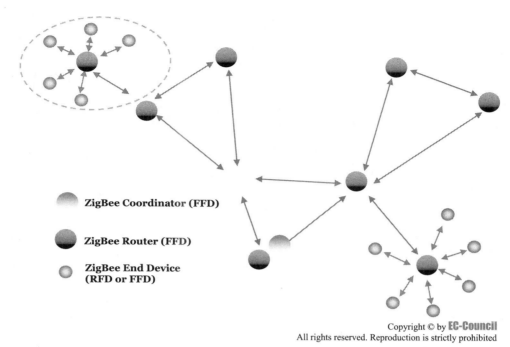

Figure 5-9   ZigBee network model.

- Router:
  - Supports the association and forwards messages to other devices
  - Unlike the coordinator, a ZigBee mesh or tree network can have multiple ZigBee routers
  - ZigBee star network does not support ZigBee routers; a message is sent from one end device to another via a coordinator
- End device:
  - Uses the ZigBee network for communication with the other devices
  - Has a lower memory requirement

Figure 5-9 illustrates a ZigBee network model.

Characteristics of ZigBee/IEEE 802.15.4 Standards

ZigBee has the following characteristics:

- The PHY layer supports 2.45-GHz and 868/915-MHz radio bands
- The 2.45-GHz radio band has a data rate of 250 Kbps and supports 16 different channels, the 868-MHz radio band supports one channel with a data rate of 20 Kbps, and the 915-MHz radio band supports 10 channels with a data rate of 40 kbps
- It is optimized for low duty-cycle applications (<0.1%)
- It accesses the CSMA-CA channel
- It yields high throughput and low latency for low duty-cycle applications such as sensors and controls
- It requires less power
- It supports star, tree, and mesh topologies
- It has addressing of up to:
  - 18,450,000,000,000,000,000 devices (64-bit IEEE address)
  - 65,535 networks
- It has an optional guaranteed slot for applications that require low latency
- Complete handshake protocol supports transfer reliability
- Range: 50 m typical (5–500 m based on environment)

Benefits of ZigBee

A ZigBee network and APS with 802.15.4 PHY and MAC provides the following benefits:

- It reduces operational cost because the cost of the devices used is very low, and installation and maintenance cost is low
- It is easy to implement; this simplicity enables inherent configuration and redundancy of network devices to provide low maintenance
- It transfers data continuously without any failure
- It requires very low power
- It provides a suitable security level

ZigBee Security Issues

The security of the system is defined at the profile level, which specifies the type of security used in the particular network. Each layer—MAC, network, and application layers—can be secured and reduce the required storage by sharing the security keys. When security is required for the MAC-layer frames, ZigBee uses the security of the MAC layer to protect the MAC command, beacon, and acknowledgement frames. The MAC layer makes use of the Advanced Encryption Standard (AES) algorithm and defines the security suite, which protects the confidentiality, integrity, and authenticity of MAC frames. The MAC layer processes the security, but the upper layers set the keys and define the security level, controlling this processing.

The SSP is initialized and configured through the ZDO and requires the implementation of AES. SSP first sees the destination or the source, and then takes out the keys and applies the security suite to the frame. It supplies the primitives to the network layer to provide the security to outgoing frames and removes the security from incoming frames. The network layer is responsible for security processing but the upper layer controls this processing by setting the keys and identifying which security suite is used for each frame.

ZigBee uses secured MAC data frames for transmission over a single hop and uses upper layers like the NWK layer for security in multihop transmission. ZigBee uses the "trust center" as a device in the network that distributes the security keys to each device. Each key is linked with a single security suite; the MAC frame header contains a bit that specifies whether security for a frame is enabled or disabled.

Fixed Wireless Broadband Technologies

Fixed wireless broadband technologies are LMDS (local multipoint distribution service), MMDS (multichannel/multipoint distribution service), cellular/PCS (personal communication system), DBS (direct broadcast satellite), and digital terrestrial. This section discusses LMDS and MMDS.

Advantages of fixed wireless broadband technologies are:

- Provide alternate, wireless means for delivering broadband services to businesses and residences
- Suitable for areas with poor or nonexistent wired infrastructure
- Lower infrastructure costs compared to wired
- Faster deployment than laying cable/fiber
- Scalable and easy relocation
- High data rates

LMDS

LMDS (local multipoint distribution service) is a new type of stationary (fixed) broadband line-of-sight, point-to-multipoint microwave system (Figure 5-10). It operates at high microwave frequencies, 24 GHz and above (28–31 GHz), and can deliver at a very high capacity, depending on the associated technologies. It is designed for a mass subscriber marketplace.

The LMDS network provides point-to-point services using its cells placed in an area of about 2–3 miles in diameter. The LMDS connections involve the cell phone towers and trunk connections with a data rate in the range of 150–620 Mbps. There are no current standards established for the deployment of the LMDS.

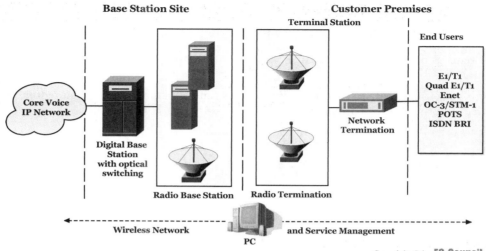

Figure 5-10 LMDS configuration.

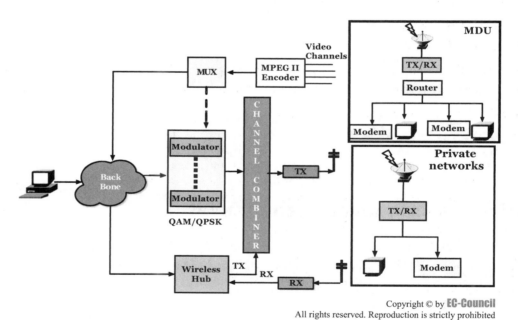

Figure 5-11 MMDS system for digital video and wireless Internet.

LMDS networks can provide these two-way broadband services:

- Video
- High-speed Internet access
- Telephony services

MMDS

The multichannel multipoint distribution service (MMDS) frequencies, located in the 2.1-GHz to 2.7-GHz band, allow two-way voice, data, and video streaming (Figure 5-11). The frequency in which the MMDS operates, within the range of 2–10 GHz, is less than that of the LMDS. The MMDS frequencies operate in one way, analog wireless cable TV broadcast service. The MMDS transmitting tower covers a diameter of approximately 35 miles.

Features	LMDS	MMDS
Frequency range	28–31 GHz	2.5–2.7 GHz
Data rate	Typically up to 45 Mbps	Typically 0.5–3 Mbps
Distance	Up to 5 miles	Up to 35 miles
Modulation techniques	TDMA, FDMA, CDMA	TDMA, FDMA, CDMA, OFDM
Target markets	Large and medium enterprises	Residential, small enterprise
CPE* costs	High	Low to medium

* a device that connects a customer to an access circuit or a cable modem

Table 5-2   LMDS versus MMDS

Advantages of using MMDS include:

- If the underutilized spectrum is digitalized, it becomes increasingly valuable and flexible
- MMDS, along with ITFS channels, offers video entertainment programming to subscribers
- System implementation is fast and cheaper
- MMDS services generate revenue with the one-way distribution technology

Key applications are:

- Originally designed for local television and distribution of business data
- Broadband services to residential and small businesses where DSL or cable is not available

Table 5-2 compares the features of LMDS and MMDS.

IDEN

First introduced in 1994, Motorola's Integrated Digital Enhanced Network (IDEN) brought to the market next generation wireless solutions designed for a variety of vertical market mobile business applications. Today, IDEN wireless handsets are used in a number of work environments ranging from manufacturing floors to executive conference rooms as well as mobile sales forces.

Motorola IDEN handset users are finding new applications and determining unique communication solutions every day to help their businesses progress and grow. For example, Motorola's IDEN solution provides the ability for you to hold a conference with a large number of people, with only the push of a button, helping you remove time-wasting and costly individual calls.[1]

Streamlining Communications into One Digital Handset

Four-in-one IDEN technology offers business users to take advantage of advanced wireless technologies with one pocket-sized digital handset that combines: two-way digital radio, digital wireless phone, alphanumeric messaging, and data/fax capabilities leveraging Internet access technology. IDEN technology gives you the freedom to go anywhere while still keeping track of what's important to not only your business but your personal life as well.

Motorola's IDEN solution truly simplifies your life by streamlining all of your communications tools.

More Than a Wireless Phone

"IDEN technology provides you more than just a wireless phone. It's a Motorola complete communications system that you hold in your hand, combining speakerphone, voice command, phone book, voice mail, digital two-way radio, mobile Internet and e-mail."

---

[1] http://IDENphones.motorola.com/IDENHome/common/what_is_IDEN.jsp

CDPD

CDPD (Cellular Digital Packet Data) is a wireless data transmission technology targeted toward mobile professionals. The technology comprises an Intermediate System (IS), Mobile Data Intermediate System (MD-IS), Mobile Data Base Station (MD-BS), and a Mobile End Station (M-ES) (Figure 5-12).

Functioning of CDPD

During transmission across cellular telephone channels, there are instances when the channel is **idle**. In fact, industry research indicates that over 30% of air time, even during heavy traffic, is unused. CDPD technology is able to **detect and use** these otherwise wasted moments by packaging data in small packets and sending it in short "bursts" during the idle time. As a result, the cellular channel works more efficiently, and voice and data transmissions are unaffected. CDPD is based on the same communications protocol as the Internet, so mobile users have access to the broadest range of information.[2]

Its features include:

- Uses unused cellular channels (in the 800- to 900-MHz range) to transmit data in packets
- 19.2 kbps maximum throughput. Real user data is less than 12kbps
- TCP/IP-based

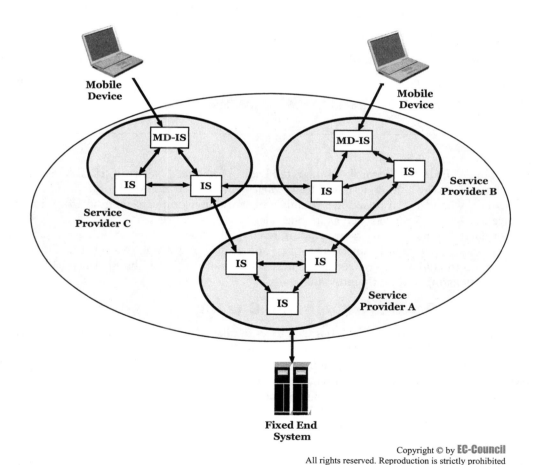

Figure 5-12   CDPD Architecture.

---

[2] http://www.arcelect.com/Cellular_Digita_Packet_Data-CDPD.htm

- Cost efficient
- Reliable, compatible
- Dedicated channels
- DSMA-CD congestion control and MAC access (***DSMA-CD***, which stands for ***Digital Sense Multiple Access with Collision Detection***, is a protocol that transmits channel and decode status flags from a base station to a mobile unit to indicate the status of the associated reverse channel. These flags signify whether it is busy or idle and whether or not there were errors.)

HSCSD

HSCSD (High-Speed Circuit-Switched Data) is a specification for data transfer over GSM networks. It has the following features:

- A circuit-switched wireless data transmission technology for mobile users at data rates up to 38.4 kbps
- Uses maximum bandwidth of 57.6 kb
- Better protocol for time-sensitive applications
- Utilizes up to four (9.6 Kb or 14.4 kb) time slots, for a total bandwidth of 38.4 kb or 57.6 kb
- Helps guarantee quality of service because of the dedicated, circuit-switched communications channel
- Used for timing-sensitive applications such as image or video transfer
- Now available in over 27 countries

PDC-P

PDC-P is the messaging system used by DoCoMo. It is a packet-switching message system utilized by NTT DoCoMo. ***DoCoMo*** is a unique network that permits subscribers to access the Internet nonstop via mobile technology. Users can send and receive e-mails, exchange pictures, conduct e-business, shop, download ringtones and wallpapers, and browse various Web sites.

PDC-P uses a maximum of three 9.6-Kb TDMA channels, on which the bandwidth is up to 28.8 Kb.

FRS

FRS (Family Radio Service) radios are an improved walkie-talkie system authorized in the United States. The FRS radios operate at less than one mile, and mostly within a visible distance. FRS radios operate in the spectrum of GMRS radios. They use FM instead of AM and have a more reliable range than license-free radios operating in the 49-MHZ band.

GMRS

The GMRS (General Mobile Radio Service) is an ultrahigh frequency (UHF) radio service used for short-distance (up to 5 miles) two-way communication in the United States. GMRS operates on any of up to eight dedicated channels (15–22) designated by the FCC. An FCC operator's license is required to use a GMRS radio. GMRS radios operate in the 462/467-MHz frequency range.

BSS

BSS (Basic Service Set) is the collection of stations that may communicate together within an 802.11 WLAN. There are two types of BSS:

- Independent Basic Service Set
- Infrastructure Basic Service Set

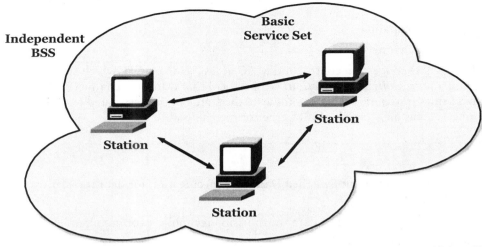

Figure 5-13   Independent BSS.

Independent BSS

An Independent BSS, or ad hoc network, is the simplest of all IEEE 802.11 networks because no network infrastructure is required (Figure 5-13). As such, an IBSS consists of one or more stations that communicate directly with each other. The abbreviation should NOT be confused with an Infrastructure BSS.

Infrastructure BSS

An Infrastructure BSS is a type of IEEE 802.11 network comprising both stations and APs (Access Points) that are used for all communication within the BSS, even if the stations reside within the same area. The method involves the station first transferring the information to the AP, which in turn forwards it to the destination station. Alternatively, should the information be destined for a wired node, the AP will forward it to the fixed network.

HPNA and Powerline Ethernet

Home Phone Networking Alliance (HomePNA)

The HomePNA™ Alliance develops triple-play home networking solutions for distributing entertainment data over both existing coax cable and phone lines. The Alliance creates internationally recognized, open and interoperable standards and best practices. By providing data rates up to 320 Mbps with guaranteed Quality of Service (QoS), HomePNA technology enables service providers to meet – and drive – the growing demand for new multimedia services such as IPTV and VoIP to the home. HomePNA technology also provides consumers with the many benefits of 'no-new-wires' home networking.[3]

Powerline Adapter

The Powerline Ethernet Adapter links your Ethernet-equipped computers and devices over your accessible, standard 110-volt electrical wiring - reducing the need for you to run cabling among them. Connect one end of the adapter into an available wall outlet and connect the other end to any available Ethernet port. The Adapter locates on any laptop or desktop, with the simplicity of Plug-and-Play technology to provide you with Internet, file, and peripheral sharing. Now you can network from virtually any room in your home or office.

Its advantages are:

- Fits any standard 2- or 3-prong wall outlet

- Offers 56-bit DES data encryption to allow for secure data transmissions

- Avoids network disruption and Powerline noise by using Power Packet-hopping frequencies to maintain network connections

---

[3] http://www.homepna.org/en/index.asp

- Installs with Plug-and-Play convenience
- Works with Windows 98 SE, 2000, Me and XP
- Life-time warranty and free 24 hour technical support[4]

Chapter Summary

- Wireless technologies represent a fast-emerging area of development and importance for providing ubiquitous access to the network.
- IrDA defines "a standard for an interoperable, universal two way cordless infrared light transmission data port."
- Bluetooth is a short-range communications technology intended to replace the cables connecting portable devices.
- Wibree is a digital radio technology that consumes ultralow power, complementing other connectivity technologies.
- Wi-Fi stands for "wireless fidelity." It is a term for certain types of wireless local area networks that use specifications in the 802.11 family.
- Hotspots provide user access to the Internet using one or more wireless access points.
- GSM makes international roaming very common between mobile phone operator, enabling subscribers to use their phones in many parts of the world.
- GPRS stands for General Packet Radio Service. It is a GSM data transmission technique that adds packet-switching protocols and shorter setup time for ISP (Internet service provider) connections.
- EDGE stands for Enhanced Data Rates for GSM Evolution. It is an advanced technology of wireless communications and an extension of GPRS.
- FDMA stands for Frequency Division Multiple Access. It defines the frequency allotted for a range of wireless cellular telephone communications into nearly 30 channels.
- TDMA is an acronym for Time Division Multiple Access. It is technology through which digital wireless transmission permits multiple users to distribute a single radio-frequency channel without interference, by assigning unique time slots to each user within the channel.
- CDMA is a "spread spectrum" technology, allowing many users to occupy the same time and frequency allocations in a given band/space.
- ZigBee is a specification for communication protocols based on the IEEE 802.15.4 standard. The ZigBee specification defines a stack protocol that allows the interoperability of wireless devices at a low cost with low power consumption for a low data-rate network.
- LMDS network topology can be point to point or point to multipoint.
- The multichannel multipoint distribution service (MMDS) frequencies, 2.5-GHz to 2.7-GHz band, allow two-way voice, data, and video streaming.
- IDEN uses speech compression and TDMA-based digital wireless technology that combines two-way radio, telephone, text messaging, and data transmission into one network.
- CDPD (Cellular Digital Packet Data) is a wireless data transmission technology targeted toward mobile professionals.
- HSCSD is a circuit-switched wireless data transmission technology for mobile users that has data rates up to 38.4 kbps.
- PDC-P is the major mobile provider in Japan. It is a packet-switching message system utilized by NTT DoCoMo.
- FRS (Family Radio Service) radios are an improved walkie-talkie system authorized in the United States.
- The GMRS (General Mobile Radio Service) is an ultrahigh frequency (UHF) radio service used for short-distance (up to five miles) two-way communication in the United States.
- BSS is a collection of stations that communicate among themselves without an AP.

---

[4] http://catalog.belkin.com

Review Questions

1. Define narrowband and broadband.

   _____

   _____

   _____

   _____

2. What is Wibree?

   _____

   _____

   _____

   _____

3. Bluetooth operates at the range of _____.

   a. 5 m

   b. 10 m

   c. 15 m

   d. 20 m

4. WISP stands for _____.

   a. Wireless Internet Standards and Protocol

   b. Wireless Internet Service Provider

   c. Wireless Instant Service Protocol

   d. Wireless Interface for Secure Processes

5. What are the different subscriber services supported by GSM?

   _____

   _____

   _____

   _____

6. Narrowband interference occurs in _____.

   a. FDMA

   b. TDMA

   c. CDMA

   d. GSM

7. Discuss advantages and disadvantages of FDMA and TDMA technologies.

   _____

   _____

   _____

   _____

8. Compare: frequency range, data rate, range, modulation techniques, target markets, and CPE costs of LMDS and MMDS services.

_____

_____

_____

_____

9. Define CDPD and HSCSD.

_____

_____

_____

_____

10. How do the different components of ZigBee communicate with each other?

_____

_____

_____

_____

Hands-On Projects

Please attempt the following exercises to reinforce what you have learned in this chapter. Record your observations or process notes for later reference.

1. Determine whether your system supports Bluetooth and infrared technologies.

2. Check for hotspots at hotels and airports when you are traveling.

3. Determine which technology your mobile phone supports: GSM or CDMA.

4. Determine whether your mobile phone is enabled for Wi-Fi. Check for Bluetooth and infrared technology support on your phone.

5. Try to configure fixed wireless broadband technologies for your network.

Chapter 6

Wireless Protocols and Communication Languages

Objectives

After completing this chapter, you should be able to:

- Discuss wireless protocols:
  - Wireless Application Protocol
  - Temporal Key Integrity Protocol
  - Shared Wireless Access Protocol
  - Extensible Authentication Protocol
  - Lightweight Directory Access Protocol
  - RADIUS
  - Wireless Robust Authenticated Protocol
  - Handheld Device Transport Protocol
  - Counter Mode with Cipher Block Chaining Message Authentication Code Protocol
  - Session Initiation Protocol
  - Simple Object Access Protocol
  - Robust Secure Network
- Discuss programming languages used in wireless devices:
  - Java 2 Platform, Micro Edition
  - Wireless Markup Language
  - Binary Runtime Environment for Wireless
  - compact HTML
  - Handheld Device Markup Language
  - VoiceXML

Key Terms

Carrier Sense Multiple Access-Collision Avoidance (CSMA-CA)   unlike CSMA-CD, which deals with transmissions after a collision has occurred, the CSMA-CA protocol acts to prevent collisions before they happen

Initialization Vector (IV)   used in cryptography to ensure that an encryption mechanism, a stream cipher, or a block cipher in a streaming mode generates a unique stream that is independent of all other streams encrypted with the same key without reapplying the cryptographic keying process

Internet Draft (ID)   working documents of the Internet Engineering Task Force (IETF), its areas, and its working groups. Unrevised documents placed in the Internet Drafts Directories have a maximum life of six months. After that time, they must be updated, or they will be deleted. After a document becomes an RFC, it will be replaced in the Internet Drafts Directories with an announcement to that effect.

Public Switched Telephone Network (PSTN)   the world's collection of interconnected, voice-oriented public telephone networks, both commercial and government owned; it is also referred to as the Plain Old Telephone Service (POTS)

Request For Comments (RFC)   a formal document from the Internet Engineering Task Force (IETF) that is the result of committee drafting and subsequent review by interested parties

Introduction to Wireless Protocols and Communication Languages

This chapter will familiarize you with wireless protocols and programming languages used in wireless devices.

Wireless Protocols

Wireless protocols are the set of rules that govern the exchange of information between wireless devices. This section will discuss the following protocols:

- Wireless Application Protocol (WAP)
- Temporal Key Integrity Protocol (TKIP)
- Shared Wireless Access Protocol (SWAP)
- Extensible Authentication Protocol
- Lightweight Directory Access Protocol (LDAP)
- RADIUS
- Wireless Robust Authenticated Protocol (WRAP)
- Handheld Device Transport Protocol (HDTP)
- Counter Mode with Cipher Block Chaining Message Authentication Code Protocol (CCMP)
- Session Initiation Protocol (SIP)
- Simple Object Access Protocol (SOAP)
- Robust Secure Network (RSN)

Wireless Application Protocol (WAP)

WAP is an important standard for information services on wireless devices such as mobile phones. WAP is the link between the mobile world and the Internet (Figure 6-1). WAP describes the wireless application environment (WAE), which allows the operator, manufacturers, and developers to create new services and applications to allow your handset (phone) to receive your e-mail or view Web pages. The WAP protocol stack was created to reduce the required bandwidth and increase the number of wireless network types that can deliver WAP content.

WAP uses the markup language known as WML (Wireless Markup Language). WML is based on XML (eXtensible Markup Language). It is used to define the content and user interface for narrow-band devices (WAP devices) such as cellular phones and pagers. WAP uses Internet standards such as XML, user datagram protocol (UDP), and Internet protocol (IP).

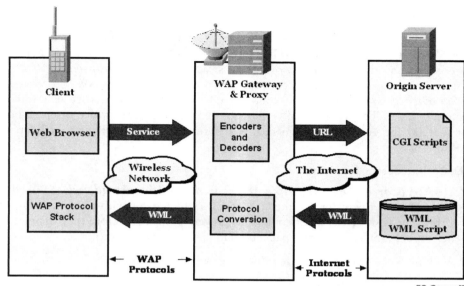

Figure 6-1   WAP model.

WAP Micro Browser

WAP Micro Browser is a Web browser that works on small wireless devices. Micro browsers are optimized to show Internet content on the small screens of handheld devices and to accommodate the low memory and bandwidth capacity of small wireless devices.

This browser can view the information written in WML. WML is made up of number of cards, with each card containing a screen of information. The collection of cards is known as a deck; this deck is the same as an HTML page. WML is case sensitive; all tabs and attributes are always in lowercase.

The Micro Browser interprets the version of JavaScript known as WMLScript, which is a complement to WML. With the help of WMLScript, the user can access user agent facilities, check user input, and execute user agent software.

Temporal Key Integrity Protocol (TKIP)

TKIP is an element of the IEEE 802.11i encryption standard used in WPA. TKIP was designed as the next generation of Wired Equivalent Privacy (WEP). TKIP eliminates the drawbacks of WEP by offering per-packet key mixing, a rekeying mechanism, and a message integrity check. It ensures that each data packet has been sent with its own encryption key.

Some features of TKIP are:

- Secret key created during four-way handshake authentication
- Dynamically changes secret key
- Function used to create new keys based on the original secret key created during authentication
- *Initialization vectors (IVs)* increased to 48-bits. IVs are used in cryptography to ensure that an encryption mechanism, a stream cipher, or a block cipher in a streaming mode generates a unique stream that is independent of all other streams encrypted with the same key without reapplying the cryptographic keying process.
- First 4 bits indicate QoS traffic class
- Remaining 44 bits are used as a counter
- Over 500 trillion keystreams possible
- Initialization vectors are hashed
- Harder-to-detect keystreams with the same initialization vectors

Shared Wireless Access Protocol (SWAP)

SWAP is a protocol built by the HomeRF Working Group. It is used for wireless voice and data networking in the home. SWAP works at the 2400-MHz band at 50 hops per second. (A hop is an intermediate connection in a string of connections linking two network devices; when a packet is transferred from one router to another, the hop occurs.) The data transmission rate is between 1 Mbps to 2 Mbps. SWAP operates together with the *PSTN (Packet Switched Telephone Network)* for voice telephony and the Internet via cordless telephone and wireless LAN technologies. PSTN is the world's collection of interconnected, voice-oriented public telephone networks, both commercial and government owned. It is also referred to as the Plain Old Telephone Service (POTS).

SWAP supports:

- TDMA interactive data transfer

- *CSMA/CA (Carrier Sense Multiple Access-with Collision Avoidance)*: SWAP helps CSMA/CA with high-speed packet transfer. Unlike CSMA-CD, which deals with transmissions after a collision has occurred, the CSMA-CA protocol acts to prevent collisions before they happen. In CSMA/CA priority is higher for acknowledgement of packets than other network data.

In a SWAP network with cordless handheld devices, the user can:

- Activate the electronic devices by voice

- Access the Internet at home from anywhere

- Transfer fax, voice, and e-mail messages

Extensible Authentication Protocol (EAP)

EAP is described by RFC 2284. (A *Request for Comments [RFC]* is a formal document from the Internet Engineering Task Force [IETF] that is the result of committee drafting and subsequent review by interested parties.) It is used by the 802.1x standard for authentication framework. It allows users to pass security authentication data between RADIUS (Remote Authentication Dial-In User Service), AP, and the wireless user. EAP is a cost-effective, worldwide authentication framework that is frequently used in wireless networks and point-to-point connections. It can also be used in a wired network. 802.1x combines this protocol with other standards such as RADIUS and TACACS+ (Terminal Access Controller Access Control System).

EAP supports multiple authentication methods:

- Token cards and smart cards

- Kerberos

- One-time passwords

- Certificates

- Public-key authentication

Figure 6-2 illustrates EAP's authentication and key distribution.

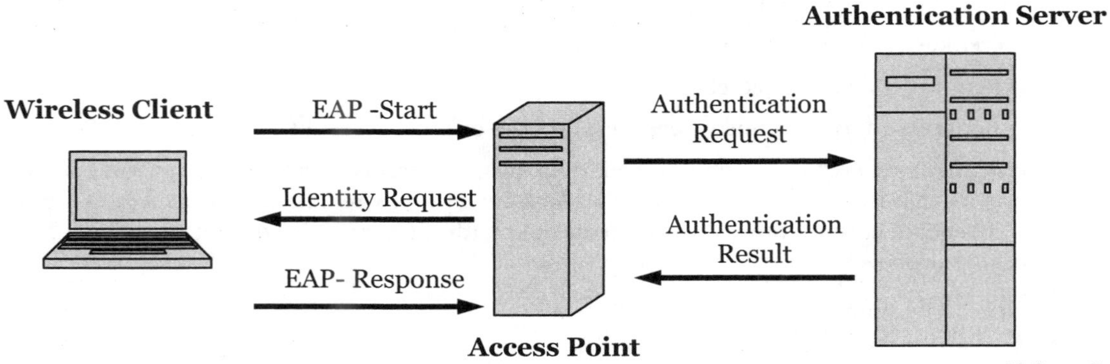

Figure 6-2   Authentication and Key distribution by EAP.

Variants of EAP are Lightweight EAP (LEAP), Protected EAP (PEAP), EAP MD5, and EAP-TLS (Transport Layer Security). LEAP and PEAP are discussed in the following sections.

The Lightweight Extensible Authentication Protocol (LEAP)

The Lightweight Extensible Authentication Protocol (LEAP) is a proprietary, closed solution that offers username and password-based authentication between a wireless client and a RADIUS server. LEAP conducts mutual authentication. It is used with the IEEE 802.1x standard for LAN port access control.

Key features of LEAP are:

- It provides assurance to the client that the access point is authorized
- It employs per-session keys that need to be changed regularly
  - Makes the collection of a pad or weak **IVs** more difficult
  - Secret key can be changed before the collection is complete
- The user is authenticated, rather than the hardware
- MAC address access control lists are not needed
- LEAP requires an authentication server (RADIUS) to support the access points

Protected Extensible Authentication Protocol (PEAP)

PEAP is an 802.1x authentication type for wireless LANs. PEAP is supported by Cisco Unified Wireless Network. It functions with WPA and WPA2 networks. PEAP is based on an Internet Draft presented by Cisco Systems, Microsoft, and RSA Security to ITEF. *Internet Drafts (ID)* are working documents of the Internet Engineering Task Force (IETF), its areas, and its working groups. Unrevised documents placed in the Internet Drafts Directories have a maximum life of six months. After that time, they must be updated, or they will be deleted. After a document becomes an RFC, it will be replaced in the Internet Drafts Directories with an announcement to that effect.

PEAP provides:

- Strong security
- User database extensibility
- Support for one-time token authentication
- Support for password change or aging

PEAP has the following security features:

- Relies on Transport Layer Security (TLS) to allocate unencrypted authentication like EAP-Generic Token Card (GTC) and one-time password (OTP) support.
- Utilizes server-side, public-key infrastructure (PKI)-based digital certification authentication.
- Permits authentication to an enlarged suite of directories, including Lightweight Directory Access Protocol (LDAP), Novell NDS, and OTP databases.
- Makes use of TLS to encrypt all user-sensitive authentication data.
- Supports password change and aging.
- Never exposes the logon username in the EAP identity response.
- Is not susceptible to dictionary attacks.
- Gives dynamic privacy security when combined with TKIP or AES.

Lightweight Directory Access Protocol (LDAP)

The X.500 Directory Service model is the best model for services provided by various operating systems. It consists of a central repository of operating system information and management functionalities. The LDAP, which is an information database and querying protocol, is based on the X.500 Directory service model. It works to combine the details of system and application services to make them compatible and to make it easier to configure data related to application programs, security, and user accounts, etc., on the local network.

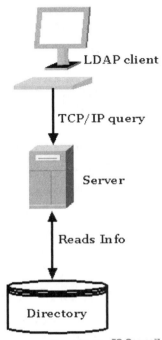

Figure 6-3   LDAP architecture.

The design of LDAP does not support large numbers of user entries and user databases, but it is a hierarchal database in the form of records with fewer entries. The directory structure of LDAP is similar to the file structure in Windows. The use of small, simple records provides faster access. LDAP is not compatible with large databases such as Oracle, Sybase, DB/2, and SQL Server. Figure 6-3 illustrates the LDAP architecture.

The LDAP servers available are few but include:

- DS Series LDAP Directory (AIX) designed by IBM
- Innosoft's Distributed Directory Server designed for Linux
- Netscape Directory Server designed for Linux
- OpenLDAP server designed for Linux
- Sun Microsystems' Directory Services designed for the Solaris platform
- SLAPD designed by the University of Michigan

Novell's eDirectory and Lotus Domino use the directory services of the LDAP protocol as an interface to communicate with directories that work with the LDAP. Microsoft's Active Directory supports LDAP use in querying and application program interfaces to interact with LDAP.

Users of LDAP communicate with its directory server for verification of authenticity and validity. The bind function is performed to validate the client. If the bind is successful, the user is connected to the server. The permissions of the user and the type of authentication mechanism are chosen and passed to the server. LDAP authorizes the clients with ACL (Access Control List).

When authenticating users, LDAP stores details of user accounts, permissions, and access limitations. If the user is determined to be valid via verification by the authentication method, LDAP identifies the user's details and loads the user's database privileges.

Benefits of LDAP are:

- Can be used as an application server to collect details such as personal data and contact information from the directory.
- Answers the client's queries that are in its repository, with the help of its search engine.
- The DNS servers store information in the LDAP record hierarchy.
- Used as an interface or gateway to exchange data between incompatible applications.

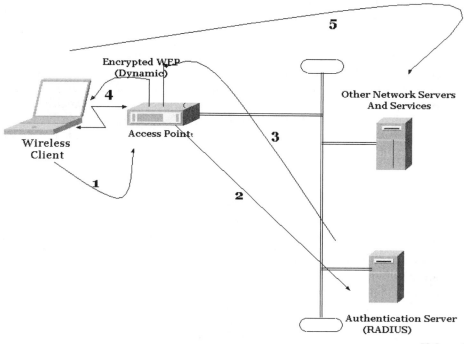

Figure 6-4   RADIUS sequence.

- Operating systems can use it to convey information to various resources and elements of the OS.
- Consists of various APIs to authenticate the users, details of the network host, location of files and directories, and details of frequently used applications.
- Systems services such as RADIUS and Kerberos use LDAP to store location details.

RADIUS

The RADIUS protocol is an organized protocol that is used to access the network. The following is the process to access the network through RADIUS (Figure 6-4):

- Enter username and password
- User information is transferred through a NAS (Network Access Server) to a RADIUS server
- The RADIUS server checks the details against the database
- Based on the settings configured by the network administrator, access is granted to the user

In a WLAN, the AP acts as NAS. RADIUS stores data in its internal database or an external database such as Active Directory or Novell Directory Services, which are similar to databases used by the LDAP. RADIUS is a user-based authentication mechanism. Hardware authentication mechanisms are carried out through MAC addresses and shared keys such as the WEP. Switching from hardware- to user-based authentication ensures scalability and security of the WLAN. RADIUS implemented in a wired network makes it easy to use in a wireless network of the same organization. WLANs that use 802.1x security solutions have employed RADIUS as an effective authentication mechanism.

Benefits of using RADIUS are:

- Authenticity does not rely on hardware
- Economical
- Decreases operating costs for the administrators when data to authenticate is upgraded, changed
- Accounting, assessment, and reporting are supported features

- Warns against unauthorized access of the network
- Can be used with VPN in a wireless network (as in 802.1x security solutions)

The distinction between the wireless VPN implementation of RADIUS and the user-based implementation is the type of NAS devices used and the authenticating protocol. The RADIUS server deals with the type of supporting protocol. The security mechanism should be built in a manner to block the attempts of intruders. Configuring Kerberos (an authentication system designed to enable two parties to exchange private information across an open network using a ticketing system) in a wireless network can ensure the security is up to the standards of the remote users. The 802.11i was developed to enhance standards for security and to overcome the shortcomings of 802.11. Kerberos efficiently approaches the standards defined in the 802.11i.

Configuration

The scalability and effectiveness of the wireless network that deploys RADIUS depends on the decisions regarding where and how to place the RADIUS servers in the network. RADIUS servers are deployed according to the network environment (such as for a single site), corporate network that is remotely accessed, or a combination of multiple network architectures. To set up a RADIUS server, take these issues into account:

- *Central authenticity and security*: A RADIUS server is configured on a central network or network hub to which individual networks connect for authentication. This configuration avoids the high cost of configuring the RADIUS server on every network, some of which may have few users and therefore may not be worth the effort. The central RADIUS server handles the authentication and security of these networks. It manages the querying of users, maintains the user account details, and stores accounting information for billing at the central site. The availability of a central site in a wireless network is an issue because the reliability of the network depends on the security provided to the central site. In a distributed network environment utilizing a central RADIUS server, the load is distributed, resulting in an increase of performance with less bandwidth usage.

- *Mixture of architectures*: The networks, which depend on a central RADIUS for authentication, may be of different types that may not be compatible with others. If certain networks are not reliably connected to the central site on which the RADIUS server is configured, then it will be necessary to install the RADIUS server separately for such networks even though they may consist of few users. The RADIUS servers that are configured are distributed servers, which secure the network and ensure consistency, integrity, and security of the network. 802.1x has the advantage of being flexible in distributed environments.

- *Distributed sites*: The distributed-site security using central authentication consists of WLAN APs in every individual network to validate its users, whose database is in the central site or operating hub of the distributed network. RADIUS servers manage the APs, WLAN, and remote access to the network. The RADIUS server authenticates the local users of the network, establishes secure network connectivity to the users, and stores the accounting information related to the user. Bandwidth availability to the RADIUS server in the central site is the major issue. There is no requirement for RADIUS servers on every location of the satellite, or network, or AP cluster. It may be beneficial, but potential problems should be dealt with prior to selecting and deploying it.

  The network connectivity of the user depends on the availability of a connecting link between the distributed network and the central hub. If the link is down, a connection cannot be established. Rekeying is necessary for users who disconnect from the network when it is down, which ensures security of connectivity. The RADIUS/AAA servers' duty is to initially authenticate the users and then periodically calculate the cryptographic keys for better security. A large number of WLANs can cause congestion on the network. This congestion can be eliminated by configuring the RADIUS/AAA servers in the WLANs that have increasing numbers of users. This situation usually occurs in reliable, fast network links and distributed environments where the user database is stored in a central repository accessible by the distributed network. Here, the WLAN users are validated with tokens.

- *Distributed autonomous sites*: In distributed autonomous networks, the database is present on the individual networks; user information is not stored in the central database. Either one or more RADIUS servers are configured in the autonomous networks to handle the WLAN and remote access. In this situation there is no requirement for a central RADIUS server as there is in central sites. The RADIUS servers perform user validation in the current network by setting WLAN connections and storing accounting information. As the WLAN users increase, the number of RADIUS servers that handle the overhead can be increased to improve the performance and security of the site. The autonomy provided to the network makes it easy to deploy the databases that use LDAP, but is not reliable for databases such as SQL, which cannot be replaced easily.

- *Single-site deployments*: In single-site network deployment, the users of WLAN are present on the same site where a central database is maintained to validate the users. More than a single RADIUS server is employed to locate the user details, manage the validation of users, secure connection establishment, and manage the WLAN and remote access. Users of WLAN can be validated with the available server databases. Addition of RADIUS/AAA APs increases the scalability of the network and makes it simple to authenticate users through the back-end database. If the users of WLAN increase, it is recommended to employ a distributed site deployment.

Wireless Robust Authenticated Protocol (WRAP)

WRAP is the encryption protocol that was used by the 802.11i standard. WRAP was the original AES-based proposal for 802.11i, but it was replaced by CCMP. WRAP is an optional component of RSN; it is based upon the Offset Codebook (OCB) mode of AES for encryption and integrity.

Handheld Device Transport Protocol (HDTP)

HDTP is a protocol optimizer for HDML-coded data. It acts as an application protocol and a session-level protocol for operations between clients and servers. HDTP supports the same applications as HTTPS (HTTP over SSL), such as:

- Extensible request methods
- Typing and cooperation of data representation
- Message privacy, reliability, and authentication

HDTP has been optimized for handheld devices and low-performance networks in the following ways:

- Datagram-based, rather than stream-based, allocating for a simpler underlying protocol stack.
- Encodes header names and other well-known values wherever possible.
- Session frameworks decrease transmission of redundant data.
- Implementation in use of security and cipher algorithms on small devices.

HDTP provides the following security features:

- Authentication, privacy, and integration
- Counteracting playback attacks

Counter Mode with Cipher Block Chaining Message Authentication Protocol (CCMP)

The CCMP (Counter Mode with Cipher Block Chaining Message Authentication Protocol) is the encryption protocol and the reliability mechanism in the 802.11i standard. It is based on the CCM mode of the AES encryption algorithm. CCMP is compulsory for anyone who implements RSN (Robust Secure Network).

CCMP uses 128-bit keys, with an initialization vector of 48 bits for reply (attack) avoidance. The two components of CCMP are:

- Counter Mode (CM): supports data privacy
- Cipher Block Chaining Message Authentication Code (CBC-MAC): supports data integrity and authentication

A disadvantage of CCMP is that it cannot be used with a device that does not have sufficient CPU power.

Session Initiation Protocol (SIP)

SIP is a protocol for multimedia conferences over IP. It is an ASCII-based protocol that can help with the creation, modification, and termination of calls between two or more terminals. SIP helps in MSN and other session-oriented applications that require interaction.

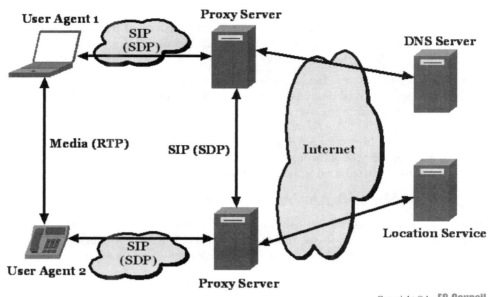

Figure 6-5   SIP components and protocols.

Key functions of SIP are:

- *Name mapping and interaction*: It contains the translation of a client's descriptive information to SIP location information.
- *Capabilities negotiation*: The different media capacities of the applicant are decided by SIP in order to declare suitable usage of media facilities during the session.
- *Participant management*: This function allows applicant management by enabling applicants to control the inclusion of newcomers into a session or the exit of an existing applicant during a session.
- *Capabilities management*: SIP is able to observe media capabilities during a session and thus make suitable changes when required. This dynamic ability will adjust the client's relations with other clients by changing the session dynamically to reflect a compounded matrix of capabilities.

These are the components of SIP (see Figure 6-5):

- *User Agent Client (UAC)*: This component determines the data necessary for the request: protocol, the port, and the IP address of the UAS to which the request is being sent.
- *User Agent Server (UAS)*: This component receives the request from UAC, and responds to it.
- *Proxy Server*: This component acts as a mediator between UASs and UACs. It services the requests or forwards them to other UASs or UACs for servicing.
- *Redirect Server*: This component allocates for redirection, which allows users to temporarily vary geographic position and remain in contact through the same SIP identity.
- *Registrar server*: This component makes it possible for users to change a contact address. It sends a REGISTER request of change of address to the registrar server, which then accepts the request and records the user's new address.

Simple Object Access Protocol (SOAP)

SOAP is an XML-based protocol. It is used for the exchange of information in a decentralized, distributed environment. SOAP increases interoperability, making it easy to transfer a request from a client to server by using XML and HTTP Web formats. It is a high-level way for devices to tell other devices to do the things over the Internet.

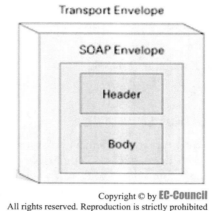

Figure 6-6 The three parts of SOAP.

SOAP consists of the following three parts (Figure 6-6):

- An envelope that describes a framework for explaining the inside matter of the message and how to process that message.
- A set of encoding rules for expressing instances of application-defined data types.
- Convention for representing remote procedure calls and responses. All encoding is in XML.

Applications of SOAP are:

- Business-to-business integration: It enables businesses to extend their applications.
- Distributed applications: Applications such as databases are stored on one server and the other operation is done by clients across the Internet.

Robust Secure Network (RSN)

RSN is the protocol that is used in 802.11 for maintaining secure communication over a wireless network. A wireless network that uses RSN with TKIP instead of CCMP is known as a Transition Security Network (TSN). RSN is also known as WPA2.

In general:

- $TSN = TKIP + 802.1x = WPA1$
- $RSN = CCMP + 802.1x = WPA2$

The RSN protocol works as follows:

- The wireless NIC sends a Probe Request to the wireless access point.
- The wireless access point replies by sending a Probe Response with an RSN Information Exchange (IE) frame.
- The wireless NIC requests authentication, which takes place by using any standard method.
- The wireless access point gives the authentication for the wireless NIC.
- The wireless NIC transmits an Association Request with an RSN Information Exchange (IE) frame.
- The wireless access point sends an Association Response.

Programming Languages Used for Wireless Communication

The following languages are designed specifically for mobile devices:

- Java 2 Platform, Micro Edition (J2ME)
- Mobile Information Device Profile (MIDP)

- Wireless Markup Language (WML)
- Binary Runtime Environment for Wireless (BREW)
- compact HTML (cHTML)
- Handheld Device Markup Language (HDML)
- VoiceXML

Java Platform, Micro Edition (Java ME)

J2ME is a Java-based runtime platform created by Sun Microsystems. It is targeted for devices that are small, stand-alone, network connectable, or embedded, such as cellular phones or personal digital assistants (PDAs). J2ME allows users to use the Java language and related tools to create programs for small mobile wireless devices.

J2ME contains a virtual machine and set of APIs (Application Programming Interfaces) that help to run the encoded program in the mobile devices. J2ME is a version of Java that is adapted to fit and have characteristics that are set for devices having a smaller footprint, such as mobile devices and other consumer products that use a smart card.

J2ME technology has two main components: configuration and profile.

Configuration

The J2ME platform has a modified configuration per profile. It consists of a virtual machine and set of class libraries that includes APIs. It supplies the base functionality for a certain range of devices that allocate the same features, such as network connectivity. A configuration might be considered for devices that have memory less than 512 KB.

The two types of J2ME configuration are:

1. *Connected Limited Device Configuration (CLDC)*: Uses a set of application programming interfaces and K (kilobyte) virtual machines for resource-constrained devices.

2. *Connected Device Configuration (CDC)*: Uses the conventional Java Virtual Machine because it maintains profiles that have a requirement for more characteristics and can contain larger memory footprints; devices such as digital television receivers, residential gateways, and screen phones use the CDC.

Profile

Profile is the set of Java APIs that have special function and ability to create a complete runtime environment to run a particular program in a specific device. Profiles are the collection of higher-level APIs that describe the application life-cycle model, the user interface, and some special properties of constant storage and access to the device. Figure 6-7 illustrates the J2ME schema.

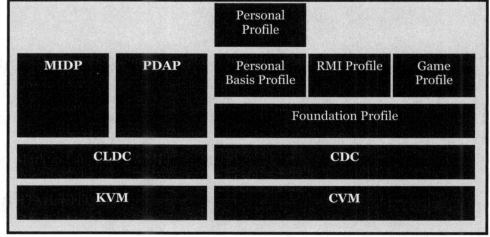

Figure 6-7   J2ME schema.

Connected Limited Device Configuration (CLDC)

The CDLC is the basic component of the J2ME architecture. It uses a set of application programming interface and K (kilobyte) virtual machines for resource-constrained devices. When the CDLC is combined with a profile like MIDP (Mobile Information Device Profile), it gives a better Java platform for the applications. This allows applications to run on devices with limited memory, processing power, and graphical capabilities.

The goals of CLDC are:

- To reduce footprint requirements to levels appropriate for mass-market use.
- To make application portability easier by abstracting local system operations into standardized APIs.
- To extend device functionality by allocating dynamic downloading of applications into the device.

The target devices which are used have the following requirements:

- A 16- or 32-bit processor with a clock speed of 16 MHz or more
- Minimum 160 KB of nonvolatile memory stored for the CLDC libraries and virtual machine
- Minimum 192 KB of total memory available for the Java platform
- It must consume little power, as it often operates on battery power
- It has connectivity to some types of networks often with a wireless, intermittent connection, and limited bandwidth

Mobile Information Device Profile (MIDP) The MIDP (Mobile Information Device Profile) is the important part of the J2ME platform. It is a set of APIs that are implemented with CLDC. When MIDP combines with CLDC, it gives a complete runtime environment for application devices such as mobile phones. The application can run on devices with limited memory, processing power, and graphical capabilities.

These are the features of MIDP:

- *Rich user interface capabilities*: MIDP applications provide the base for highly graphic and instinctive applications. MIDP applications are installed and run locally, and work in both networked and unconnected modes.
- *Extensive connectivity*: MIDP provides leading connectivity standards, containing HTTP, HTTPS, datagrams, sockets, server sockets, and serial ports. MIDP provides the Short Message Service and Cell Broadcast Service capabilities of GSM and CDMA networks.
- *Multimedia and game functionality*: A game API adds game-specific functions and the Mobile Media API (MMAPI) package adds video and other multimedia functions to MIDP applications.
- *Over-the-air provisioning*: One of the main advantages of MIDP is its ability to install and update applications dynamically and securely, over the air.
- *End-to-end security*: MIDP provides a strong security model that complies with open standards and protects the network, applications, and mobile information devices.

The MIDP specifications are:

- *MIDP 1.0*: The original version that gives core application functionality required by mobile applications, including a basic user interface and network security.
- *MIDP 2.0*: A modified version of the MIDP 1.0; it contains features such as a better user interface, multimedia and game functionality, better extensive connectivity, and end-to-end security.

Wireless Markup Language (WML)

WML is based on XML (eXtensible Markup Language). It is used to define the content and user interface for narrow-band devices (WAP devices) such as cellular phones and pagers. WML is designed with the limitations of small devices in mind. These limitations are:

- Small display and restricted user input facility
- Narrow-band network connection
- Restricted memory and computational resources

WML allows the text part of Web pages to be accessible on cellular telephones and personal digital assistants (PDAs) via wireless connection. WML differs from HTML in following cases:

- WML is created for wireless applications with a screen a few lines of text long, and approximately an inch wide
- WML is case sensitive, with all tabs and attributes always in lower case
- Unlike HTML, in WML there is no separate text. All the text is held in the WML element. HTML only displays that data.

WML is supported by every mobile phone browser.

Binary Runtime Environment for Wireless (BREW)

BREW is one of the main platforms available for mobile developers. BREW is a collection of APIs that allow developers to produce software applications for wireless devices. C, C++, or Java platforms can be used for writing BREW applications.

The components of BREW are:

- BREW Thin Client.
- BREW stands between the application and the wireless device on-chip operating system, allowing programmers to develop applications without coding for the system interface.
- BREW Distribution System (BDS): a wireless data services delivery and billing environment. Leveraging open and extensible technology, BDS enables network operators to rapidly deploy wireless data services to subscribers network wide via mobile devices.

compact Hypertext Markup Language (cHTML)

cHTML is a part of HTML. It is made for small application devices such as PDAs and cellular phones. Small-device applications have many hardware restrictions such as less memory, low storage capacity, low-power CPU, monocolor display screen, and the absence of keyboard or mouse, so there is a need for a simple form of HTML. cHTML supports GIF (Graphics Interchange Format) images, and uses four buttons instead of two-dimensional cursor movements.

The principles of cHTML are:

- *Depends totally on current HTML W3C recommendation*: cHTML is a subset of HTML, so it inherits the flexibility and portability of standard HTML.
- *Light specification*: cHTML is designed for use in devices with less memory and low-power CPUs; frames and tables occupy too much memory, so they are excluded from cHTML.
- *Can be viewed on small, monocolor display*: cHTML assumes a smaller display space for 2 colors, typically black and white, and offers flexibility for display screen size.
- *Easily operated by user*: It is designed in such a way that all basic operation is done by four buttons: Cursor forward, Cursor backward, Select, and Back/Stop.

Handheld Device Markup Language (HDML)

HDML is designed to make Web sites portable. The user can see the Web site on mobile phones, PDAs, and other small devices. This language needs the runtime the user agent to make it useful. HDML is Openwave's proprietary language; it is displayed on mobile phones that use the Openwave browser. HDML, created before the WAP standard, uses Openwave's Handheld Device Transport Protocol (HDTP).

The factor that gives the runtime environment to HDML is known as *user agent*. This agent displays and allows the user to interact with cards of information. The card is the basic building block of HDML content; a collection of cards is known as a deck.

Voice Extensible Markup Language (VoiceXML)

VoiceXML is designed for developing audio dialogs that characterize synthesized speech, digitized audio, and recording of spoken input, telephony, and mixed-initiative conversations. This language is created for making Internet content and data accessible via voice and phone. It is a common language for content, tool, and platform providers.

Features of VoiceXML are:

- Minimizes client/server communications by identifying multiple interactions per document.
- Protects application authors from low-level and platform-specific elements.
- Supports service portability across implementation platforms. VoiceXML is a common language for content providers, tool providers, and platform providers.
- Easy to apply to simple interactions, but it provides language characteristics to support complex dialogs.

The scope of VoiceXML explains the man-machine communication provided by a voice response system. It consists of:

- Output of synthesized speech (text to speech)
- Output of audio files
- Identification of spoken input
- Recording of spoken input
- Telephony characteristics like call transfer and disconnect

Chapter Summary

- Wireless protocols are a set of rules that govern the exchange of information between wireless devices.
- WAP is an application communication protocol inherited from Internet standards.
- The Micro Browser interprets the version of JavaScript known as WMLScript. It is a complement to WML.
- TKIP eliminates the drawbacks of WEP by offering per-packet key mixing, a rekeying mechanism, and a message integrity check.
- SWAP operates together with the PSTN (Packet Switched Telephone Network) for voice telephony and the Internet via cordless telephone and wireless LAN technologies.
- EAP is an 802.1x standard that allows developers to pass security authentication data between the access point (AP) and wireless client.
- LEAP conducts mutual authentication. It is used with the IEEE 802.1x standard for LAN port access control.
- PEAP relies on Transport Layer Security (TLS) to allocate nonencrypted authentication like EAP-Generic Token Card (GTC) and one-time password (OTP) support.
- The design of LDAP does not support a large number of user entries and user databases, but is a hierarchal database in the form of records with fewer entries.
- The distinction between the wireless VPN implementation of RADIUS and the user-based implementation is the type of NAS devices used and the authenticating protocol.
- WRAP is an encryption protocol in the 802.11i standard; it is based on the Offset Codebook (OCB) mode of AES.
- HDTP is a protocol optimizer for HDML-coded data; it acts as an application and session-level protocol for operations between clients and servers.
- CCMP is the encryption protocol and the reliability mechanism in the 802.11i standard.
- SIP helps in MSN and other session-oriented applications that require interaction.
- SOAP enables businesses to extend their applications, and the make use of those applications, or allows other companies to use them.
- RSN is the protocol that is used in 802.11 for maintaining the secure communication over a wireless network.
- Java 2 Platform, Micro Edition (J2ME) is targeted at small, standalone, or connectable consumer and embedded devices.
- WML is an XML language that is used to specify the content and user interface for WAP devices.
- BREW is a set of APIs that enable developers to create software applications for wireless devices.

- cHTML gives support to GIF (Graphics Interchange Format) images, and uses four buttons instead of two-dimensional cursor movements.
- HDML is designed to make Web sites portable.
- VoiceXML is designed for developing audio dialogs that characterize synthesized speech, digitized audio, and recording of spoken input, telephony, and mixed-initiative conversations.

Review Questions

1. What are the different protocols used for wireless communication?

_____

_____

_____

_____

2. Define initialization vector.

_____

_____

_____

_____

3. Explain the role of WAP protocols in a WAP system.

_____

_____

_____

_____

4. How does TKIP enhance the security of a WAP system?

_____

_____

_____

_____

5. WAP supports the _____ markup language.
   a. compact HTML
   b. HDML
   c. WML
   d. VoiceXML

6. What is the WAP Micro Browser?

_____

_____

_____

_____

7. What are the different protocols used for authenticating wireless communication?

_____

_____

_____

_____

8. Explain how RSN protocols work.

_____

_____

_____

_____

9. _____ defines the basic set of application programming interfaces and Java virtual machine features in the J2ME environment.

  a. PDAP

  b. MIDP

  c. CDC

  d. CLDC

10. List the various programming languages used for wireless communication.

_____

_____

_____

_____

Hands-On Projects

Please attempt the following exercises to reinforce what you have learned in this chapter. Record your observations or process notes for later reference.

1. Determine the protocols supported by your wireless network.

2. Check whether your wireless communication is secure. Employ the security protocols.

3. Determine the wireless communication protocols supported by your mobile phone.

4. Check which programming platform your mobile phone supports.

5. Determine the markup language supported by your mobile phone.

Chapter 7

Wireless Devices

Objective

After completing this chapter, you should be able to:

- Discuss the wireless devices that make up a typical wireless infrastructure

Key Terms

Gain   a measure of the increase in signal amplitude produced by an amplifier

Radiator   a heating element that transfers thermal energy

Resonator   a hollow, metallic device whose dimensions allow the echoing oscillations of electromagnetic waves, used to increase volume

Service set identifier (SSID)   the sequence of characters or code that is attached to each packet of the wireless network, which is useful to identify the packet that is covered in a particular network when there are a number of networks present; the code can contain a maximum of 32 alphanumeric characters. All wireless devices can communicate with each other if they have the same SSID. SSID is used for unique identification of a set of wireless network devices that work in a given "service set."

Subscriber identity module (SIM)   a small card containing the telephone number of the subscriber, encoded network identification details, the PIN, and other user information such as the phonebook—all the information that is necessary to activate a phone; a SIM can be shifted from phone to phone

Universal mobile telecommunication system (UMTS)   the third-generation standard after GPRS; in this broadband system, packet-based transmission of text takes place. It transfers digitized voice, video, and multimedia at a data rate up to 2 Mb/s. It is based on WCDMA (Wideband Code Division Multiple Access) and offers a set of services to mobile phone users located all over the world.

Waveguide technology   analyzes the ways of transferring electromagnetic waves from a speaker to the air and the conductors used to carry EM waves from one point to another

Introduction to Wireless Devices

A typical wireless infrastructure comprises devices that connect to the network. They include: antennas, access points, mobile stations, base station subsystems, network subsystems, base station controllers, terminals, mobile switching centers, wireless modems, and wireless routers.

Antennas

An antenna is a device that is designed to transmit and receive electromagnetic waves (generally called radio waves). An antenna is a collection of metal rods and wires that capture radio waves and translate them into electrical current. The size and shape of antennas are designed according to the frequency of the signal they are designed to receive. An antenna that *gains* (a measure of the increase in signal amplitude produced by an amplifier) high frequency is highly focused, but a low-gain antenna receives or transmits over a large angle. A transducer translates radio-frequency fields into AC current and vice versa.

There are two basic types of antennas:

- Omnidirectional antennas
- Directional or unidirectional antennas

Types of Antennas

Apart from the basic types of antennas (directional and omnidirectional), there are others, including aperture, leaky wave, reflector, monopole, dipole, Yagi, log-periodic, and active.

- *Directional*: Radio signals are concentrated in a particular direction.
- *Omnidirectional*: Radiate or receive equally in all directions.
- *Aperture*: Have a physical opening through which the propagation of electromagnetic waves takes place. They were developed from waveguide technology. **Waveguide technology** analyzes the ways of transferring electromagnetic waves from a speaker to the air and the conductors used to carry EM waves from one point to another.
- *Leaky wave*: Fundamentally, a perforated waveguide obtained from millimeter wave (mm-wave) like dielectric guides, microstrip lines, coplanar and slot lines.
- *Reflector*: Used to concentrate EM energy that is radiated or received at a focal point; they are generally parabolic.
- *Monopole*: Simple antenna that is omnidirectional (in azimuth). If it is one half of a wavelength long, it then has a gain of 1.64 (or $G = 2.15$ dBi) in the horizontal plane. It is one half of a dipole placed in half space, with a perfectly conducting, infinite surface at the boundary.
- *Dipole*: Two wires that are kept either horizontally or vertically and pointed in opposite directions. One end of the wire is connected to a radio and the other is suspended in free space. Dipole is a straight, level antenna separated at its center by a line to a transmitter or receiver.
- *Yagi*: Also called an aerial antenna, it is the most directive antenna. It is generally used where gain and directivity are required.
- *Log-periodic*: Provides gain and directivity over a large bandwidth; consists of a number of dipole elements.
- *Active*: Consists of a small whip antenna that supplies incoming RF to a preamplifier, whose output is then connected to the antenna input of a receiver. These antennas are designed to receive.

Directional Antennas

Directional antennas radiate radio waves in a somewhat constrained area. They are not as versatile as omnidirectional antennas but are useful for fixed locations. These antennas are used when the distance between the transmitter and receiver is no more than a few hundred meters. The amount of information that can be transferred can be high because the wavelength used in these antennas is very small (10^{12} to 10^{14}).

Directional antennas are designed for concentrating the radio signals in a particular direction. In this design, antenna gain and the direction are closely related. Directivity is the measure of power density the antenna radiates in the direction of strongest emission; thus, the directional attenna is controlling the RF energy pointed in a certain direction. The amount of RF energy remains constant but spreads over a small area, thus increasing the signal strength. The antenna gain is measured in decibels or in dipole (dBd).

Omnidirectional Antennas

Omnidirectional antennas radiate electromagnetic energy uniformly in all directions. They usually radiate strong waves in two dimensions, but not as strongly in the third. These omnidirectional antennas are effective for irradiating areas in which the location of other wireless stations will vary with time. A good example of omnidirectional antennas are the ones used by radio stations. These antennas are very effective for radio signal transmission because the receiver may not be stationary. Therefore, listeners get the signal regardless of the direction.

Omnidirectional antennas radiate or receive equally in all directions. As it does not support a specific direction, it is also known as "nondirectional." During transmission the radiated signal has similar strength in every direction, which is helpful in broadcasting a signal to all the stations of that area. While receiving, all the signals are received equally.

Aperture Antennas

These antennas have a physical opening through which the propagation of electromagnetic waves takes place (Figure 7-1). These types of antennas are developed from waveguide technology. The particular pattern they emit has a short main beam that denotes high gain.

Transmission lines are created for transmission of high-power microwave EM signals (wavelength in centimeters), which are generated from strong microwave sources such as magnetrons and klystrons. These antennas are suitable for a frequency range between 1 and 20 GHz.

For a fixed aperture size, the main beam pattern becomes short as the frequency increases. These types of antennas are used in aircraft and spacecraft applications.

Leaky Wave Antennas

These antennas are obtained from millimeter wave (mm-wave) like dielectric guides, microstrip lines, coplanar and slot lines. These antennas are useful for applications with frequencies of more than 30 GHz. It includes the infrared frequency range. Periodical breaks are established at the end of the guide, which results in large radiation leakage.

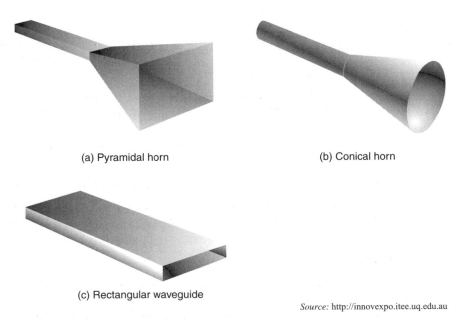

(a) Pyramidal horn

(b) Conical horn

(c) Rectangular waveguide

Source: http://innovexpo.itee.uq.edu.au

Figure 7-1 Aperture antennas.

Reflector Antennas

Reflector antennas are used to concentrate EM energy that is radiated or received at a focal point. They are generally parabolic.

A parabolic cylinder mirror transmits the rays from a main line source into a group of parallel rays. In 1888, Heinrich Hertz used these parabolic reflectors for the first time for radio waves. Corner reflectors are used very rarely.

Large reflectors have high gain and directivity, but they are difficult to manufacture, mechanically weak, and heavy. They are used in radio telescopes and satellite communication.

Plain reflectors provide maintenance of the radio link for non-line-of-sight conditions.

Antenna Functions

The functions of an antenna are as follows:

- *Transmission line*: Antennas transmit radio waves from one point to another or receive radio waves. This power transmission takes place in free space through natural media such as air, water, and earth. Antennas avoid power reflection.
- *Radiator*: Antennas radiate energy powerfully. This radiated energy is transmitted through a particular medium. In this application the antenna should be comparable to a half wavelength.
- *Resonator*: A hollow metallic device whose dimensions allow the echoing oscillations of electromagnetic waves; it is used to increase volume. The use of the resonator is necessary in the broadband application. It is unavoidable. Resonance means increasing sound—attenuate means weaken— in a broadband application. If resonance occurs, it must be mitigated.
- Resonances which occur must be attenuated.

Antenna Characteristics

The characteristics of antennas are as follows:

- *Operating frequency band*: Antennas operate at a frequency band between 960 MHz and 1,215 MHz.
- *Transmit power*: Antennas transmit power at a 1,200-watt peak and 140-watt average.
- *Typical gain*: Gain is the ratio of power input to the antenna to the power output from the antenna. The gain is measured in decibels (dBi). The typical gain is 3.0 dBi.
- *Radiation pattern*: The radiation pattern of antenna is in a 3-D plot. This pattern generally takes two forms: elevation and azimuth.
- *Directivity*: The directivity gain of an antenna is the calculation of radiated power in a particular direction. It is generally the ratio of radiation intensity in a given direction to the average radiation intensity.
- *Polarization*: The orientation of electromagnetic waves from the source. There are a number of polarizations including; linear, vertical, horizontal, circular, circular left hand (LHCP), and circular right hand (RHCP).

Access Points (AP)

APs are the hardware devices or software used to connect wireless users into a wired network for communication. They act as a bridge or hub between a wired LAN and a wireless network; they are generally connected to the wired network. An AP may also be called the "base station." APs are necessary for providing strong wireless security, and also are used for increasing the physical range of the services that the wireless users access. The range of an AP is increased with the help of repeaters, which amplify the network's radio signals. APs use IP addresses for configuration.

Operating Modes of APs

An AP is a piece of wireless communications hardware that creates a central point of wireless connectivity. Similar to a "hub," the access point is a common connection point for devices in a wireless network. Wireless access points must be deployed and managed in common areas of the campus, and must be coordinated with the telecommunications and network managers.

The operating modes of APs are as follows:

- *Access-point mode*: In this mode, an AP acts as a hub or a station to which wireless clients are connected. In access-point mode, an AP never wirelessly discloses its own connection to the LAN; it must be hardwired to a switch or other node.

- *Repeater*: In this mode, APs are used for increasing the range of the wireless network. Repeaters receive the signal from an AP, amplify that network's radio signals, and transmit them to the wireless clients.

- *Bridge*: This mode is used for connecting two separate LAN networks for communication. In the bridge mode, APs must be wired to a switch or other network devices.

- *Multipoint bridge*: In this mode, more than two access points are connected to each other to form a wireless link between them.

- *Wireless client*: In this mode, an AP provides a wireless connection between the separate LAN sector and another LAN.

PC Cards

A PC Card is a credit card–sized peripheral that adds memory, mass storage, and I/O capabilities to computers in a rugged and compact form. Previously, these cards were called PCMCIA (Personal Computer Memory Card International Association) Cards. They were later called PC Cards, PC Card Hosts, PC Card Software based on the new technology.

The PC Card interface uses ISA-style or PCI parallel bus connections. The PC Card interface uses 68-contact pin and socket connectors automatically.

Throughput of the PC Card interface is as follows:

- CardBus (32-bit burst mode)
  - Byte mode: 33 Mbytes/sec
  - Word mode: 66 Mbytes/sec
  - DWord mode: 132 Mbytes/sec
- 16-bit memory transfer (100-ns minimum cycle)
  - Byte mode: 10 Mbytes/sec
  - Word mode: 20 Mbytes/sec
- 16-bit I/O transfer (255-ns minimum cycle)
  - Byte mode: 3.92 Mbytes/sec
  - Word mode: 7.84 Mbytes/sec

The PC Card standard provides three types of PC Cards (Type I, II, and III), which have the same length and width and use the same 68-pin connector, but have different thicknesses. In the case of an electrical or software interface, a thin card can be used in a thick slot, but a thick card cannot be used in a thin slot. The size of the bigger card prevents it from fitting into the smaller slot. Any card can hypothetically be used for any device, based on the difference in sizes and the needs of different applications.

PC Cards have the following applications:

- *Type I*: Used for memory devices such as RAM, flash, OTP, and SRAM cards.
- *Type II*: Used for I/O devices such as data/fax modems, LANs, and mass storage devices.
- *Type III*: Used for devices whose components are thicker, such as rotating mass storage devices.
- *Extended*: Allows the addition of components that must remain outside the system for appropriate operation, such as antennas for wireless applications.

The PC Card standard defines the operation of PC Cards at two different voltages: 3.3 V and 5.0 V. To prevent 3.3 V cards from being inserted into wrong slots, a "key" is defined on the edge of the PC Card connector, which operates only at 5.0 V.

Wireless Cards

The wireless network card locates and communicates with the AP with a powerful signal to give the user network access. A powerful signal commonly yields better and quicker connection to the network. Wireless network cards should be Wi-Fi-certified by the Wireless Ethernet Compatibility Alliance (WECA). As there will be numerous future additions to the wireless standards, it is suggested that the wireless card be upgraded via a firmware upgrade, so they will be able to handle new features. A wireless network interface card (WNIC) is different than a network card, which works only with an 802.11 network. A WNIC works on the physical and data link layer of the OSI model.

A WNIC is a fundamental component of a wireless desktop computer. This card uses an antenna for communicating through microwaves. A WNIC in a desktop PC is generally located in the PCI slot. A WNIC can function in two modes:

- *Infrastructure*: Access point is required
- *Ad hoc*: Access point is not required

In an infrastructure mode, the WNIC needs an access point. The WNIC sends data to other wireless nodes through the access point, which acts as the central hub. Each wireless computer in an infrastructure mode links to an access point. While linking to an access point under the infrastructure mode, it must use the same SSID. If the access point is configured for WEP, the same WEP key or other authentication fields must be used.

The **service set identifier (SSID)** is the sequence of characters or code that is attached to each packet of the wireless network. This is useful to identify the packet that is covered in a particular network when there are a number of networks present. The code can contain a maximum of 32 alphanumeric characters. All wireless devices can communicate with each other as long as they have the same SSID. SSID is used for unique identification of a set of wireless network devices that works in a given "service set."

In an ad hoc mode, the WNIC does not need an access point because it can interface directly with all other wireless computers. When configuring the node in an ad hoc mode, be sure that other subordinate nodes have the same channel and matching SSID.

Wireless Modem

Wireless modems are the devices used to connect computers to a WLAN without using cable wiring. The modem is connected to a wireless network instead of to a telephone system. When users connect to the wireless modem, they connect directly to the ISP (Internet service provider) and can then access the Internet.

Wireless modems function at a speed similar to dialup modems. Wireless modems provide cellular, satellite, or Wi-Fi protocols to connect to a WLAN that supports the Internet service. Some wireless modems connect directly to the PDA or the laptop.

The wireless modem interface consists of a PCMCIA (Personal Computer Memory Card International Association) card. A PCMCIA wireless modem card is used in a laptop, which provides access to the Internet through public "hotspots." The following are three different physical configurations possible for a PCMCIA card:

1. *CompactFlash card*: Provides a suitable way to communicate with PDAs, tablets, and other portable devices.
2. *USB (Universal Serial Bus)*: An external peripheral interface standard that is used for communication between a computer and external peripheral devices.
3. *Serial port*: One of the computer interfaces. Before internal modems became common, external modems were connected to computers via serial ports.

The following are examples of wireless voice networks that are used by some wireless data networks:

- *CDPD (Cellular Digital Packet Data)*: An arrangement that gives wireless access to the Internet and other packet-switched networks. It provides TCP/IP and connectionless network protocol (CLNP).
- *GSM GPRS (General Packet Radio Service)*: An arrangement for data transfer on TDMA and GSM networks.
- **Universal Mobile Telecommunication System (UMTS)**: Third-generation standard after GPRS. In this broadband system, packet-based transmission of text takes place. It transfers digitized voice, video, and multimedia at a data rate up to 2 Mb/s and is based on WCDMA (Wideband Code Division Multiple Access). It offers a set of services to mobile phone users located all over the world.
- *GSM EDGE (Enhanced Data GSM Environment)*: An arrangement for data transfer on GSM networks.

Wireless modems have the following features:

- *Modem speed*: The speed of the wireless modem is nearly the same as dialup modems.
- *Protocol(s) supported*: Wireless modems support protocols such as Ethernet, CPCD, GPRS, ISDN, EVDO, Wi-Fi, etc.
- *Frequency band*: Wireless modems have frequency bands of 900 MHz, 2.4 GHz, 5 GHz, 23 GHz, VHF, and UHF.
- *Radio technique*: Wireless modems use the direct sequence spread spectrum or frequency-hopping radio techniques.
- *Channels*: A number of channels are available for transmission and reception.
- *Signal strength*: The signal strength is highest in this type of modem.
- *Full duplex*: Wireless modems support full-duplex capability.

Wireless Router

A wireless router is a simple router with a wireless interface. It is a device that connects wireless networks. This router connects the network and operates at the network layer of the OSI model. It is a regular IP router with 802.11 interfaces that contain antennas.

Connected users can share files, pictures, peripherals, and printers with everyone else on the network. Wireless routers have filtering capacity. However, they are not as secure as wired networks.

An example of a wireless broadband router is the WR850GP, which has these features:

- Wireless users are free to roam anywhere
- Installation wizard makes networking simple
- Able to extend the users and devices by connecting wirelessly
- Wireless performance is 35% more than standard 802.11g networking
- Data rates up to 54 Mbps

Using a Wireless Router as an AP

Take the following steps to configure a wireless router as an AP:

- *Step 1*: Unplug the PC from the wired connection and plug it into a LAN port of a secondary router.
- *Step 2*: With the help of a default LAN IP address and default password, use the browser to access a secondary router.
- *Step 3*: To assign a LAN IP to a new device, use the commands winipcfg in Windows 9x or "ipconfigrelease/renew" in Windows 2000/XP on a PC.
- *Step 4*: Perform the following tasks on the secondary router:
  - Modify the default password so it contains a combination of at least eight numbers/letters/symbols.
  - Change the ESSID to a unique name and create all important wireless configurations.
- *Step 5*: Go to the LAN setup page in AP.
  - Turn the DHCP service off.
  - Alter the LAN IP of the AP from the default, so it lies in the range of the subnet of the primary router but outside the range of the dynamic LAN IP of the primary router.
- *Step 6*: Reconnect the PC to the wired connection and repeat the method of getting a new LAN IP. You may have to reboot the PC.
- *Step 7*: Connect the AP to the router, LAN port to LAN port directly or through the switch/ patch panel.
- *Step 8*: It may be necessary to reboot one or both the routers. However, one of them should be capable of allocating LAN Ips wirelessly and connecting at this point. Make sure that the Wi-Fi card is properly configured.

Wireless USB

The wireless USB is a natural extension of a USB, which connects peripherals and consumer electronic devices to a host PC. It is based on Ultra Wide Band (UWB) technology that supports a 480-Mbps data rate over a distance of two meters (approximately 6.6 feet). If the speed slows to 110 Mbps, then UWB will travel farther (up to 10 meters, or approximately 30 feet). Based on the speed limit, the distance can be calculated. The less speed applied, the more area it covers. This technology is functional for home or office environments.

The fundamental relationship in a wireless USB is the "hub and spoke" topology. The host initiates all the data traffic among the devices that are connected to it, and assigns time slots and data bandwidth to each device. These relationships are referred to as clusters. The connections between the wireless USB host and the wireless USB device are point to point and direct. The difference between a wired USB device and one that is wireless is that in a wired USB device, hubs are not present in the connection topology. The wireless USB host can reasonably connect a maximum of 127 wireless USB devices.

Wireless USB clusters exist together within a spatial environment with minimum interference, thereby allowing a number of other wireless USB clusters to be present within the same radio cell.

Wireless USB technology has the following attributes:

- Simple and low-cost implementation
- Point-to-point connection topology that supports up to 127 devices. It follows the same host-to-device architecture as used for wired USBs.
- Consists of high spatial capacity in less area, which allows access to multiple devices concurrently at high bandwidth
- Plays the dual role model where, in addition to being a WUSB device (e.g., a digital camera connected to a computer), it can function as a host with limited capabilities (e.g., transferring pictures if connected to a printer)

Wireless USB specifications include the following requirements:

- Mutual authentication in device and host connections
- World-class security as a standard and nonremovable feature for all certified wireless USB devices
- Asymmetric, host centric model that maintains the USB model of cheap or simple devices and confines the complexity to the host

Wireless Game Adapter

A wireless game adapter fixes a video game console to a Wi-Fi home network to allow Internet or head-to-head LAN gaming. It is available in 802.11b and 802.11g ranges, which are used for home networks. An example of an 802.11g wireless game adapter is the Linksys WGA54G. It is connected to a wireless router either by using an Ethernet cable or Wi-Fi. Ethernet cables provide the most consistency and best performance. Wi-Fi is preferred for its convenience.

Wireless game adapters include setup software that has to be installed on one computer to complete the startup configuration of the device. Wireless game adapters are constructed with the correct network name (SSID) and encryption settings.

Wireless Game Adapter: WGE111 54 Mbps

The WGE111 54 Mbps Wireless Game Adapter links the gaming console to a wireless network, eliminating the need for wires. It is attached to the game console's Ethernet port to link. In the case of LAN (ad hoc) gaming, two or more WGE111 units are used to link two game consoles.

An external switch enables the user to select easily between Internet and LAN modes for either online or LAN gaming. In LAN gaming, WGE111 connects a game console to other WGE111 units having no wireless networks. Because of its compact size it is easy to carry to LAN parties and gaming events.

Specifications:

- *Dimensions*: 80 × 120 × 32.5 mm (3.14 × 4.72 × 1.19 in)
- *Weight*: 32 g
- *Status LEDs*: Power (green), Internet (green), AdHoc (blue), Ethernet (green)

- *Standards compliance*: 802.11g
- *Interface*: RJ-45
- *Security*: 64/128-bit WEP encryption

Wireless Print Server

A wireless print server allows one or two printers to be shared across a Wi-Fi network. Wireless print servers for home networks are usually available in 802.11b and 802.11g.

When using USB 1.1 or USB 2.0, the wireless print server is connected to printers by a network cable. A wireless print server can connect to a wireless router over Wi-Fi by itself, or it can be attached with an Ethernet cable.

To complete the startup of the device, the print server products must provide setup software on a CD-ROM for installation on a computer. Also, the print server requires each computer to have client software installed. The advantages of a wireless print server are:

- Printers can be located anywhere within the range of a wireless network
- Does not require a computer to be turned on in order to print
- Does not require a computer to manage all print jobs, which can bog down its performance
- Administrators can change computer names and settings without reconfiguring the network print settings

Wireless Range Extender

A wireless range extender increases the distance over which a WLAN signal can spread, helps overcome obstacles, and improves overall network signal quality. Wireless range extenders are available in different forms as range expanders or signal boosters. They work as a communication or network repeater, selecting and reflecting Wi-Fi signals from a network's base router or access point. If range extenders were connected directly to the primary base station, the network performance of the device would be low. They connect wirelessly to a Wi-Fi router or access point, allowing them to work with a limited set of other equipment.

Wireless Internet Video Camera

A wireless Internet video camera allows video and audio data to be recorded and transmitted through a Wi-Fi computer network. It is available in 802.11b and 802.11g ranges. It works by serving up the data streams to any computer connected to it.

It contains a built-in Web server, allowing computers to easily connect through it using either a standard Web browser or special client/user interface. Through authorized computers and proper security information, video streams of the cameras are easily viewed over the Internet. Wi-Fi Internet video cameras are connected through a wireless router by using either Ethernet cable or a wireless connection. Wireless Internet video cameras come with software that must be installed to configure the device.

The features of a wireless Internet video camera are:

- Resolution of the captured video images (for example, 320 × 240 pixels, 640 × 480 pixels and other image sizes)
- Contains motion sensors, which have the ability to send e-mail alerts when new activity is detected and captured
- Images can be time-stamped
- Contains built-in microphones and jacks for external microphones and audio support
- Supports Wi-Fi security such as WEP or WAP

Bluetooth Connectivity Devices

Bluetooth offers connectivity for several devices. Bluetooth is an open wireless protocol for exchanging data over short distances from fixed and mobile devices.

Air2Net Bluetooth PC Card

Air2Net Bluetooth Wireless PC Card is designed for mobility and faultless connections between a laptop and other Bluetooth devices. The Bluetooth PC Card acts in accordance with Bluetooth 1.1 standards and enables legacy laptop PCs with Bluetooth wireless connectivity. Its wireless specifications are:

- *Frequency Band/Bandwidth*: 2.4 GHz to 2.4835 GHz
- *Antenna*: 0dBi embedded antenna
- *Transmission Speed*: 460 Kbps
- *Channels*: 79 channels (United States, Japan, and Europe)
- *Transmit Power*: 4 dBm maximum
- *Receiver Sensitivity*: -70 dBm <0.1% BER

Interfaces/Ports and Media:

- *Host Interface*: PC Card
- *Interfaces/Ports*: 1 × wireless Ethernet
- *Connectivity Media*: Wireless

Bluetooth Combo Print Adapter

Bluetooth Combo Print Adapter allows any Bluetooth computer or PDA to send print jobs to a USB or parallel printer wirelessly. It acts in accordance with USB 1.1, IEEE 1284, and specifications of Bluetooth 1.1. It supports data transmission rates up to 723 Kbps and a wireless access range up to 330 ft (100 meters). It supports both Pico-net and Scatter-net, which allow a printer to be shared with up to seven PCs or PDAs. It supports HCRP (Hardcopy Cable Replacement Profile) and SPP (Serial Port Profile) that reside on flash memory. It contains complete receiver and transmitter functions.

Its wireless specifications are:

- *Wireless Technology*: Bluetooth
- *Frequency Band/Bandwidth*: 2.402 GHz to 2.4835 GHz ISM band
- *Antenna Range*: 330 ft
- *Transmission Speed*: 723 Kbps
- *Transmit Power*: 20 dBm

Interfaces/Ports:

- 1- × 4-pin USB Type A printer
- 1- × 36-pin Centronics parallel printer

Wireless Media Gateway: WMG80

The WMG80 wireless media gateway, stores and allows the user to share digital data from today's digital media entertainment, including videos, music, Internet, and pictures. It is connected to network media adapters to function as an in-home, networked, media storage device. WMG80 has an 80-GB hard drive to store the digital media, and also two USB ports and an internal print server, which provides the support for USB printers. The WMG80 setup is quick and easy because it has a setup wizard.

Figure 7-2 illustrates a wireless media gateway setup.

The features of WMG80 are:

- *Access photos, videos, music, and more on demand*: It stores family media contents on a media gateway that is accessible to the whole family. Those contents can be instantaneously shared with others—even when they are in different rooms of the house—when it is connected with the wireless media adapter.

- *Robust security keeps data secure*: NAT and SPI firewalls ensure that the networked data is safe from Internet intruders. Wireless security includes 64-bit/128-bit WEP and MAC address filtering.

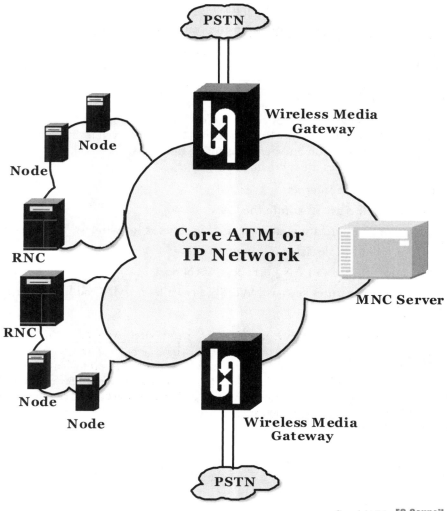

Figure 7-2 Wireless media gateway.

- *Create a wireless network for home or office*: Establish the LAN and share single peripherals such as high-speed broadband connection, files, and printers among all the computers.

- *Extremely fast sharing of content to network devices*: It contains zero waiting time. It transfers the data with 802.11g wireless connectivity for up to five times the speed of 802.11b wireless networks. With a 54-Mbps signaling rate, the family can enjoy video, music, and pictures almost instantly.

Wireless Presentation Gateway: D-Link DPG-2000W

The D-Link DPG-2000W wireless presentation gateway, connects a standard VGA cable to almost any projector or monitor. It uses 802.11g technology for displaying presentations on monitors or on a screen using a over projector. It includes presentation session manager software that allows multiple presenters one-click access to the monitor or projector for faultless delivery of presentations. The presentation session manager software automatically allocates an IP address to the DPG-2000W to match the wireless settings for added convenience and easier access.

Features of the D-Link DPG-2000W wireless presentation gateway are:

- Can communicate with any wireless laptop or computer

- Supports IEEE 802.11g wireless standards having transfer speeds of up to 54 Mbps

- Provides for real-time display of images, applications, and presentations

- Compatible with virtually any presentation projector or monitor
- Web-based administration utility for customization options, configuration settings, and firmware upgrade

Hotspot Gateway

The Hotspot Gateway device provides confirmation, authorization, and accounting for a wireless network. It keeps deliberately harmful users away from the private network, even if they break the encryption. It is specified as an all-in-one hotspot solution and performs many functions.

Hotspot Gateway provides the following features:

- Secure gateway to the Internet
- High-speed wireless access within the LAN
- Authentication, authorization, and accounting services for wireless or wired clients
- Support for point-of-sale ticket or receipt printing
- A combination of up to 4 LAN ports or 4 WAN ports
- Supports security features such as NAT, SPI firewall, and MAC address filtering to make the environment secure

GSM Network Devices

The Global System for Mobile Communication (GSM) is the most popular cellular network. GSM is different from its predecessors in that both the signaling and speech are transmitted in digital form. As with other cellular networks, GSM allows roaming, which means users can operate their phones all over the world. Most GSM networks operate in either the 900-MHz or 1800-MHz bands. GSM uses a variant of linear predictive coding (LPC) that reduces the bit rate. GSM uses GMSK-type modulation.

The GSM network system consists of the following devices:

- Mobile Station
- Base Station Subsystem
  - Base Station Controller
  - Base Transceiver Station
- Network Subsystem
  - Mobile Switching Center
  - Home Location Register
  - Visitor Location Register
  - Authentication Center
  - Equipment Identity Register

In a GSM network, the mobile station communicates across the Um Interface (air interface) with a base station transceiver in the same cell. The base station subsystem (BSS) consists of a base station controller (BSC) and one or more base transceiver stations (BTSs). The network subsystem consists of: the mobile switching center (MSC), home location register, visitor location register, authentication center, and equipment identity register.

Mobile Station

The mobile station (MS) includes the mobile equipment (ME) and the *subscriber identity module (SIM)*. A SIM is a small card that contains the telephone number of the subscriber, encoded network identification details, the PIN, and other user information such as the phonebook—all the information that is necessary to activate a phone. A SIM can be shifted from phone to phone. The mobile stations communicate with the base transceiver station (BTS), in the base station subsystem (BSS), through the Um Interface (air interface). ME is a physical device such as a telephone or PC. This ME is individually identified by the International Mobile Equipment Identity (IMEI). The SIM contains the International Mobile Subscriber Identity (IMSI).

MExE (Mobile Station Application Execution Environment)

MExE is a working group in the 3G Partnership Program (3GPP). MExE performs secure downloads of applications and content for mobile computing and e-commerce.

MExE is not limited to a GSM network only; it is organized for a wide variety of networks. MExE includes a complete application environment for mobile devices containing Java Virtual Machine (JVM). MExE describes various technology requirements known as "class marks."

These class marks are based on the following:

- *Classmark 1*: Based on the Wireless Application Protocol (WAP); it provides simple and cheap data access over slow- or high-latency links.

- *Classmark 2*: Based on Personal Java Environment and Java phones; it uses the standard Internet technology and provides strong applications and flexible MMIs.

- *Classmark 3*: Based on CLDC and MIDP applications of J2ME.

Base Station Subsystem

The BSS consists of two main components, the base transceiver station (BTS) and the base station controller (BSC). BTS and BSC communicate through the Abis interface. The BTS contains the radio transceiver, which describes the cell and also handles the radio link protocols with the mobile station. In wide areas a number of BTSs are required, making it necessary that BTSs are rugged, reliable, portable, and inexpensive.

BSC handles the radio sources for one or several BTSs. It also manages the radio channel setup, frequency hopping, and handover technique. The BSC connects the MS and the mobile switching center (MSC). BSS communicates with the MS via the Um Interface.

Base Station Controller (BSC)

The BSC is the part of the BSS that communicates with the BTS through the Abis interface. BSC is part of the wireless system's infrastructure that controls one or more cell sites' radio signals, thus reducing the load on the switch. The BSC connects the MS and MSC.

BSC is used for handling the radio sources for one or several BTSs, managing the radio channel setup and frequency hopping, and managing the handover technique.

Base Transceiver Station (BTS)

The BTS contains an antenna and a transceiver, which handle the radio interface with the mobile phone communication system. It is the first entity in GSM networks to detect the mobile signal. It can communicate with either a mobile phone or a PCS phone.

It is connected to the BSC over a T1/E1 line, which encrypts and decrypts the communication. The transceiver signal strength of the BTS defines the limitations of the mobile phone.

The functions of BTSs differ from vendor to vendor. BTSs are equipped with radios that modulate the layers of the air interface. To increase the performance of a BTS, frequency hopping is used.

Network Subsystem

The network subsystem (NS) acts as a link between a cellular network and a Public Switched Telecommunications Network (PSTN). An MSC is the main element of the NS. Services such as registration, authentication, location updating, and handover are provided with different functional entities that together form a NS.

Signaling between various units in the NS is accomplished via the Signaling System number 7 (SS7), which utilizes trunk signaling in ISDN. NS manages the handoff between cells in different BSSs. The NS includes several entities such as HLR, VLR, AuC, and EIR (Figure 7-3).

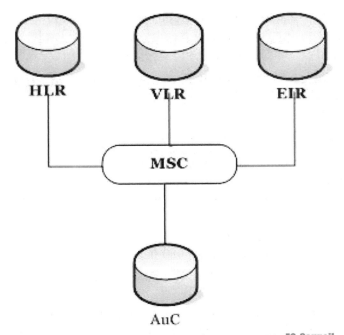

Figure 7-3 Network subsystem.

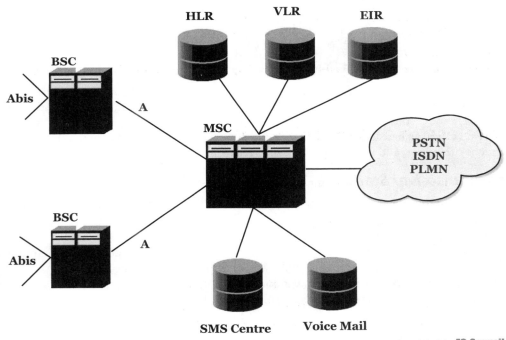

Figure 7-4 Mobile switching center.

Mobile Switching Center

The MSC is the part of the GSM network that performs switching functions and handles communication between PSTN and mobile phones (Figure 7-4). It works as a simple switching node of PSTN or ISDN. MSC is the main component of the NS.

MSCs are defined by various names according to their work:

- *Gateway MSC (GMSC)*: Detects the currently located Visited MSC called by the subscriber. The mobile-to-mobile and PSTN-to-mobile calls are routed through the GMSC.
- *Visited MSC*: Where a user is currently located.
- *Anchor MSC*: Where the handover takes place.
- *Target MSC*: The MSC towards which a handover should take place.

MSC provides the following functionality to a GSM:

- With HLR (Home Location Register) and VLR (Visitor Location Register), provides the call routing and roaming ability of GSM
- Provides the functions necessary for managing mobile subscriber, registration, authentication, and location updating
- Used for call handover and calls routed to the subscriber
- Manages the mobility management operations

Mobile Switching Center Databases The MSC has databases where information about the subscriber is stored:

- *Home Location Register (HLR)*: The HLR consists of information about the subscriber that is recorded into the respective GSM network, with the current location of the mobile subscriber. This location is generally in the form of a signaling address of the VLR connected with a MS. There is one HLR with each GSM network.
- *Visitor Location Register (VLR)*: VLR consists of select information about the subscriber, currently in physical range of the HLR, which is important for call control and provision of subscribed services.
- *Authentication Center (AuC)*: This database contains a copy of the secret key present in each subscriber's SIM card that is helpful for authentication and encryption.
- *Equipment Identity Register (EIR)*: This database consists of a set of all valid mobile equipment, where every mobile station is found with the help of its International Mobile Equipment Identity (IMEI).

Add Wireless to a Wired Network

Follow this procedure to connect a wireless network to a wired network (Figure 7-5):

- Requirements for connection:
  - Desktop PCs, laptops, or tablet PCs provided with wireless LAN access cards
  - One or more wireless access points
- Procedure:
  - Connect a wireless access point to the wired network:

    This access point then transfers the signal wirelessly to all other wireless networks.
  - Ensure all of your computers are wirelessly equipped:

    The computers that are connected to the wireless network must support the wireless LAN protocol called Wi-Fi (802.11).
  - Configure the SSID on your access points and wireless computers:

    Wi-Fi access points use the SSID to distinguish a particular wireless network from another. And remember to make changes in the SSID immediately for security.
  - Configure your access point and cards for maximum security:

    Before using a wireless network, carefully examine the security options and configuration.

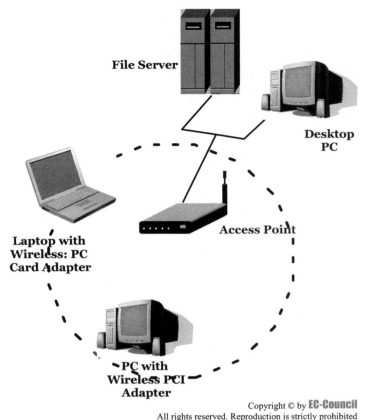

Figure 7-5 Add wireless to a wired network.

Chapter Summary

■ Antennas are important for sending and receiving radio waves. They convert electrical impulses into radio waves and vice versa. There are two basic types of antennas: omnidirectional and directional.

■ An access point is a piece of wireless communication hardware that creates a central point of wireless connectivity. Similar to a hub, the access point is a common connection point for devices in a wireless network.

■ A PC Card is a credit card–sized peripheral that adds memory, mass storage, and I/O capabilities to computers in a rugged and compact form.

■ The wireless network card locates and communicates to the access point with a powerful signal to give the user network access.

■ Wireless modems are devices that are used to connect computers to a WLAN without using cable wiring. The modem is connected to a wireless network instead of to a telephone system.

■ A wireless router is a simple router with a wireless interface. It is a device that connects wireless networks. This router connects the network, and operates at the network layer of the OSI model. It is a regular IP router with 802.11 interfaces that contain antennas.

■ Wireless gateways include wireless media gateways, wireless presentation gateways, and the Hotspot Gateway.

■ GSM devices include: mobile station, base station subsystem, and network subsystem.

■ The mobile Switching Center (MSC) is the main element of the NS. Services such as registration, authentication, location updating, and handover are provided with different functional entities that together form a network subsystem.

Review Questions

1. What is the subscriber identity module (SIM)?

   _____

   _____

   _____

   _____

2. What are the different types of antennas discussed in this chapter?

   _____

   _____

   _____

   _____

3. In _____ mode, the access point functions to extend the range of the wireless network.
   a. repeater
   b. bridge
   c. multipoint
   d. wireless client

4. Explain the steps to configure a wireless router as an access point.

   _____

   _____

   _____

   _____

5. The central element of the network subsystem is the _____.
   a. mobile station (MS)
   b. base station controller (BSC)
   c. mobile switching center (MSC)
   d. home location register (HLR)

6. What are the features of a wireless modem?

   _____

   _____

   _____

   _____

7. List the technical prerequisites defined by MExE.

   _____

   _____

   _____

   _____

8. What is the Hotspot Gateway and how does it work?

_____

_____

_____

_____

9. Discuss the various functions of a mobile switching center.

_____

_____

_____

_____

10. How can wired and wireless networks be configured to work together?

_____

_____

_____

_____

Hands-On Projects

Please attempt the following exercises to reinforce what you have learned in this chapter. Record your observations or process notes for later reference.

1. Determine the type of antenna present in your wireless network.

2. Find the access point position in your classroom.

3. List some of the devices used in a mobile communication network.

4. Try to configure your wireless modem and wireless router.

5. Try to configure your wireless router as an access point.

Chapter 8

Fundamentals of RFID

Objective

After completing this chapter, you should be able to:

- Explain the fundamentals of RFID, including its components, system architecture, applications, standards, security and privacy threats, countermeasures to those threats, and vendors

Key Terms

Active RFID tag   RFID tag that requires power

Passive RFID tag   RFID tag with no internal power supply

RFID   an automatic identification technique that stores and retrieves data using devices known as RFID tags, or transponders

RFID antenna   packed with the transreceiver and a decoder; emits radio signals that activate the tags

RFID collisions   tag collision in RFID systems occurs when numerous tags are energized by the RFID tag reader at the same time; reader collision in RFID systems occurs when the coverage area of one RFID reader overlaps with another reader

RFID system architecture   includes a controller, a premises server, and an integration server

RFID tag   an electronic device that can be included in or attached to any product, animal, or person for its identification with the help of radio waves

RFID tag reader   a device that is used to manipulate and examine RFID tag data

Introduction to Fundamentals of RFID

Paul Brennan, an electrical engineer at University College London, was the leader of a project that featured RFID technology called Optag. Optag is designed to improve airport security; it can track the movements of suspected passengers, and security personnel can block those passengers from entering restricted areas.

Another application of RFID technology is in place at the Lahey Clinic Medical Center in Burlington, Massachusetts, which is a medical facility in the Boston area. It employs more than 480 physicians and 4,600 nurses, therapists, and other support staff. For many years, employees have wasted their time searching for equipment, because they did not have efficient and effective ways to track it.

In 2000, Edward Bortone, director of materials services and security, turned to GE Healthcare, which handles the facility's clinical engineering needs, including the maintenance of medical equipment. GE Healthcare in collaboration with PinPoint developed a real-time locating system (RTLS) using active (battery-powered) RFID tags. GE Healthcare and PinPoint installed interrogators (readers) in a portion of the facility and tagged more than 500 mobile assets; companion software allows the clinic to track the location of those assets in real time.

The upgraded asset-tracking system is linked to GE Healthcare's AssetPlus maintenance software, so the Lahey Clinic receives alerts when assets are due for regular cleaning or maintenance. Bortone believes the new system will allow nurses to spend more time with patients and less time searching for equipment.

RFID (radio-frequency identification) tags can be used to track people, products, equipment, etc. This chapter will explain RFID technology—its components, applications, and vulnerabilities.

RFID (Radio-Frequency Identification)

RFID is an automatic identification technique that stores and retrieves data using devices known as RFID tags, or transponders. RFID transmits the identity of an object in the form of a unique serial number with the help of radio waves. RFID wireless transmission of data takes place between the data-carrying devices and its reader. The power needed for operating the electronic devices is transferred through the reader by the contactless technique.

RFID System Components

The basic components of the RFID systems are tags, tag readers, and antennas.

RFID Tag

An *RFID tag* is an electronic device that can be included in or attached to any product, animal, or person for its identification with the help of radio waves. RFID tags are also called transponders; they can store and remotely retrieve data. Chip-based RFID tags contain silicon chips and antennas. In an RFID system, each object is equipped with a small and inexpensive tag that contains a transponder with a digital memory chip that is given a unique electronic product code.

The RFID tags read these tags and process them according to the needs of a particular application. Tags transfer data that gives identification or location information or specifics about the tagged product, such as price, color, and date of purchase.

There are two main types of RFID tags: passive and active.

Passive RFID Tags

Passive RFID tags have no internal power supply. They are smaller in size because they do not require an on-board power supply. They measure 0.15 mm × 0.15 mm with a thickness up to 7.5 micrometers, which is thinner than paper. They are small enough that they do not require batteries and have unlimited life spans.

The incoming radio-frequency signals generate a minute electrical current in the antenna, which is sufficient for the CMOS integrated circuit (IC) in the tag to power up and transmit a response. Passive tags signal the carrier from the reader, showing that the antenna supports using power from the incoming signal. It also has the capacity to transmit outbound. A passive RFID tag is not only an ID number, but it also consists of nonvolatile EEPROM for storing additional data. Passive tags have a practical read distance, depending on the size of the antenna and the selected radio frequency, which ranges from about 10 millimeters up to 6 meters.

Active RFID Tags

Active RFID tags require power. They have their own internal power source that can be used to power any integrated circuit (IC) that creates an outgoing signal. They are able to transmit higher power as compared to passive tags. Active tags have the ability to conduct sessions with the reader, so they are more reliable than passive tags. Passive tags must rely on the power of the reader to transmit data. If a reader is not present, the passive tag cannot communicate any data, where active tags can communicate in the absence of a reader. Due to their higher-power transmitting ability, they are more effective in "RF-challenged" environments such as water or metal or at longer distances.

The practical range of active tags is hundreds of meters. Some active tags have sensors; for example, temperature logging that can be used in concrete maturity monitoring or for monitoring the temperature of perishable goods. Active tags have larger memories compared to passive tags, so they are able to store extra information sent by the transceiver. The battery has a lifespan of up to 10 years.

Chipless RFID Tag

A chipless RFID tag does not use IC technology to store information. These tags make use of fibers or materials that reflect the reader's signals back. The return signal is unique, and it is used as an identifier. The fibers are available in different shapes such as thin threads, fine wires, or even labels or laminates. The cost of these fibers ranges from 10 cents to 25 cents per unit. Chipless tags are unable to transmit a unique serial number, so they are less usable in the supply chain. They are used as an anticounterfeiting measure with documents.

Chipless RFID tags are used in various environments different from those using RFID tags with electronic circuitry. They work over a wider temperature range and are less sensitive to RF interference.

Tag Readers

An **RFID tag reader** is a device that is used to manipulate and examine RFID tag data. It has an antenna that emits radio waves and the tag responds to those waves. It has four different ranges:

1. Nominal read range
2. Rogue scanning range
3. Tag-to-reader eavesdropping range
4. Reader-to-tag eavesdropping range

The RFID tag perceives the reader's activation signal when it passes through the reader's electromagnetic zone. Readers are mounted to a fixed location or they can be handheld. The tag reader emits radio waves in a broad range depending on the radio frequency used and the power output. They decode the encoded data in the tag's IC and pass the data to the host computer for processing.

RFID Stations

An RFID station consists of an RFID reader and antenna. The RFID reader is connected to a PC and works as the barcode scanner. It handles communication between the information system and the RFID tag. An antenna is connected to the RFID reader; the size of the antenna depends on the communication distance required for a given system's performance. The antenna activates the RFID tags and emits wireless pulses to transfer the data. RFID stations read the information present in the RFID tags and update it with new information. It usually consists of application software designed for the particular task. It performs the filtering operations and reduces the unnecessary duplicate reading of the same tag.

RFID Antenna

An **RFID antenna** is packed with the transreceiver and a decoder. It emits radio signals that activate the tags. It reads the data from the tag and with some of the tags it can write the data to the tag.

RFID System Architecture

Figure 8-1 illustrates the **RFID system architecture**, which includes a controller, a premises server, and an integration server.

RFID Controller

An RFID controller is used in a store or distribution-center environment. It supports the following functions:

- Provides connectivity that is either synchronous or asynchronous
- Provides software deployment, which includes device drivers, filters, aggregators, and dynamically loading software modules

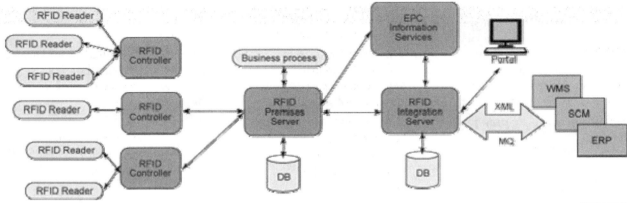

Figure 8-1   RFID system architecture.

- Ensures security that authenticates the readers at the edge
- Filters duplicates, noise, and incomplete reads

RFID Premises Server

An RFID premises server is used in stores or distribution centers. It supports the following functions:

- Adds persistence for storing all incoming RFID events from the controllers
- Controls all the attached RFID controllers by passing commands and data to the network with the help of synchronous or asynchronous communication
- Provides limited support to process management
- Acts as a gateway into EPC (Electronic Product Code) information services accessed either locally or remotely
- Uses a straightforward HTTP or database lookup method that involves service federation or database joins
- Sends and receives commands and data from the server with synchronous or asynchronous methods, and behaves like a gateway to the RFID integration server

RFID Integration Server

The RFID integration server supports the following functions:

- Offers process integration, which includes sophisticated management, cross-LOB or cross-enterprise process management, and application integration
- Improves RFID data from existing sources by cleaning and validating the data
- Integrates business-to-business (B2B) processes that offer the use of RFID-related data to partners along the supply chain
- Integrates various GUIs, so that data from RFID sources is displayed along with sources of other new or existing data
- Enables customers to select a wide range of software products to replace servers or to implement their own processes

RFID Frequencies

Table 8-1 lists RFID frequencies and their applications.

Frequency Band	Characteristics	Typical Applications
Low 100–500 KHz	Short-to-medium read range Inexpensive Low reading speed	Access control Animal identification Inventory control
High 10–15 MHz 850–950 MHz	Short-to-medium read range Potentially inexpensive Medium reading speed	Access control Smart cards
Ultrahigh 2.4–5.8 GHz	Long read range High reading speed Line of sight required Expensive	Railroad car monitoring Toll collection systems Vehicle identification

Table 8-1   RFID frequencies and applications

Applications of RFID Systems

RFID systems are commonly used in following cases:

- Passport data scanning
- Transport payments
- Product tracking
- Automotive vehicle identification
- Animal identification
- Person identification
- Food production control
- Vehicle parking monitoring
- Toxic waste monitoring
- Valuable objects insurance identification
- Asset management
- Access control

RFID system applications are generally described as track and trace applications. These applications provide functionality and benefits for product authentication. RFID also supports the data collection process. Instead of wondering what is in the warehouse, RFID helps track the details of every unit until it leaves the warehouse. RFID enables secure data transmission. Data from independent suppliers is carried on the tags and uploaded into the central system.

Many companies follow just-in-time (JIT) practice, in which components are used when they are delivered, so there is no storage time. Such a practice can result in out-of-stock situations. RFID eliminates such problems, because it helps track and maintain accurate inventory levels.

RFID is used in retail and manufacturing processes too, allowing delivery of products directly from the factory to the retail center.

RFID Standards

RFID standards deal with the following:

- Air Interface Protocol – the way in which tags and readers communicate
- Data Content – organization of data

- Conformance – tests that endorse compliance of products to the standard
- Applications – how the products are used

There are two major RFID standardization organizations:

- ISO, which has developed RFID standards for automatic identification and item management
- EPC Global (Auto-ID Center)

ISO RFID Standards

ISO has established the RFID standard for automatic identification and item management. This standard is also called the ISO 18000 series. It covers air interface protocols to track goods in the supply chain. It includes the main frequencies used in the RFID system around the world.

ISO RFID standards are divided into seven parts:

1. 18000~V1: A generic parameter for air interfaces for globally accepted frequencies.
2. 18000~V2:
   - Covers the air interface for 135 KHz
   - Is unaffected by presence of water
   - Short range, a few centimeters
3. 18000~V3:
   - Covers air interface for 13.56 MHz
   - Thin, flexible form factor
   - Read/write capability
   - Like 18000~V2, also unaffected by water
   - Has a mid range, 70 – 125 cms
4. 18000~V4:
   - Covers the air interface for 2.45 GHz
   - Has the ability to propagate
   - Has long range in active version (100 m+)
   - Affected by water
   - Read/write capability
   - Small antenna and Bluetooth-capable
5. 18000~V5:
   - Covers the air interface for 5.8 GHz
6. 18000~V6:
   - Covers the air interface for 860 MHz to 930 MHz
   - Has the ability to propagate
   - Has high data rates
   - Read/write capability
   - Relatively large antenna
7. 18000~V7:
   - Covers the air interface at 433.92 MHz
   - Has long range of many meters
   - Has high data rate
   - Read/write capability

EPC Standards

EPC was started by the MIT Auto ID Center.

- EPC is a data content/access system.
- EPC data fits into ISO data carriers.

EPC standards are for class 0 (R0) and class 1 (WORM) tags:

- Class 1 defines the standards for simple, passive, and read-only backscatter tags with one-time field-programmable, nonvolatile memory.
- Class 0 defines the standard for read-only tags that were programmed at the time the microchip was made.

Class 1 and Class 0 have a couple of shortcomings; they are not interoperable and are incompatible with ISO standards.

RFID Collisions

There are two kinds of *RFID collisions* in the execution of RFID technology: tag collision and reader collisions.

RFID Tag Collision

Tag collision in RFID systems occurs when numerous tags are energized by the RFID tag reader at the same time. It also occurs by reflecting these signals back to the reader simultaneously. When a large number of tags are read together in the same RF field, then it is difficult for the reader to differentiate the signals, as tag collision confuses the reader.

To separate the individual tags, different systems have been invented, which vary from vendor to vendor. For example, when a reader identifies a tag collision, it sends a gap pulse signal. After receiving this signal, each tag asks a random-number counter to determine the interval before sending its data. Tags then send their data separately, as each one gets a unique number interval.

RFID Reader Collision

Reader collision in RFID systems occurs when the coverage area of one RFID reader overlaps with another reader. This collision causes two problems:

1. *Signal interference*: This problem arises when RF fields of two or more readers coincide and interfere. It is solved by having the readers programmed to read different times. This technique is known as Time Division Multiple accesses (TDMA), which results in reading the same tag twice.

2. *Multiple reads of the same tag*: This problem arises when the same tag is read only once by the overlapping readers. It is solved by allowing the given tag to be read only once by the programmed RFID system.

RFID Security and Privacy Threats

RFID is a noticeable target for misuse. Wireless identification is a powerful capability, and RFID reveals a physical object's nature and location with the help of wireless identification. It works as a medium for various activities such as managing supply chains, tracking livestock, preventing counterfeiting, controlling building access, supporting automated checkout, developing smart home appliances, locating children, and foiling grave robbers. Following are some of the vulnerabilities of RFID tags:

- *Sniffing*: RFID tags are designed to be legible by any compliant reader, so the sniffer can collect RFID data easily by overhearing something on the wireless RFID channel. The collected tag data may reveal information. Reading the data also occurs by reflecting the signals back to the reader simultaneously.
- *Tracking*: RFID tags without unique identifiers facilitate tracking by forming constellations, which are recurring groups of tags that are associated with an individual.
- *Spoofing*: Attackers imitate the genuine RFID tags by writing suitably formatted data on blank RFID tags. Tag cloning is a type of spoofing attack that produces illegal copies of lawful RFID tags.

- *Replay Attacks*: Relay devices can intercept and retransmit RFID queries, which offenders can use to abuse various RFID applications. RFID-enabled license plates and e-plates are examples of current RFID systems that are vulnerable to attack by a relay device.

- *Denial-of-Service*: Thieves exploit the RFID technology and back-end databases by removing tags from the items entirely or by placing them in a foil-lined booster bag that blocks RFID readers' query signals and temporarily deactivates the items. Another way of attacking is to flood the RFID system with data.

Protection Against RFID Attacks

Modern RFID security solutions consist of the following:

- *Cryptography*: Developers have established a lightweight version of the symmetric key and public key cryptography to protect the tags from attacks. Public key–based Basic Access Control for digital passports is the first RFID-specific identification technique.

- *Detection and evasion*: Consumers who can detect unauthorized RFID activity can take their own evasive maneuvers. Devices such as *C't* magazine's RFID Detektor and FoeBuD's Data Privatizer help users to identify nearby RFID activity. Devices such as RFID Guardian interpret RFID scans and log their meaning. RFID evasion can be made more active by RFID blocking in a distributed or centralized way.

- *Temporary deactivation*: RFID tags can be deactivated to protect them from threats. Faraday cage technique can be used to temporarily deactivate the tags, like RF-deflecting metallic sleeves that can be issued with digital passports. On-tag mechanisms are also available for tag deactivation. EPC global tags have a password-protected feature that deactivates the tags permanently. There are some expensive tags that have a password-protected function that deactivates the tag temporarily and then reactivates it.

- *Other techniques*: There are several techniques available to protect RFID devices from attacks. Modify the RFID tag identifiers' appearance and data periodically, which will prevent unauthorized tag access. Trusted RFID readers or an on-tag pseudorandom number generator refreshes the names periodically present in RFID tags' pseudonyms.

RFID Malware

Malware is malicious software that disrupts or harms computer systems. Threats arise when hackers or criminals cause valid RFID tags to behave in unexpected ways. If certain vulnerabilities exist in the RFID software, an RFID tag can be infected with a virus. When an unsuspecting reader scans an infected tag, there is a danger of the tag exploiting a vulnerability. The three classes of malware are worms, viruses, and exploits.

RFID Worms

RFID worms abuse the network connection through self-replication. They spread by attacking online RFID services and tags. RFID worm code causes unprotected RFID servers to download and execute the files from a remote location. The software that is infected by a worm infects the new RFID tags by replacing the data with a copy of RFID worm code.

RFID Viruses

RFID viruses self-replicate the code to new RFID tags separately and without the need for a network connection. These viruses do not have a payload, so the workings of back-end RFID systems are modified or interrupted. Newly infected RFID tags infect other RFID systems if they use same software system.

RFID Exploits

RFID exploits are harmful RFID tag data that attack the parts of the RFID system that are vulnerable. When an RFID reader scans a tag, it anticipates getting the information in a reliable format. Therefore, a malicious person can write incorrect data content or data with an incorrect format, thus corrupting the RFID reader's software and database.

Three types of RFID exploits are SQL injection, client-side scripting, and buffer overflow.

SQL Injection

Systems use databases to store information that is read and written from tags. If middleware does not process the data read from the tag correctly, it is possible to exploit the database by executing SQL code on the tag. This process is called SQL injection.

Client-Side Scripting

Many middleware systems use Web-based components to provide a user interface or query databases in different parts of the world. These Web-based components are susceptible to attacks. If a Web browser is used to display the attacks either directly or indirectly through the database, it is likely to abuse the dynamic features offered by modern browsers by including JavaScript code on the tag. This exploit is called client-side scripting.

Buffer Overflow

Buffer overflow is exploiting the limited memory of RFID tags by reading more data than expected and causing its buffer to overflow. The code that binds the RFID reader interface with middleware is written in a low-level language such as C or C++, which are vulnerable to buffer overflows. RFID tags with limited memory can cause buffer overflow, even if the middleware expects to read a small amount of data.

Defending Against RFID Malware

Following are some methods to defend against RFID malware:

- Secure the user accounts and database accounts.
- Disable or remove unnecessary features.
- Stop database attacks.
  - To avoid SQL injection, data that is copied into an SQL statement must be validated and constrained using database API functions.
  - Do not copy data into SQL statements; use prepared and parameter-binding statements.
  - New versions of MySQL database allow the programmer to enable multiple queries.
  - Handle the GetCurrentQuerys-style functionality to limit the likelihood of attacks.
- Stop Web-based attacks.
  - Insert escaping data into HTML pages to prevent client-side scripting.
  - Proper bypassing or disabling avoids SQL injection.
- Stop glue-code attacks.
  - Check the buffer bounds to prevent buffer overflows.
  - Tools such as Valgrind and Electric Fence prevent buffer overflow.
  - Use the programming language to perform the checks automatically.

RFID Security

RFID communication should be secure in order to maintain privacy of communication and to avoid manipulation of the information stored on the tags. A security bit is present on the reserved memory block of the tag. The tag should be set so the security bit is always turned on. Following are some security strategies:

- *Random Transaction IDs on Rewritable Tags*: To understand this concept, consider the example of library settings. For every check-out, the reader selects a new random number r, reads the tag data D, and stores the (r, D) pair in a back-end database. The RFID reader then deletes the D from the tag and writes r. For every check-in, the library reader reads r, checks the respective D from the database, and writes D back to the tag.
- *Improved Passwords via Persistent State*: Persistent passwords stored in RFID tags are vulnerable to eavesdropping attacks. It has been observed that the communication from tag to reader is more difficult to eavesdrop on than communication from reader to tag. To enhance the security of these passwords,

RFID tags send a nonce (alert) to readers. This nonce is necessary to recover the passwords of the tags. An attacker needs to pick up this nonce to eavesdrop on passwords, which make these attacks difficult.

- *Scheme for Mutual Authentication of Tag and Reader with Privacy for the Tag*:
  - *PRF (Pulse Repetition Frequency) Private Authentication Scheme*: This technique uses a shared secret and the PRF to protect the messages during communication between tag and reader.
  - *Tree-Based Private Authentication*: A new tree-based protocol has been built up to provide private authentication. This tree scheme employs a single security parameter k for each reader and tag.
  - *A Two-Phase Tree Scheme*: A two-phase tree scheme employs two phases for tree-based authentication. In the first phase, it runs the tree scheme with R1 and T1 (reader and tag instances) created with a constant security parameter, and identifies the tag. In the second phase, as the tag is detected, the reader and tag can execute R1 and T1 with k as a security parameter.

All the methods described previously provide the security to protect tags from read/write activities.

RFID and Privacy Issues

RFID can be used to compromise personal privacy by the following:

- Hides the RFID tags and uses them for stealth hacking
- Uses a unique identifier provided by the RFID for the purpose of profiling and identifying consumer patterns and behaviors
- Makes use of hidden readers for stealth tracking and extracting personal information

The main privacy concern about the RFID system is the capability of tracking anybody anywhere without permission. Due to the small size of the RFID tags, it is possible to hide the tags so that no one is aware of the tag's presence.

When a company collects data with the help of RFID, it has to comply with some laws. It has to obtain permission and meet legal requirements for gathering and storing various kinds of personal data. A company is also required by law to safeguard that stored personal information.

Any organization making use of RFID should first be sure that it is aware of its privacy obligations under various federal and local laws before starting the collection of data, to avoid any legal complications later.

Some methods to avoid the attacks are as follows:

- *RSA Blocker Tags*: These tags are the same in size and appearance as the RFID tags. They help to maintain privacy by spamming, so that any reader who tries to scan the tags without permission becomes confused and believes that there are many tags in its proximity.
- *Kill Switches*: New RFID tags are being shipped with a kill switch that disables the RFID tags. Due to this disabling, there is no possibility of stealth tracking and profiling the person with the product containing the dead tag.

RFID Vendors

- *UPM-Kymmene*: A Finnish company whose RFID inlay and tag division takes a flexible approach to the products designed and manufactured
- *Symbol Technologies Inc.*: One of the companies that organize the Electronic Product Code (EPC)-compliant RFID solutions.
- *AXCESS International Inc.*: Provides active and semiactive RFID and real-time location systems (RTLS) solutions for enterprise asset management, physical security and productivity, vehicle access, and supply chain efficiencies.
- *CIO Decisions*: Provides RFID for midmarket enterprises; its mission is to serve information as needed by CIOs and senior IT executives.

- *Imprivata, Inc.*: This authentication and access management appliance company solves complex problems such as managing employee identities, strengthening corporate security, and achieving regulatory compliance.
- *Infosys Technologies Limited*: Defines designs, delivers IT-enabled business solutions, and supplies RFID tags.
- *Intermec Technologies Corporation*: Provides wireless networking equipment and RFID systems that aim to solve companies' real-world problems; it establishes, manufactures, and integrates technologies that identify, track, and manage supply chain assets. Core technologies consist of RFID, mobile computing and data collection systems, bar-code printers, and label media.
- *KeyTone Technologies*: A global provider of enterprise solutions and an RFID vendor with offices in the U.S., Japan, U.K., and India.
- *Weber Marking Systems*: Supplies built-in and auxiliary reject systems to identify and segregate improperly encoded tags; it also offers smart labels for use in their own RFID printers and a range of preencoded labels and tags to satisfy associated identification applications.
- *IBM*: Big Blue has made RFID a top priority, adding the technology to its manufacturing operations and rolling out industry-specific RFID deployment services and RFID test labs.
- *Hewlett-Packard*: One of the vendors of the RFID, HP is transitioning to the next generation of RFID technology called EPC Gen 2. HP has been using RFID technology to identify and track pallets and boxes of various products shipped to select Best Buy and Wal-Mart distribution centers.
- *Sokymat*: A Swiss company, it produces one of the largest tags in the world. It provides RFID solutions for logistics, access control, and animal identification.
- *Cisco*: As companies increase RFID deployment, the router will require a network that can intelligently handle a lot of new data and Cisco plans to meet that need.
- *Omron*: A Japanese electronics vendor that focuses on making UHF systems for the supply chain, starting with the creation of the RFID Business Development Group.

Chapter Summary

- Radio-frequency identification (RFID) is an automatic identification method.
- An RFID tag is an electronic device that holds data.
- There are two kinds of RFID tags: passive and active.
- An RFID reader is a device that is used to interrogate an RFID tag.
- RFID stations can read and update information stored in the RFID tag.
- RFID system architecture includes a controller, a premises server, and an integration server.
- RFID applications are generally described as track and trace.
- RFID standards define the air interface protocol, data content, conformance, and applications.
- The two major RFID standardization organizations are ISO and EPC Global.
- Two kinds of collisions occur in RFID technology: tag and reader.
- Tag collisions occur when numerous tags are energized by the reader at the same time.
- Reader collisions occur when the coverage area of two readers overlaps.
- RFID technology is vulnerable to various kinds of attacks, including sniffing, tracking, spoofing, replay, and denial of service.
- The protective measures against RFID attacks are cryptography, detection and evasion, temporary deactivation, and other techniques.
- RFID technology can also be vulnerable to malware such as worms, viruses, and exploits.

Review Questions

1. Define radio-frequency identification.

   _____

   _____

   _____

   _____

2. Explain the roles of the various components of an RFID system.

   _____

   _____

   _____

   _____

3. List the various applications of RFID identification.

   _____

   _____

   _____

   _____

4. A/An_____ offers process integration, including sophisticated, cross-LOB or cross-enterprise process management, and application integration.
   a. RFID premises server
   b. RFID integration server
   c. RFID controller
   d. antenna

5. What is the role of standards in an RFID system? List the various RFID standards.

   _____

   _____

   _____

   _____

6. Explain the EPC standards used for RFID.

   _____

   _____

   _____

   _____

7. What are RFID collisions?

   _____

   _____

   _____

   _____

8. RFID malware is transmitted and executed via a/an _____.

    a. exploit

    b. worm

    c. virus

    d. RFID tag

9. Discuss the major security and privacy threats posed by RFID technology.

    _____

    _____

    _____

    _____

10. Explain the various measures available to protect an RFID system from attacks.

    _____

    _____

    _____

    _____

Hands-On Projects

Please attempt the following exercises to reinforce what you have learned in this chapter. Write down your observations or process notes for later reference.

1. Locate RFID tags in your nearest shopping mall.

2. Determine the types and class of RFID tags used for tracking goods in the mall.

3. Try to identify the components used in an RFID system.

4. Determine the frequency band used by an RFID system deployed in the mall.

5. Try to determine if the users' privacy is safe. Is there any hidden tag for stealth tracking?

Chapter 9

Wireless VoIP

Objective

After completing this chapter, you should be able to:

• Define and discuss wireless VoIP, including its advantages and disadvantages

Key Terms

H.323 signaling protocols   used to make a VoIP call, these protocols define how various components of the VoIP system will interact with each other

ITU-T   widely used standards for telecommunications equipment and systems

Real-Time Transport Protocol (RTP)   an Internet standard protocol used for network transport functions for transmission of real-time data from audio, video, and multimedia applications

Session Initiation Protocol (SIP)   an application-layer control (signaling) protocol for initiating, managing, and terminating sessions between two or more endpoints

Voice over Internet Protocol (VoIP)   used to route voice over the Internet or through any other Internet protocol–based network, it allows users to make voice calls using an Internet connection

Voice over WLAN (VoWLAN)   a technique for transmitting voice information over a wireless broadband network in a digital form

Wireless VoIP   VoIP running over a wireless LAN (WLAN); it combines VoIP with the Internet and wireless networks based on 802.11 standards

Introduction to Wireless VoIP

Voice over Internet Protocol (VoIP) technology is used to route voice over the Internet or through any other Internet protocol–based network. It allows users to make voice calls using an Internet

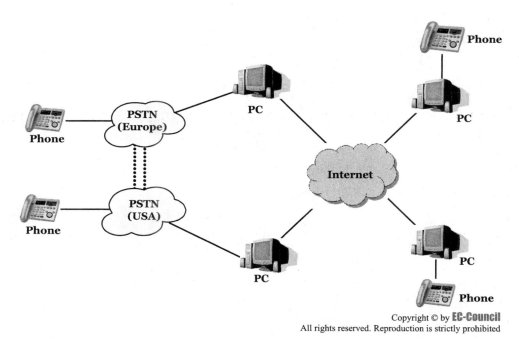

Figure 9-1 VoIP system.

connection. With a VoIP system users can make a call from a computer, special VoIP phone, or traditional phone with an adapter to another computer or phone. Protocols used to carry voice over Internet are generally known as Voice over Internet Protocols.

VoIP technology has revolutionized communication. It offers substantial savings to end users as available underutilized Internet infrastructure can be used to carry calls. VoIP technology is currently in its development stage, and better, faster, more cost-effective, and reliable communication systems lie in the future. The main advantage VoIP offers over PSTN phone lines is its mobility. Users can roam the world and still make/receive calls with an Internet connection, whereas you cannot make or receive PSTN calls from any place other than where the PSTN connection is established.

VoIP technology works in three basic steps:

1. *Digitalizing voice in data packets*: Analog voice is first converted to digital data by using analog-to-digital converters so that it can be sent through an IP-based network.

2. *Sending data packets to destination*: Data packets are sent to their destinations using Internet protocols and Internet infrastructure.

3. *Reconverting data packets into voice at destination*: Data packets are converted to voice at the destination using digital-to-analog converters. These converters convert digital signals to regular analog phone signals.

Figure 9-1 illustrates the VoIP system.

VoIP Technology

This section discusses the technology required for VoIP communication.

Analog-to-Digital Conversion

In a VoIP communication, analog voice data is first converted to digital data packets using analog-to-digital converters so that it can be sent across an IP network. The major advantage of digital data packets is that their flow can be controlled easily. Digitalized data can be filtered, monitored, or encoded in other formats in order to conform with available standards and protocols.

Compression Algorithms

Compression algorithms are required to compress data in order to overcome the problem of bandwidth shortage. Digital data is compressed into standard formats for faster transmission while also ensuring protocol compliance.

Real-Time Transport Protocols (RTP)

Real-time Transport Protocols are used to encapsulate raw data packets into TCP/IP stacks so they can be sent over IP. VoIP uses UDP protocols for data transfer instead of TCP because TCP protocols are more resource intensive. UDP-IP packets consist of RTP packets that contain VoIP data packets.

Resource Reservation Protocol (RSVP)

RSVP is a signaling protocol used within VoIP technology. It requests a certain amount of bandwidth and latency in every network hop that supports it. RSVP is used to manage the quality of VoIP services.

Quality of Service (QoS)

The term quality of service (QoS) encompasses all methods and policies used for real-time data streaming to facilitate interactive voice data exchange. Some QoS methods are listed below:

- High values in the Type of Service field in IP protocol indicate low urgency, and low values represent more real-time urgency.
- Queuing packets methods:
  - FIFO (First In, First Out) allows passing of data packets in arrival order.
  - WFQ (Weighted Fair Queuing) is a fair passing of packets. Available bandwidth is fairly divided for passing of different types of data packets. For example, if FTP, UDP, and TCP data packets are in the queue, an equal number of data packets of each will pass.
  - CQ (Custom Queuing) allows users to decide the priority of data packets.
  - PQ (Priority Queuing) sets up a number of queues with different priority levels. Data packets of a queue with higher priority level will pass first.
  - CB-WFQ (Class Based Weighted Fair Queuing) divides data packets into classes and each class is associated with a bandwidth value.
- Shaping capability is the limit of bandwidth available for download and upload of data packets
- Congestion avoidance uses techniques such as RED (Random Early Detection) to avoid data flow congestion in network.

H.323 Signaling Protocol

H.323 signaling protocols are used to make a VoIP call. These protocols define how various components of the VoIP system will interact with each other.

Software Support for VoIP

The VoIP terminal or gateway requires software for voice-to-packet conversion, which is discussed in this section.

Voice Processing Module

The voice processing module runs over a Digital Signal Processing (DSP) unit. It prepares voice data for transmission over an IP network. Various components of the voice processing module and their functions are listed below:

- PCM Interface
  - Receives samples from the telephony (PCM) interface
  - Forwards them to the appropriate VoIP software module for processing
  - Performs continuous phase resampling of output samples to the analog interface

- Echo Cancellation Unit
  - Performs echo cancellation on sampled, full-duplex voice port signals in accordance with the ITU G.165 or G.168 standard
- Voice Activity/Idle Noise Detector
  - Saves bandwidth by suppressing packet transmission when voice signals are not present
- Tone Detector
  - Detects dual-tone multifrequency (DTMF) signals and discriminates between voice and facsimile signals
- Tone Generator
  - Generates DTMF tones and call-progress tones under the command of the operating system
- Facsimile Processing Module
  - Provides a facsimile relay function by demodulating the PCM data, extracting the relevant information, and loading the scan data into packets
- Packet Voice Protocol Module
  - Encapsulates the compressed voice and fax data for transmission over the data network
- Voice Playout Module
  - Buffers the packets that are received and forwards them to the voice codec for play out

Call Processing (Signaling) Module

- Detects the presence of a new call and collects addressing information
- Monitors the telephone network interface to collect incoming commands and responses
- Terminates signaling protocols (e.g., E&M) and extracts information
- Maps signaling information into a format that can be used to establish a session across the packet network

Packet Processing Module

- Processes voice and signaling packets
- Adds appropriate transport headers before submitting data packets to the IP network
- Converts signaling information from telephony protocols to the packet signaling protocol

Network Management Module

- Provides management/agent functionality, which enables standard management systems to perform remote fault, accounting, and configuration management
- Provides ancillary services such as support for security features, access to dialing directories, and remote access support

Mobile VoIP

Mobile VoIP is a technology by which voice calls are transported as IP packets over the radio and core network of a service provider (Figure 9-2). It combines VoIP systems with a VoWi-Fi-enabled multiradio mobile device. The basic difference between a normal circuit-switched mobile voice call and a mobile VoIP call is that a mobile VoIP call uses IP protocols and packet-switched data networks for call transportation. Calls made by a wireless mobile device that travels through an IP network are known as mobile VoIP calls. A calling mobile device should be connected to the service provider's network.

Mobile VoIP technology enables cell phone operators to route calls over the fixed VoIP network, which helps them to cut costs. The advantage for users is that they can roam and hand over calls across the mobile and WLAN networks with uninterrupted connectivity.

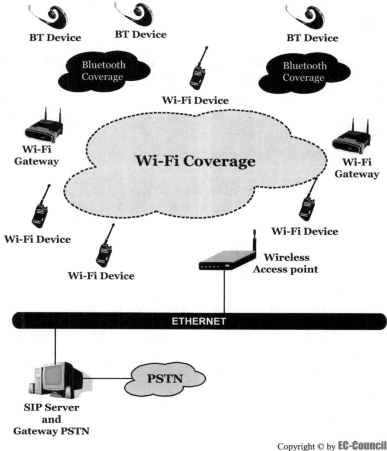

Figure 9-2   Mobile VoIP architecture.

VoIP over BreezeACCESS VL

BreezeACCESS VL is a high-capacity broadband wireless access (BWA) solution designed to provide high-end IP services. It provides a constant network connection for high-speed and reliable Internet access. BreezeACCESS helps provide secure VPN services running in virtual LANs based on IEEE 802.1Q and 802.3ad Q-in-Q.

BreezeACCESS VL uses wireless packet-switched data technology to support:

- Fast Internet access
- Virtual private networks
- VoIP
- Hotspot feeding

The cell architecture of BreezeACCESS VL enables it to be expanded and restructured according to the user's needs. Multiple cells with many access points can be installed in case of high bandwidth requirement, whereas areas with lesser bandwidth requirements can be served by a microbase station with a standalone access point.

BreezeACCESS VL operates in Time Division Duplex (TDD) mode, using Orthogonal Frequency Division Multiplexing (OFDM) modulation with Forward Error Correction (FEC) coding. The multipath resistance capacity of OFDM enhances the robustness of BreezeACCESS and supports: adaptive modulation, use of ARQ, automatic power control, best AU selection, automatic clear-channel selection, automatic bandwidth search, and different redundancy options.

The BreezeACCESS VL system supports various traffic prioritization mechanisms to facilitate delay-sensitive, network-based applications such as VoIP. In addition, BreezeACCESS VL configuration can be optimized for VoIP by:

- *Wireless link prioritization*: Helps configure the parameters that affect the process of accessing wireless media and transmitting high- and low-priority packets
- *QoS through priority queuing*: Supports low-, mid-, and high-priority queuing
- *Admission control*: Dynamic resource allocation protocol of BreezeACCESS VL sets the upper limit for the number of calls according to the number of voice ports in the cell and the operator's service policy
- *Bandwidth management*: Manages bandwidth and controls traffic that each station can forward to the wireless link; helps avoid congestion at any particular point of network
- *Sector load*: The transmit/receive throughput an access unit is providing; depends on average modulation used for sending and receiving the packets and interferences

Voice over WLAN (VoWLAN)

Voice over WLAN (VoWLAN) is a technique for transmitting voice information over a wireless broadband network in digital form (Figure 9-3). This technique uses the IEEE 802.11 set of specifications for transporting the data over wireless local area networks and the Internet. It is known as the "VoWi-Fi" or "Wi-Fi VoIP."

VoWLAN uses voice-enabled wireless devices. Generally, it uses a PDA or Wi-Fi handset that looks and performs like a cell phone. These devices send voice data as a discrete data packet and not as an analog stream. Sometimes software-based phones, such as a soft phone that resides on devices such as a laptop or desktop computer, can be used.

The VoWLAN system routes the call from a phone to the WLAN access point, and then to a VoIP gateway or IP PBX. The call is sent to its exact destination in the private network or on the Internet or PSTN.

The VoWLAN system enables all standard functions and messaging applications that are available on VoWLAN devices, such as wired phones.

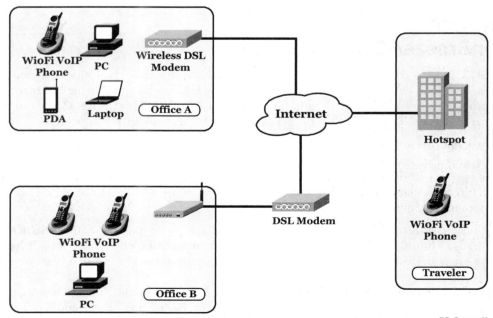

Figure 9-3   VoWLAN call routing.

Characteristics of VoWLAN

In VoWLAN voice and data can be transmitted over single network. Wireless VOIP combines VOIP with Internet wireless 802.11 successors such as:

- *802.11e:* Defines QoS measures that prioritize voice traffic using two techniques; wireless multimedia (WMM) and WMM scheduled access
- *802.11r:* Specifies a fast roaming protocol to reduce the packet loss when a person moves to another access point within the WLAN
- *802.11k:* Consists of the radio resource management protocol to allow a handset to find out the conditions of the WLAN and select the best available path for data transmission

VoIP is designed to interoperate clearly with the POTS (Plain Old Telephone System) network. However, they do not communicate as effectively with one another. PC-based software solutions such as Skype can interoperate with other VoIP systems via conversion to and from the POTS network.

Limitations of VoWLAN

The following are some of the limitations of VoWLAN:

- Inconsistent voice performances and quality of service because IP packets are lost or may be delayed over long distances or at any point in a network that is highly congested
- Security requires encryption and authentication, which are not widely available in the VoWLAN
- It has the availability of broadband connection over the Internet
- It is relatively easy to snoop on VoIP calls and even change their content because VoIP solutions do not support encryption
- It is not possible to make phone calls during a power outage
- It causes a delay in message delivery to the destination, and has little possibility to minimize such delay
- During the transmission of the packets, there are maximum chances of loss of packets due to congestion
- Variation in delay causing jitter
- Due to echo, there are impedance mismatches at the receiving end

Wireless VoIP

Wireless VoIP is VoIP running over a wireless LAN (WLAN). It combines VoIP with the Internet and wireless networks based on 802.11 standards. Wireless VoIP enables users to save money because making a call using it comes at a low cost when compared to making a standard mobile phone call. In many parts of the world where GSM coverage is not adequate but Wi-Fi networks are available, wireless VoIP can play a major role in facilitating cost-effective and reliable communication. Users with a VoIP-enabled handset need to be in the range of a WLAN access point or Wi-Fi zone to make and receive calls over the Internet.

Wireless VoIP is finding its way into various industries, such as health care and retail, where mobility of the workforce is a critical factor in production. Concerns about speed and security, however, are hindering the adoption of wireless VoIP by many industries. Wireless standards are in their development stage and, as of now, do not guarantee scalability, security, and quality of service. But wireless VoIP is likely to offer a better, cheaper, and more reliable communication in the near future. Success of services such as Skype and wireless VoIP equipment, from various VoIP vendors, that complies with wireless standards encouraged early mass adoption of wireless VoIP technology.

Wireless VoIP Deployment

A typical deployment of wireless VoIP consists of:

- *Broadband Internet connection:* Required to serve the growing demand for bandwidth for multimedia services and a large volume of data transfer
- *VoIP gateway box:* A simple SIP gateway providing point-to-point connectivity

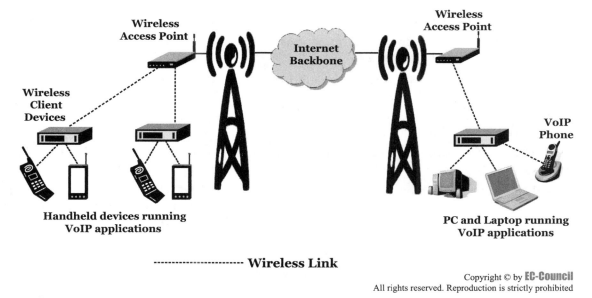

Figure 9-4   Wireless VoIP.

- *Analog telephone adapter (ATA) box*: Used for analog-to-digital conversion and vice versa
- *VoIP call manager application*: Provides software support for managing VoIP services

Figure 9-4 shows various components of a wireless VoIP system.

Advantages of Wireless VoIP

The major benefits of wireless VoIP are as follows:

- Cost is less compared to other traditional calling systems. Because the calls get routed over the data network internally or over the Internet externally, the mobile telephony costs are either eliminated or decreased.

- Increases functionality because wherever users are connected to the Internet, their incoming calls are automatically routed to the VoIP phone.

Limitations of Wireless VoIP

Some major limitations of wireless VoIP are:

- VoIP on LANs is deployed mostly in corporate environments where wireless VoIP may pose problems of scalability. Wireless standards are still in the development stage, so various components used in a wireless VoIP system developed by different vendors may not be compatible.

- Quality of service (QoS) is not as good as with wired networks. Standards and protocols used in the current wireless industry do not focus much on quality of service, whereas wired networks have established standards to support a better quality of service. However, the emerging 802.11e standard is being developed for QoS support for LAN applications, which may help achieve managed service levels for wireless data, voice, and video communication.

- Setting up a wireless network requires more resources than a wired network. In the long run, a wireless VoIP will be cost effective, but it requires a large, one-time investment. Fewer vendors in the market and complexity of wireless standards and protocol implementation are the reasons behind the high setup cost of a wireless network.

- A wireless VoIP is vulnerable to more threats because of numerous access points within a network and unstable standards. Security is the major issue hindering the growth of the wireless industry. Although there are various techniques available to secure a wireless network to a certain level, a wireless network is always more vulnerable than a wired network.

Standards and Protocols

Standards ensure compatibility and interoperability among devices from different manufacturers. They play a major role in the successful implementation of a wireless VoIP. The absence of any stable standard has stunted the development of wireless VoIP equipment. The proprietary devices developed by various companies serve only a specific purpose and may not be compatible with other systems. This lack of compatibility increases the setup cost of a wireless VoIP system.

The main challenge in deploying a wireless VoIP is to find a suitable IP telephony signaling protocol that can handle various VoIP services for call management, conference calling, and call transfers. These protocols should be able to establish a secure and reliable communication between different components of wireless VoIP systems.

The major signaling standards and protocols for wireless VoIP are:

- *ITU-T*: Widely used standards for telecommunications equipment and systems
- *H.323*: Specifies the components, protocols, and procedures for a wireless VoIP deployment
- *SIP*: An application-layer signaling protocol for creating, modifying, and terminating sessions
- *MGCP*: A protocol for handling signaling and session management

ITU-T and H.323

ITU Telecommunication Standardization Sector (ITU-T) coordinates standards for telecommunications on behalf of the International Telecommunication Union (ITU).

H.323 is the ITU-T recommendations that define "packet based multimedia communications systems" and a distributed architecture for VoIP. H.323 standards define components, protocols, and procedures for providing multimedia communication services over a packet-based network. H.323 can carry audio codecs G.711, G.722, G.723, G.728, and G.729 for VoIP. These protocols allow information exchange between the following components of a packet-switched network:

- Terminals
- Gatekeepers
- Gateways
- Multipoint control units (MCUs)
- Proxy servers

H.323 architecture enables the following types of information exchange (Figure 9-5):

- Audio (digitized) voice
- Video (digitized)
- Data (files or image)
- Communication control (exchange of supported functions, controlling logic channels, etc.)
- Controlling connections and sessions (setup and tear down)

Session Initiation Protocol (SIP)

Session Initiation Protocol (SIP) is an application-layer control (signaling) protocol for initiating, managing, and terminating sessions between two or more endpoints. According to the official RFC definition, "SIP makes use of elements called proxy servers to help route requests to the user's current location, authenticate and authorize users for services, implement provider call routing policies, and provide features to users." SIP also provides a registration function that allows users to upload their current locations for use by proxy servers. Because registration plays an important role in SIP, a user agent server that handles a REGISTER is given the special name *registrar*. It is an important concept that the distinction between types of SIP servers is logical, not physical.

SIP is widely used as a signaling protocol for VoIP, along with H.323 and others, enabling Internet telephone calls, multimedia distribution, and multimedia conferencing services.

SIP is lightweight; it has only six methods, which reduces the level of complexity. It is transport independent; it can be used with UDP, TCP, and ATM. It is a text-based protocol, so it has low overhead.

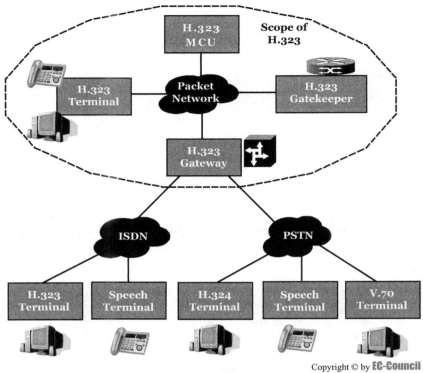

Figure 9-5   H.323 architecture.

SIP provides the following services for system and proxy service communications:

- Call forwarding
- Called and calling number delivery, where numbers can be in any naming scheme
- Personal mobility (the ability to reach a called party under a single, location-independent address even when the user changes terminals)
- Terminal-type negotiation and selection: A caller can be given a choice of how to reach the party (e.g., via Internet telephony, mobile phone, an answering service, etc.)
- Terminal capability negotiation
- Caller and called number authentication
- Blind and supervised call transfer
- Invitations to multicast conferences

Figure 9-6 illustrates SIP architecture.

Media Gateway Control Protocol (MGCP)

MGCP also known as H.248 and Megaco, is an internal protocol used within a distributed VoIP system that appears to the outside world as a single VoIP gateway. This is a standard protocol used for handling signaling and session management processes. These protocols are used to establish communication between a media gateway and media gateway controller. Media gateways are devices that convert data from a circuit-switched network format to a packet-switched network format. Media gateway control protocols are used to initiate, maintain, and end sessions between two or more endpoints.

MGCP is a client-server protocol used by telephony providers in order to have more control over subscribers. MGCP was designed as a combination of Internet Protocol Device Control (IPDC) and Simple Gateway Control Protocol (SGCP). It is an application-layer protocol and works in a master/slave architecture where the media gateway controller is master and the media gateway is slave. The media gateway controller directs the media gateway to initiate a session with a particular endpoint and controls the entire session.

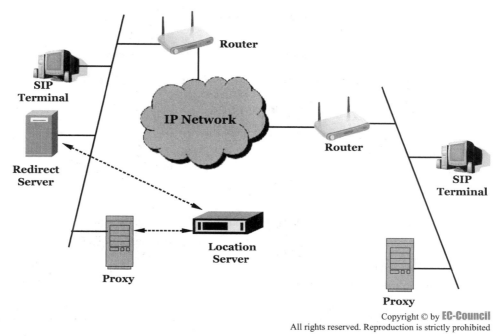

Figure 9-6 SIP architecture.

MGCP is endorsed by the Internet Engineering Task Force (IETF) as Megaco (RFC 3015) standards and by the Telecommunication Standardization Sector of the International Telecommunication Union (ITU-T) as Recommendation H.248.

The architecture of an MGCP implementation includes the following components:

- *Call Agent*: Acts as a software switch for a VoIP network. It directs media gateways and signaling gateways.

- *Media Gateway (MG)*: Performs the conversion of media signals between the format supported by circuit-switched networks and the format supported by packet-switched networks

- *Signaling Gateway (SG)*: The network component responsible for translating signaling messages between IP and PSTN

Real-Time Transport Protocol (RTP)/RTP Control Protocol (RTCP)

RTP defines a standardized packet format to deliver audio and video over the Internet and is used in communication and entertainment systems involving streaming media and video teleconference applications. RTP Control Protocol (RTCP) partners with RTP in delivering and packaging multimedia data, but does not transport the media itself. RTP carries the media streams and RTCP monitors the transmission statistics and quality-of-service information.

RTP

Real-Time Transport Protocol (RTP) is an Internet standard protocol used for network transport functions for transmission of real-time data from audio, video, and multimedia applications. This protocol enables high-bandwidth-demanding, real-time services such as media on demand, and interactive services such as Internet telephony. RTP was developed by the Audio-Video Transport Working Group of the International Engineering Task Force (IETF) and first published in 1996 as RFC 1889, which was superseded by RFC 3550. These protocols support both unicast and multicast applications.

RTP is the foundation of VoIP technology. It can be used efficiently for streaming media, videoconferencing, and push-to-talk services. RTP uses UDP protocols as it is mainly used for applications where time delay plays a critical role in quality of service instead of data packet loss.

RTP was designed to provide the following services:

- *Payload type identification*: Identification of data being carried
- *Sequence numbering*: PDU sequence number
- *Time stamping*: Presentation time of the content being carried in the PDU
- *Delivery monitoring*

RTCP

Real-Time Transport Control Protocol (RTCP) provides control information for an RTP flow. It helps RTP deliver and package multimedia data. RTCP collects information about a media connection, such as number of bytes and data packets sent, number of lost packets, and round-trip delay.

RTCP provides the following services:

- Gives feedback on the quality of data distribution
- Carries a persistent, transport-level identifier for an RTP source, called the canonical name or CNAME
- Controls the RTCP packet flow rate in order for RTP to scale up to a large number of participants
- Conveys minimal session-control information

Both RTP and RTCP are designed to be independent of the underlying transport and network layers. Figure 9-7 illustrates MGCP and RTP architecture.

MediaPro: VoIP and Video Analyzer

MediaPro is a real-time, hardware-based, multiprotocol, multitechnology video and VoIP tester and analyzer, and SIP and H.323 analyzer. It is multiple-protocol-enabled, and capable of analyzing a wide variety of VoIP signaling protocols and media codecs.

The MediaPro Voice over IP analyzer and Voice over IP tester are VoIP analysis and VoIP testing tools capable of performing countless VoIP and IP video measurements such as MOS, PMOS, PESQ, VoIP quality measurements, call quality analysis, and SIP analysis.

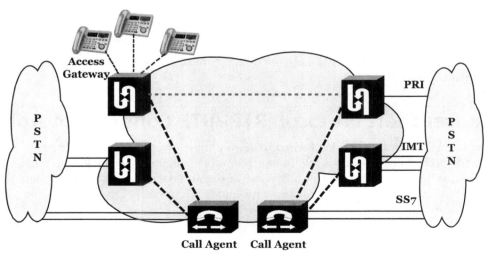

Figure 9-7   MGCP/ RTP architecture.

VoIP Tester and Video Tester Main Advantages

- Provides high-performance, real-time capture capability using dedicated hardware
- Provides an embedded jitter buffer analysis
- Evaluates voice quality using PESQ, PAMS, and PMOS
- Supports multi-VoIP signaling, including SIP, Megaco, MGCP, H.323, H.225, RAS, RTP, CRTP, RTCP, H.245, and SKINNY
- Calculates enhanced jitter and interpacket delay using an automatic expected-packet-length mechanism
- Allows transparent playback, taking into account jitter, packet loss, silence suppression, and packet order
- Provides statistics reports and graphs
- Flexible hardware filters enable line rate filters
- Provides enhanced filtering capabilities, including calling party number, called party number, source and destination IP addresses
- Provides automation capabilities through MasterScript, a powerful scripting tool
- Supports conversion to and from Sniffer or Ethereal format[1]

323Sim: H.323 Simulator

The 323Sim is an H.323 simulator – a VoIP call generator that enables developers and service providers to benchmark, load-test, and verify proper protocol implementation in Voice over IP equipment under heavy stress. Focused on protocol flexibility, this H.323 simulation tool can stress every type and aspect of any network entity implementing the H.323 protocol.

Main Advantages

- Generates up to 6,000 simultaneous calls per server with unlimited scalability
- Sends and receives H.323 voice and video calls and interacts with other H.323 entities
- Simulates a few different load traffic profiles: ramp, Poisson, and normal distributions
- Provides fine-grain control over call setup rates and parameters
- Displays call activity and completion statistics such as setups, releases, active calls online, and QoS
- Transmits RTP packets (encoded in various codec formats) for gateway load testing
- Supports H.261, H.263, and MPEG-4 video streams
- Tests DTMF integrity
- Enables activation of specific portions of the call setup process (RAS, Q.931, or H.245) for pinpoint testing
- Supports fast start connections and early H.245
- Supports tunneling mode H.245 using H.225 signaling
- Supports objective voice quality measurement in collaboration with other components
- Enables RTP generation using the copper 10/100/1,000-Mbps line interface module
- Provides automatic test capabilities through MasterScript, a powerful scripting tool
- Supports H.323 V4
- Supports many various codec types
- Supports alternate gatekeepers
- Tests integrity of gatekeeper communication procedures under stress by enabling RAS message generation[2]

Unlicensed Mobile Access (UMA)

UMA technology was established by wireless companies to control traffic over the cellular networks and Wi-Fi. It allows access to GSM and GPRS mobile services over the unlicensed spectrum, which also includes Bluetooth and Wi-Fi. It accesses GSM and GPRS mobile services with the help of IP-based broadband connections.

Features of UMA are:

- Allows the faultless transmission of mobile voice and data services
- Provides a similar mobile identity on cellular RAN and unlicensed wireless networks
- Provides faultless transitions, including roaming and handover between cellular RAN and unlicensed wireless networks
- Maintains the investment in existing/future mobile core network infrastructure
- Independent of underlying unlicensed spectrum technology such as Wi-Fi and Bluetooth
- Transparent to existing, standard CPE devices such as access points, routers, and modems
- Uses the standard "always on" broadband IP access networks such as DSL, cable, T1/E1, broadband wireless, and FTTH
- Provides security equivalent to current GSM mobile networks
- Has no impact on the operation of cellular RAN

Wireless VoIP Gateway

A wireless VoIP gateway converts circuit-switched (PSTN) voice or fax traffic to an IP network from a traditional PBX. Then the data is transferred across the LAN/WAN to another gateway to convert it back into a format compatible with the recipient phone. Sometimes VoIP gateways are used to route VoIP traffic based on routing tables and translate between different VoIP protocols. It is a flexible network device that provides a high-speed broadband Internet connection and toll-quality telephone voice for either wired or wireless hosts, at home or at the office.

It combines an ADSL modem, 802.11g access point, and VoIP gateway. It allows the PC to access 2.4-GHz networks that have a high-performance data rate of up to 54 Mbps. It also gives cost-effective voice over Internet service at the same time.

Other features of VoIP gateways are voice compression and decompression, packetization, control signaling, and call routing. The critical capabilities that purchasers demand from VoIP gateways include easy deployment and integration with existing PBX and IP infrastructure, flexible call routing, true H.323 and SIP survivability, PSTN failover, efficient multiplexing, efficient NAT traversal, and analog device support. VoIP gateways include multiple deployment actions that are either software or hardware based. Hardware-based VoIP gateways are deployed in the form of standalone boxes, chassis cards, or modules. Software-based VoIP gateways are not deployed in any action.

Several manufacturers offer high-quality wireless VoIP gateways. The last section of this chapter includes a list of vendors for gateways and wireless IP phones, which we discuss in the next section.

Wireless IP Phone

With the help of 802.11 standards, a wireless IP phone converts voice signals into IP packets. These standards are used for transmission over a Wi-Fi network.

The core subsystems include:

- *RF transceiver/power amplifier*: Makes the frequency translation between RF and base-band signals
- *Media access control (MAC)/base-band processor*: Implements 802.11a/b/g MAC functionality and provides complete modem functionality
- *DSP/microcontroller/OMAP*: Executes VoIP call controls, voice processing, and handset user interface
- *Memory*: Stores executing code and data/parameters
- *Peripheral interface*: Allows the user to communicate with the system network and control video/audio I/O sources, and carries voice/data communication

- Voice CODEC: Interfaces with the handset microphone and speaker to digitize the base-band voice signal
- *Power conversion*: Allows power from the AC adaptor or USB to be converted to run various functional blocks

Check the list in the VoIP Vendors section later in this chapter for vendors of wireless IP phones.

Challenges to Building Successful Wireless VoIP Products

The major challenges in building successful wireless VoIP products are as follows:

- *Voice Prioritization – QoS*: Only two wireless QoS schemes, SpectraLink Voice Prioritization and Symbol Voice Prioritization, are supported by currently available VoIP equipment. Therefore, if not using one of those, another QoS solution would have to be developed, which would be very costly and time consuming.
- *Out-of-range detection*: VoIP protocols are unable to detect out-of-range conditions. A mobile device may go out of range or may stop working due to a dead battery. These conditions should be detected beforehand and quickly for normal functioning of VoIP.
- *Encryption*: Higher levels of security place high demands for maintaining good voice quality. There is always a trade-off between security and QoS issues. Various encryption methods and algorithms such as WEP (40/128 bit), TKIP (rapid-rekey), WPA, MIC, 802.11i, VPN, and AES, used for wireless security, are not designed to keep QoS in focus.
- *Authentication*: Popular wireless authentication/security schemes do not support the highest-quality wireless voice implementations.
- *Codec compression*: Codec compression technologies such as G.723, G.726, and G.729 are hardware dependent. Due to this dependency, the target device needs to be specifically designed for VoIP, which increases the cost of wireless VoIP deployment and decreases the compatibility of various devices used.
- *PBX integration*: Integration of PSTN with PBX requires some gateway products, which often results in protocol conflicts due to a lack of standards in the VoIP industry.
- *Acoustical voice quality*: Popular mobile devices are not designed from an acoustical perspective to deliver quality sound and require headsets to support VoIP.

Attacks on Wireless VoIP

Wireless VoIP can be attacked in the following ways:

- *Identity and Service Theft*:
  - *Phreaking*: A type of hacking that performs service theft. It steals service from a service provider.
  - *Eavesdropping*: A type of hacking that leads to identity theft. The hacker can achieve control over billing information, voice mail, or the calling plan by stealing credentials and other information such as names and passwords.
- *Viruses and Malware*: Soft phones and software using wireless VoIP are susceptible to malware and viruses. They can be exploited by malicious code attacks because they run on devices such as PCs and PDAs.
- *DoS (Denial of Service)*: A DoS attack is denying access to a device or network service by overloading the network or consuming all the bandwidth. DoS attacks degrade the service of VoIP by flooding a target with unnecessary SIP call-signaling messages.
- *SPIT (Spamming over Internet Telephony)*: Spamming is the abuse of e-mail systems to send unsolicited, undesired bulk e-mails to many recipients against their wishes. Each VoIP account has a related IP address, allowing spammers to send their voice mails to thousands of IP addresses. These spam messages may contain viruses and malware.

- *Phishing over VoIP*: Phishing attacks attempt to acquire confidential information from the receiver by sending voice mail and making it appear that it came from a trustworthy entity.
- *Call Tampering*: This attack is carried out by interfering with a phone call when it is in progress. It can be performed by adding noise packets to the communication stream. It results in the degradation of the quality of a call.
- *Man-in-the Middle Attack*: In a man-in-the-middle attack, the attacker injects call-signaling SIP messages into the communication stream and impersonates one of the calling parties.

VoIP Vendors

VoIP services and products are offered by the following vendors.

Avaya

- Avaya, Inc. is an American telecommunications company that specializes in VoIP, contact center, and mobile voice and data technology
- For additional information, visit its official site: *http://www.avaya.com/*

Cisco

- Cisco Systems, Inc. is a worldwide leader in networking for the Internet that designs and sells networking and communications technology and services. Cisco's IP-based networking solutions are the foundation of these networks
- For additional information, visit its official site: *http://www.cisco.com/*

D-Link

- D-Link is a worldwide leader and award-winning designer, developer, and manufacturer of networking, broadband, digital electronics, voice, and data products
- For additional information, visit its official site: *http://www.dlink.com/*

DrayTek

- DrayTek manufactures a range of ISDN routers, terminal adaptors and PBXs, and routers for broadband, cable, and ADSL technology. Since its establishment in 1997, DrayTek has focused on providing comprehensive remote-access solutions for small office and home users
- For additional information, visit its official site: *http://www.draytek.com/*

IBM

- IBM is a multinational computer technology corporation that manufactures and sells computer hardware, software, infrastructure services, hosting services, VoIP, and consulting services in areas ranging from mainframe computers to nanotechnology
- For additional information, visit its official site: *http://www.ibm.com/*

Intrado

- Intrado provides the core of the nation's 911 network and innovative emergency communications services and mobility solutions that transform communications and help save lives. The company's unparalleled industry knowledge and experience reduce the effort, cost, and time associated with providing reliable information for 911, safety, and mobility applications
- For additional information, visit its official site: *http://www.intrado.com/*

Linksys

- Linksys, a division of Cisco Systems, Inc., is a global leader in wireless and Ethernet networking for consumer and SOHO users. Linksys is best known for its broadband and wireless routers, but it also manufactures Ethernet-switching and VoIP equipment
- For additional information, visit its official site: *http://www.linksys.com/*

NETGEAR

- NETGEAR has been a worldwide provider of technologically advanced, branded networking products since 1996. Their mission is to be the preferred customer-driven provider of innovative networking solutions for small businesses and homes
- For additional information, visit its official site: *http://www.netgear.com/*

Nortel

- Nortel is a recognized leader in delivering communications capabilities that enhance the human experience, ignite and power global commerce, and secure and protect the world's most critical information. Serving both service provider and enterprise customers, Nortel delivers innovative technology solutions encompassing end-to-end broadband, VoIP, multimedia services and applications, and wireless broadband, designed to help people solve the world's greatest challenges
- For additional information, visit its official site: *http://www.nortel.com/*

Sophos

- Sophos is a company that makes security software such as antivirus, antispyware, and antispam for desktops, e-mail servers, and other network gateways
- For additional information, visit its official site: *http://www.sophos.com/*

Symbol

- Founded in 1975, Symbol has for over 30 years led the way in providing full-service, integrated enterprise mobility solutions. It designs, develops, manufactures, markets, integrates, and supports a family of portable, batch and wireless transaction-based workforce automation systems
- For additional information, visit its official site: *http://www.symbol.com/*

Teletronics

- Since 1986, Teletronics has been a pioneer in developing cost-effective products and solutions for the ever-evolving broadband wireless industry. The company is focused on becoming a leading total solution provider of high-capacity broadband wireless data, voice, and video solutions
- For additional information, visit its official site: *http://www.teletronics.com/*

Chapter Summary

- VoIP is the routing of voice over the Internet or through any other IP-based network.
- VoIP allows you to make a call directly from a computer, a special VoIP phone, or a traditional phone using an adapter.
- Wireless VoIP is VoIP running over a wireless LAN (WLAN).
- IP telephony signaling protocols are required to handle features such as call management, conference calling, and call transfers.
- UMA enables access to GSM and GPRS mobile services over unlicensed spectrum, including Bluetooth and Wi-Fi.

- A VoIP gateway converts circuit-switched (PSTN) voice or fax traffic from a traditional PBX to an IP network.
- A wireless IP phone converts voice signals into IP packets using 802.11 standards for transmission over a Wi-Fi network.

Review Questions

1. Define VoIP, mobile VoIP, and wireless VoIP.

   _____

   _____

   _____

   _____

2. _____ specifications are used for seamless transitions (roaming and handover) between cellular RAN and unlicensed wireless networks.

   a. SIP

   b. MGCP

   c. RTP

   d. UMA

3. What are the advantages and disadvantages of wireless VoIP over wired VoIP?

   _____

   _____

   _____

   _____

4. _____ is a real-time, hardware-based, multiprotocol, multitechnology video and VoIP tester and analyzer, and SIP and H.323 analyzer.

   a. KisMAC

   b. Airsnort

   c. MediaPro

   d. Airopeek

5. What are the BreezeACCESS VL systems?

   _____

   _____

   _____

   _____

6. List the major challenges to building a successful wireless VoIP product.

   _____

   _____

   _____

   _____

7. Discuss the different types of security attacks on a wireless VoIP system.

_____

_____

_____

_____

8. What measures can be taken to protect wireless VoIP systems from different attacks?

_____

_____

_____

_____

9. Is there any tool to analyze the performance and capacity of a wireless VoIP system?

_____

_____

_____

_____

10. List the major wireless VoIP vendors.

_____

_____

_____

_____

Hands-On Projects

Please attempt the following exercises to reinforce what you have learned in this chapter. Write down your observations or process notes for later reference.

1. Determine the VoIP architecture employed in your wireless network.

2. Identify all of the devices used in the wireless VoIP system of your organization.

3. Determine the standards and protocols compliance of wireless VoIP devices used in your wireless VoIP system.

4. Try to simulate protocol implementation in wireless VoIP equipment under heavy stress.

5. Try to access GSM and GPRS mobile services over an unlicensed spectrum such as Bluetooth or Wi-Fi.

Endnotes

[1]www.radcom.com (accessed June 26, 2009).

[2]www.radcom.com (accessed June 26, 2009).

Chapter 10

Wireless Security

Objective

After completing this chapter, you should be able to:

- Discuss wireless security

Key Terms

Certificates   provided by third parties for data security on mobile devices; includes the signing entity's public key digital signature.

Denial-of-service attack   an attack on a computer system or network that causes a loss of service to users by consuming the bandwidth or overloading the computational resources of the victim system

DMZ (Demilitarized Zone)   acts as a "neutral zone" between a public network and a company's private network

Man-in-the-middle attack   the attacker intercepts the identification information of both the sending and receiving parties

Social engineering   the attacker tries to trick people into revealing information that compromises a target system's security

Warchalking   a method where whackers use chalk to place a special symbol on a sidewalk or other surfaces to indicate a nearby open wireless network

Wardriving   driving through a neighborhood with a wireless-enabled notebook computer, mapping houses and businesses that have open wireless access points

Warflying   flying around in an aircraft looking for open wireless networks

Warwalking   exploring an area on foot to look for open wireless networks

WEP   an encryption standard used in 802.11's (Wi-Fi) standard

Whacker   wireless hacker

WPA wireless security that allows only authorized users to access their network; a subset of IEEE 802.11i, it provides data protection by utilizing encryption, strong access control, and user authentication

Introduction to Wireless Security

Wired and wireless network communications each have pros and cons. Wired networks offer more and better security options than wireless. A wireless network provides users the freedom to move from place to place within the network with uninterrupted connectivity.

Wired communications have more thoroughly established standards, whereas wireless standards are in the development stages. Wireless networks are much more equipment dependent than wired networks. Overall, advantages and disadvantages of wired and wireless networks can be considered according to the following points:

- *Cost*: Installing the equipment for wired networks is less expensive than equipment for wireless networks
- *Reliability*: Wired networks are more reliable than wireless networks
- *Performance*: Wired networks have better performance than wireless systems
- *Security*: Wired networks are more secure than wireless ones

Business and Wireless Attacks

"The growing corporate appetite for wireless access services is one of the factors driving the need for advanced information security services as technologies for circumventing network security systems continue to keep pace with the technologies designed to defend against them," said Allan Carey, a senior analyst with IDC's Information Security Services research program. As more and more firms go to wireless networks, the security issue deepens. Business is at high risk from *whackers* (wireless hackers) who do not need to enter the business network physically to hack, but can easily compromise the network with the help of freely available tools. ***Warchalking, wardriving, warflying,*** and ***warwalking*** are some of the ways a whacker can assess the vulnerability of a firm's network. (Warchalking is a method whereby whackers use chalk to place a special symbol on a sidewalk or other surfaces to indicate a nearby open wireless network. Wardriving is driving through a neighborhood with a wireless-enabled notebook computer, mapping houses and businesses that have open wireless access points. Warflying is flying around in an aircraft looking for open wireless networks. Warwalking is exploring an area on foot to look for open wireless networks.)

Many organizations are deploying wireless networks to allow employees to roam around a corporate campus without leaving the network. Some airports offer wireless connectivity to its travelers, so they can continue working while waiting for flight departures. Some hotels also provide such facilities to their customers. However, with ease of use comes associated risk. An attacker who is sitting miles away from the wireless network can "sniff into" the network without being noticed.

Since many large corporate data networks use wireless networking solutions, the objective should be to deploy and maintain secure, high-performance wireless LANs with a minimum amount of time, effort, and expense. Wireless networks and access points (APs) are some of the simplest and most inexpensive types of targets to footprint while also being some of the hardest to detect and scrutinize.

Types of Wireless Attacks

The most common attacks on wireless networks include the man in the middle, DoS, and social engineering.

Man-In-The-Middle Attacks

In a ***man-in-the-middle attack,*** the attacker intercepts the identification information of both the sending and receiving parties.

Eavesdropping

Eavesdropping is easy in a wireless network as there is no physical medium used for communication. An attacker in the vicinity of the wireless network can receive the radio waves on the wireless network without considerable

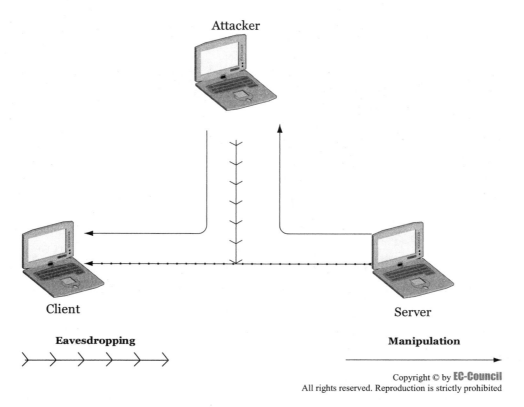

Figure 10-1   Eavesdropping and manipulation.

effort or gadgets. The entire data frame sent across the network can be examined in real time or stored for later assessment. In order to prevent whackers from getting sensitive information, the network should implement several layers of encryption. WEP, the data-link encryption, was developed only for this purpose. If a security mechanism such as IPSec, SSH, or SSL is not used for transmission, then the application data is available to anyone and it is vulnerable to attacks by whackers with an antenna. Unfortunately, WEP can be cracked with tools that are freely available on the net. Accessing e-mail using the POP or IMAP protocols is risky as these protocols pass the e-mail over the wireless network without any form of extra encryption. A determined whacker can potentially log gigabytes worth of WEP-protected traffic in an effort to postprocess the data and break the protection, making the wireless network more vulnerable to eavesdropping.

Manipulation

Manipulation is the extended step of eavesdropping. It occurs on a wireless link when an attacker is able to receive the victim's encrypted data, manipulate it, and retransmit the changed data to the victim. The attacker may change e-mails, instant messages, or database transactions. They change the destination to have the packets sent to themselves instead of the intended recipient. After the packet leaves the wireless network and is routed over the Internet to them, the encryption is no longer in place—it is for the wirelesss segment only, so they receive the data in clear text.

Figure 10-1 illustrates eavesdropping and manipulation.

Denial-Of-Service Attacks

A *denial-of-service attack* is an attack on a computer system or network that causes a loss of service to users because it is consuming the bandwidth of the victim network or overloading the computational resources of the victim system. Denial-of-service (DoS) attacks (Figure 10-2) at the application and transport layers are primarily the same, but the interaction between the network, data-link, and physical layers that increase the risk of a DoS attack on a wireless network is very different. Wireless DoS attacks are divided into three types: physical, data-link, and network.

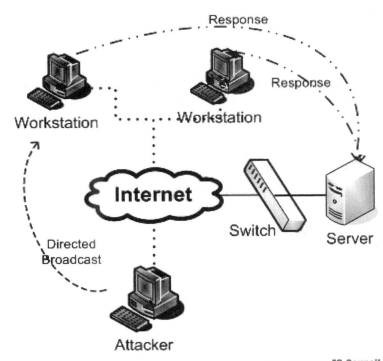

Figure 10-2 DoS attack.

Physical DoS Attacks

To conduct a physical DoS attack on a wired network, the hacker must be in close proximity to the victim's network. However, in the case of a wireless network, proximity does not matter; attackers can launch attacks miles away from the victim's network. Unlike a wired network where evidence of a physical attack is present, there are no indications or evidence of a wireless physical attack.

The 802.11 PHY specifications define a limited range of frequencies for communication. 802.11 PHY devices that use a specific PHY are constrained to these frequency ranges. Because it is easy and inexpensive to construct a device that produces a lot of noise at 2.4 GHz, an attacker can create a device that will saturate the 802.11 frequency bands with noise. Several commercial devices that are available today can bring down a wireless network with ease. If the attacker can create enough RF noise to reduce the signal-to-noise ratio to an unusable level, then the devices within range of the noise will be effectively taken offline. Many 2.4-GHz cordless phones available in the market have the capability to bring down an 802.11b network. A cordless phone can induce a noise that can drop the signal-to-noise ratio to a level that can bring down a wireless LAN (WLAN). Interference in a particular band, due to more signals or crowding of signals, can affect a wireless network. The devices cannot pick out the valid network signal from all of the random noise being generated and therefore will be unable to communicate. An attacker attempting a physical DoS attack can also use large-scale Bluetooth deployments.

Data-Link DoS Attacks

Since the data-link layer is easily accessible, DoS attacks are easy to accomplish.

The attacker forming a DoS attack at this layer does not have to worry about WEP being turned on because it will not prevent the attack. The attacker has complete access to manipulate associations between stations and access points to terminate the access to the network. If the victim network is not using WEP authentication, then it is vulnerable to spoofed APs. By spoofing the AP a hacker can block traffic from the victim's network.

If an AP is improperly using diversity antennas, the attacker can deny access to clients associated with the AP. Antenna diversity is a mechanism whereby a single radio uses multiple antennas to overcome multipath fade. If the diversity antennas do not cover the same region of space, the attacker can deny service to associated stations by taking advantage of the improper setup.

Network DoS Attacks

Because an 802.11 network is a shared medium, a malicious user can flood the network traffic, denying access to other devices associated with the affected access point. If the network allows any unauthorized user to be associated with the network, then it is more vulnerable to a network-layer DoS attack. For example, an attacker can generate a ping (ICMP) to flood the base station (BS). Because the speed on the 802.11 networks is relatively slow, a network DoS may happen accidentally due to a large transfer of files or the running of applications that require more bandwidth than allotted.

Social Engineering Attacks

Social engineering is the most prevalent form of network attacks. In this type of attack, the attacker tries to trick people into revealing information that compromises a target system's security. It is the hardest attack to defend against because it involves human nature.

WEP (Wired Equivalent Privacy)

WEP is an optional encryption standard used in 802.11's (Wi-Fi) standard. In 802.11 it is executed in the MAC layer, which is supported by radio interface card (NIC) and the access point vendor's support. WEP provides the same privacy service to the WLAN user as there is on a wired LAN.

In a WLAN when WEP is active, each packet is encrypted by taking the XOR of the original packet with an RC4 stream. These packets are created using 64-bit keys, and these keys consist of a 24-bit initialization vector and 40-bit WEP keys. An additional 4-byte integrity check value (ICV) is calculated and appended at the end of the original packet. This ICV also gets encrypted with the RC4 stream cipher. WEP that uses 128-bit keys to encrypt the data is known as WEP2.

The main goals of WEP are:

- *Confidentiality*: Prevents link layer eavesdropping
- *Access Control*: Restricts entrance to a building, room, etc., to authorized persons
- *Data Integrity*: Protects data from being changed by an unauthorized third party
- *Adaptability*: Can be used on existing hardware

WEP was introduced in 1997 but was superseded by WPA (Wi-Fi Protected Access) in 2003 because of the following vulnerabilities:

- *Key management and key size*: A wireless network that uses WEP has a single WEP key used by every node on the network. Access points and clients use the same key. 802.11 40-bit encryption is too weak of an algorithm.
- *The 24-bit IV is too small*: WEP's have IV of size 24 bits, and use the XOR binary logic operation with an RC4 cipher stream. RC4 requires a unique IV for each packet but 802.11 does not implement it that way. It reuses the IV on each packet. If the RC4 cipher stream for a given IV is found, an attacker can decrypt successive packets that used the same IV.
- *ICV algorithm*: The ICV algorithm is not appropriate. The WEP ICV is based on CRC-32. CRC-32 is an algorithm for detecting noise and common errors during transmission. It is an excellent checksum for detecting errors but a poor choice for a cryptographic hash.
- *Authentication messages can be forged easily*.

Cracking WEP

WEP can be cracked via passive or active attacks (Figure 10-3):

- *Passive Attack*: A passive attack takes place when the attacker eavesdrops on network traffic. An eavesdropper can capture network traffic for study, using available tools such as network monitor in Microsoft products and Tcpdump in Linux products. A passive attack is not always malicious in nature. Wireless communications work on frequencies that anyone can use, so it is difficult to prevent a passive attack. Passive attacks are very common on wireless networks and are difficult to detect.
- *Active Attack*: If an attacker collects enough data from a passive attack, then they start an active attack against the network. There are a number of active attacks that are the same as active attacks on a wired

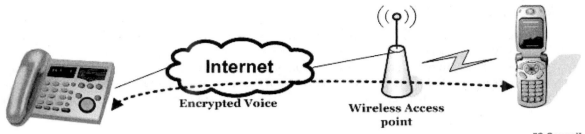

Figure 10-3 WEP cracking.

network. A simple way to prevent a wireless network from unauthorized access is to use MAC filtering. It allows only listed client stations to authenticate with the AP.

WEP Tool: WEPCrack

WEPCrack is a tool that breaks 802.11 WEP secret keys. This tool exploits the vulnerabilities in the RC4 algorithm that consists of WEP security parameters.

WEPCrack consists of three hacking applications based on the PERL language:

- *WeakIVGen.pl*: Allows the user to copy the encryption output of 802.11 networks to weaken the secret key used to encrypt the network traffic
- *Prism-getIV.pl*: Evaluates packets of information until a matching pattern is found for decrypting the secret key
- *WEPCrack.pl*: Combines the other two important outputs to decode the network encryption or to determine the secret key

SSID (Service Set Identifier)

SSID is a sequence of characters that uniquely names a wireless local area network (WLAN); the sequence is attached to each packet of the wireless network. It is useful to identify the packet that is covered in a particular network when there are a number of networks present. The code can contain a maximum of 32 alphanumeric characters. All wireless devices that communicate with each other have the same SSID. SSID is used to identify a unique set of wireless network devices works in a given service set.

The main variants of SSID are:

- *IBSS (Independent Basic Service Set)*: A service set in which wireless devices communicate with each other directly; there is no use of access points.
- *ESS (Extensible Service Set)*: A service set in which a number of Basic Service Set are joined using access points.

Beacon Frames

Beacon frames are included in the IEEE 802.11 wireless network protocol. Beacon frames are the "heartbeat" of the WLAN; they declare the presence of network, create the connection, and maintain the communication in a particular pattern. In passive scanning mode, a beacon frame helps the wireless station find the nearest wireless AP. It helps users find an available network.

Beacon frames include the following information:

- The interval of time required to transmit the frames
- The capability information that contains the requirements of the stations that want to join the network
- The basic rate set, which is the bitmap that lists the rates the WLAN supports

Each AP announces its existence a number of times per second by broadcasting beacon frames that carry the ESS name (SSID). Stations find out the APs by passively listening for beacons. Once the stations establish a suitably named AP, they send a requesting frame that contains the needed SSID. Networks without frames are known as closed networks.

The following are aspects of a closed network:

- It means SSID is not broadcasting
- Less effort at security through obscurity, so the presence of the network becomes less obvious
- BSSIDs are exposed as soon as a single frame is transferred by any member station
- Mapping between SSIDs and BSSIDs is exposed by the number of management frames that are not encrypted

Authentication Modes

Authentication is accomplished by a station providing the correct SSID or through shared-key authentication. Three scenarios for authentication are:

- Access point and all base stations share a secret encryption key:
  - Hard to deploy
  - Hard to change
  - Hard to keep secret
  - No accountability
- Requires a station to encrypt with WEP a challenge text provided by the access point
- An eavesdropper gains both the plaintext and the ciphertext
  - Perform a known plaintext attack
  - This authentication helps to crack WEP encryption

MAC (Media Access Control) Address

MAC is the unique hardware number of a device connected to a shared network medium. It is same as the Ethernet address in the Ethernet LAN. When your computer is connected to the Internet, a corresponding table transmits your IP address to the computer's physical (MAC) address on the LAN. In Figure 10-4 the ipconfig command exposes the physical address of a computer's NIC, which is used as the MAC address.

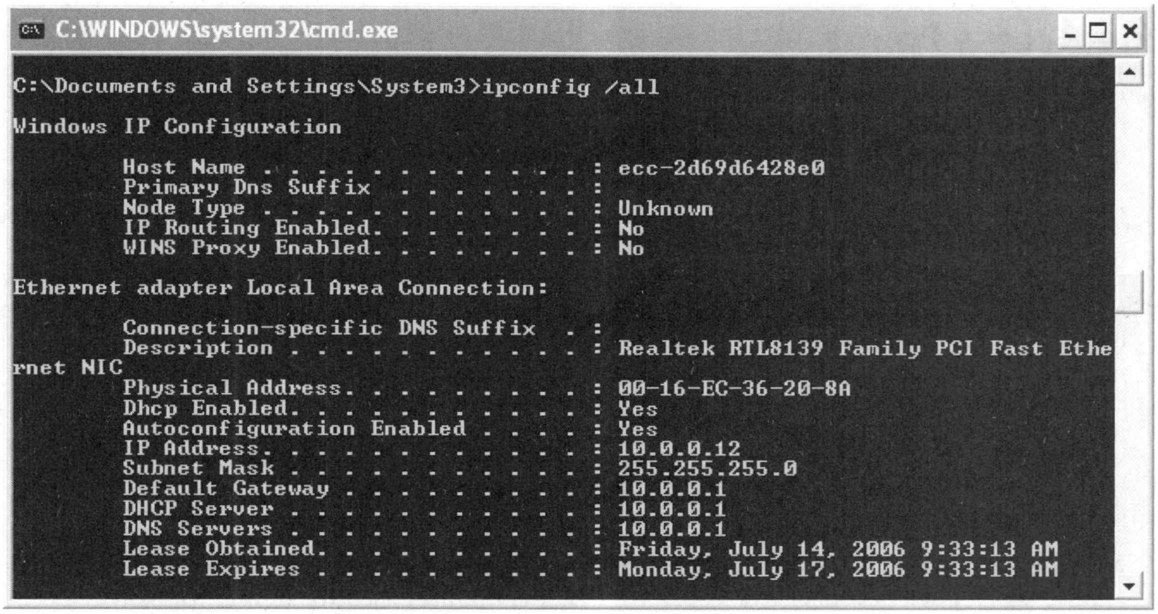

```
 C:\WINDOWS\system32\cmd.exe                                    _ □ ×

C:\Documents and Settings\System3>ipconfig /all

Windows IP Configuration

        Host Name . . . . . . . . . . . . : ecc-2d69d6428e0
        Primary Dns Suffix  . . . . . . . :
        Node Type . . . . . . . . . . . . : Unknown
        IP Routing Enabled. . . . . . . . : No
        WINS Proxy Enabled. . . . . . . . : No

Ethernet adapter Local Area Connection:

        Connection-specific DNS Suffix  . :
        Description . . . . . . . . . . . : Realtek RTL8139 Family PCI Fast Ethe
rnet NIC
        Physical Address. . . . . . . . . : 00-16-EC-36-20-8A
        Dhcp Enabled. . . . . . . . . . . : Yes
        Autoconfiguration Enabled . . . . : Yes
        IP Address. . . . . . . . . . . . : 10.0.0.12
        Subnet Mask . . . . . . . . . . . : 255.255.255.0
        Default Gateway . . . . . . . . . : 10.0.0.1
        DHCP Server . . . . . . . . . . . : 10.0.0.1
        DNS Servers . . . . . . . . . . . : 10.0.0.1
        Lease Obtained. . . . . . . . . . : Friday, July 14, 2006 9:33:13 AM
        Lease Expires . . . . . . . . . . : Monday, July 17, 2006 9:33:13 AM
```

Figure 10-4   Using the ipconfig command to expose the physical address of a computer's NIC.

In 802.11 networks, the MAC sublayer of the data-link layer (DLC) telecommunication protocol uses the MAC address for communication. There are separate MAC sublayers for every physical device. Most 802.11 access points permit the network administrator to go through a set of MAC addresses that are used for communication on the network.

MAC Sniffing and AP Spoofing

Most vendors have implemented MAC-level access controls to add security to the nature of 802.11. One way to provide added security is for the administrator to define a list of approved client MAC addresses that will be allowed to connect to the access point. Most of the access points have MAC address filtering capabilities. MAC filtering has two options, open or closed. In a closed MAC filter, only listed addresses are allowed to access the network. This option is a more secure way of accessing the network because only known cards are permitted to access the network. In an open MAC filter, the addresses listed in the filter are prevented from accessing the network. This is not always practical in large networks.

Additionally, the MAC address does not provide a good security mechanism because it is both easily observable and reproducible. Even if WEP is enabled, an attacker can easily sniff MAC addresses as they are in clear text. Moreover, it is possible to change the MAC address on a wireless card using software. An attacker can use the same option to masquerade as a valid MAC address by programming the wireless card and accessing the wireless network. Therefore, any MACs can be sniffed off the network with a wireless sniffer, and the attacker's MAC address can be changed easily in most cases. Each network card has a MAC address similar to Ethernet cards and each MAC address is unique, but the attacker can change the MAC address by using the ifconfig command. All the attacker needs to know is a trusted MAC address in the list of a particular AP. An unauthorized wireless card, which spoofs a MAC address of other legitimate users, can be detected on a wireless network. When the attacker tries to login with the spoofed MAC address, the legitimate user gets disconnected from the wireless network. Some wireless cards have logs that indicate the attempt to reset.

Wellenreiter v2

Wellenreiter is a wireless network discovery and auditing tool. It is the easiest-to-use Linux scanning tool available. There is no need to configure the card. Wellenreiter can discover networks (BSS/IBSS) and detect ESSID broadcasting or nonbroadcasting networks, their WEP capabilities, and the manufacturer automatically. DHCP and ARP traffic is decoded and displayed to give further information about the networks. An Ethereal/Tcpdump-compatible dumpfile and an application savefile will be created automatically. Using a supported GPS device and the GPSD utility, the location of the discovered networks can be charted.

Rogue Access Points

Rogue, or unauthorized, access points can allow anyone to place an 802.11-equipped device onto a corporate network, which puts them very close to mission-critical resources (Figure 10-5). With the help of wireless sniffing tools, access points for the authorized network, media access control (MAC) addresses, vendor names, or security configurations can be discovered. Then a list of MAC addresses of the authorized access points on the LAN can be created and cross-checked against the list of MAC addresses found by sniffing. An access point with a vendor name different than the authorized access points is the first alert to a possible rogue. Consider an access point a rogue if it looks suspicious, and then try to locate it using simple, known techniques like walking with a wireless access point sniffing device. Walk in the direction where the signal strength of the access point's beacon increases, which will indicate which part of the network needs to be examined. Sometimes a rogue access point may be an active access point that is not connected to the corporate network. These access points do not cause any damage to security. When an access point is found that interfaces to the corporate network, it is advisable to shut it off immediately. Centralized network monitoring devices should be used to monitor the networks.

There are two basic methods for locating rogue access points: requesting a beacon and sniffing the air.

Requesting a Beacon

A wireless device can sense the SSIDs used by nearby wireless access points as the IEEE's 802.11b standard allows. When a wireless device detects the SSID, it configures itself to connect to the wireless network. When an 802.11b-compliant network card transmits a packet or requests a beacon, all the access points in the vicinity broadcast their availability via SSID announcement. This method is effective because there is no traffic created by an SSID broadcast until it is requested. The problem with this method is that the access point must be configured to respond to these beacon requests. However, many organizations turn this option off. For this

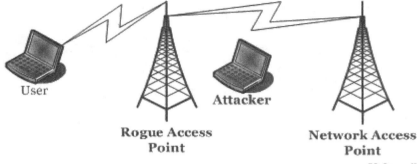

Figure 10-5   Rogue access point.

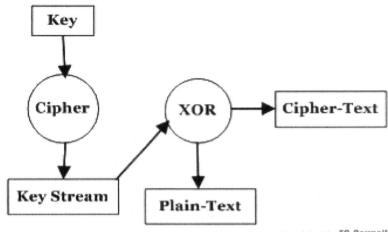

Figure 10-6   Stream cipher.

reason, this method is not very effective at finding all wireless access points. However, some users fail to turn this feature off while deploying access points. Also, wireless access points that home users use do not have the feature allowing them to turn the mechanism off.

Sniffing the Air

Another method of detecting rogue access points is by using wireless sniffing tools. Sniffing is a method to detect the presence of a wireless network. In order to passively capture the packets from the air, the receiver on the wireless card has to be in promiscuous mode. The receiver records the information of the sniffed packet, allowing the hacker to deconstruct the packets to find a way to access the network. Select a precise channel for sniffing the wireless network. 802.11b operates on 12 channels, and it is difficult to constantly switch between channels to monitor packets. In order to sniff the wireless network, there must be traffic on it.

It is technically feasible to detect an access point by sniffing traffic, but it is not practical. If the network does not have users who use unauthorized access points, then there will be no traffic to watch. In addition, if the access point is near but is not in use, then the sniffer will not find it. Sniffing is a useful method for finding out who is using the wireless access point after it has been identified. Requesting beacons, which is the process used by NetStumbler and MiniStumbler, will return the channel information that can be used later to sniff the network.

Stream Cipher

A stream cipher is one of the symmetric encryption algorithms (Figure 10-6). It is faster than a block cipher. A block cipher requires a large block of data, but a stream cipher works on smaller parts of plaintext, generally bits. A stream cipher forms a sequence of bits known as a keystream. Encryption is done by taking the XOR operation of the keystream with plaintext.

The stream cipher in which the keystream is independent of the plaintext and ciphertext is known as a synchronous stream cipher. If it is dependent on the data and its encryption, then it is called self-synchronizing. The input required for a stream cipher is the IV sent in plaintext and the secret key. The length of an IV is 24 bits, and the secret key is either 40 or 104 bits. The total length of the input is 64 or 128 bits.

Application to WEP

- The pad (stream of bits) is formed from the combination of the IV and the WEP key passed through RC4
- Knowing all the pads is the same as knowing the 40-bit or 104-bit secret

PAD Collection Attacks

A pad collection attack is a semipassive attack. It collects a set of pads and then decrypts any packet for which a pad is present. It works with 64-bit or 128-bit encryption. Pad collection needs traffic across the network. It can spread the attack over time in order to slow down possible detection.

There should be a separate pad for each encrypted packet that is transferred between an access point and a station. It is possible to make a table and skip the RC4 step by mapping pads to IVs. The stream is never longer than 1,500 bytes (the maximum Ethernet frame size). The 24-bit IV provides 16,777,216 (256^3) possible streams, so all the pads can fit inside 25,165,824,000 bytes (23.4 GB). The WEP key is not needed because once a table is completed it is as good as having the WEP key.

Steps for Hacking Wireless Networks

To combat hackers, you need to understand how they think and operate. Following are general steps a hacker might take to compromise a WLAN.

Step 1: Find Networks to Attack

1. The attacker tries to find a way to connect and communicate with the AP.
2. The attacker can use NetStumbler to map out active wireless networks in a given area.
3. Using NetStumbler, the attacker locates a strong signal on the target WLAN.
4. NetStumbler not only has the ability to monitor all active networks in the area, but it also integrates with a GPS to map APs.

Step 2: Choose the Network to Attack

1. At this point, the attacker has chosen his or her target.
2. NetStumbler or Kismet can tell whether or not the target network is encrypted.
3. Wireless networks use broadcasts, so the attacker can sniff the traffic even though he or she is not an authorized user.

Step 3: Analyzing the Network

1. The attacker analyzes the network using NetStumbler, for example:
   - WLAN has no broadcasted SSID
   - NetStumbler tells you that SSID is ZXECCOUNCIL
   - Multiple access points are present
   - Open authentication method
   - WLAN is encrypted with 40-bit WEP
   - WLAN is not using 802.1x

Step 4: Cracking the WEP Key

1. The attacker sets NIC drivers to monitor mode.

2. Begins capturing packets with Airodump.

3. Airodump quickly lists the available network with SSID and starts capturing packets.

4. After a few hours of Airodump session, launches Aircrack to start cracking.

5. WEP key for ZXECCOUNCIL is now revealed.

Step 5: Sniffing the Network

1. Once the WEP key is cracked and the NIC is configured appropriately, the attacker is assigned an IP and can access the WLAN. Now he or she has complete control of the traffic like an authorized user.

2. The attacker begins listening to traffic with Ethereal.

3. The attacker looks for plaintext protocols (in this case FTP, POP, Telnet).

NetStumbler

NetStumbler is one of the wireless security tools used for 802.11b network scanning. It does not sniff the TCP/IP protocol. Rather, it provides an easy method for enumerating wireless networks. The working principle of NetStumbler is quite simple. It transmits connection requests to all the listening access points with an SSID. The APs will each respond by sending their own SSID. Note that NetStumbler is not a passive sniffer; the traffic handled by it is visible on a victim's network. When NetStumbler is launched, it starts a capture file and searches for access points. Examples of the NetStumbler filter are:

- *Encryption Off*: Can list all the devices that are not WEP enabled, which implies that network traffic can be sniffed.

- *Encryption On*: Lists those devices that are WEP enabled.

- *IBSS (Peer)*: Allows two or more wireless cards to communicate with each other without the presence of an AP.

- *Short Preamble*: An alternative method for specifying data in the 802.11b physical layer. It is widely used for time-sensitive applications such as voice over IP (VoIP) or streaming media.

The toughest part of using NetStumbler is in locating the wireless networks.

Kismet

Kismet is a tool that is used in 802.11 layer2 as a wireless network detector, sniffer, and instruction detection system for wireless security. It can be used to notice and evaluate access points that are in the range of a computer on which it is installed.

Kismet operates with any wireless card that supports raw monitoring mode (radio frequency) and sniffs 802.11a, 802.11b, and 802.11g traffic. Kismet discovers networks by passively taking the packets together, identifying standard named networks and hidden networks, and by deducing the presence of nonbeaconing networks via data traffic.

The features of Kismet are:

- Supports the decloaking of hidden wireless networks and graphical measurement of networks with the help of GPS integration

- Provides Ethereal/Tcpdump well-suited data logging

- Provides AirSnort well-suited weak-IV packet logging

- Supports network IP range detection

- Supports producer and model detection of access points and clients

- Helps identify known default access-point configurations

- Helps in runtime decoding of WEP packets for known networks

WEP Tool: AirSnort

AirSnort is a wireless LAN (WLAN) tool that recovers encryption keys. AirSnort operates by passively monitoring transmissions, computing the encryption key when enough packets have been gathered.

802.11b, using the Wired Equivalent Protocol (WEP), is crippled with numerous security flaws. Most damning of these is the weakness described in *Weaknesses in the Key Scheduling Algorithm of RC4,* by Scott Fluhrer, Itsik Mantin, and Adi Shamir. Adam Stubblefield was the first to implement this attack, but he has not made his software public. AirSnort, along with WEPCrack, which was released at about the same time, are the first publicly available implementations of this attack.

AirSnort requires approximately 5–10 million encrypted packets to be gathered. Once enough packets have been gathered, AirSnort can guess the encryption password in under a second.

AirSnort runs under Windows or Linux, requires that your wireless NIC be capable of RF monitor mode, and that it pass monitor mode packets up via the PF_PACKET interface. Cards known to do this are:

- Cisco Aironet
- Prism2-based cards using wlan-ng drivers or Host-AP drivers
- Orinoco cards and clones using patched orinoco_cs drivers
- Orinoc cards using the latest Orinoco drivers >= 0.15 with built-in monitor mode support
- Windows: Any card supported by Airopeek[1]

WPA

WPA is the first generation of wireless security that allows only authorized users to access their network. WPA depends on the subset of IEEE 802.11i. For Wi-Fi networks WPA acts as a powerful, standards-based, interoperable security technology. It provides powerful data protection by utilizing encryption, strong access control, and user authentication (Figure 10-7). WPA uses 128-bit encryption keys and dynamic session keys to provide the wireless network's privacy and enterprise security.

Two types of WPA are:

- *WPA-Personal*: This version makes use of a set-up password and prevents unauthorized network access
- *WPA-Enterprise*: Confirms the network user through a server

The features of WPA are:

- *WPA authentication*: WPA needs 802.1x authentications. WPA makes use of a preshared key for the environment without Remote Authentication Dial-In Use Service (RADIUS) infrastructure, and uses Extensible Authentication Protocol (EAP) and RADIUS for environments with RADIUS infrastructure.

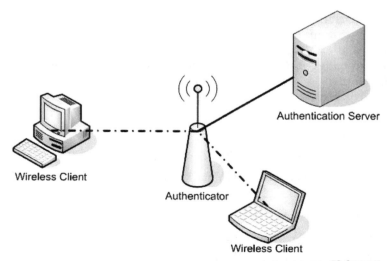

Figure 10-7 WPA.

- *WPA key management*: With WPA, rekeying of both unicast and global encryption keys is necessary. For a unicast key, the Temporal Key Integrity Protocol (TKIP) changes the key for each frame. However, for a global key, WPA allows the AP to announce the changed key to connected wireless clients.

- *Temporal key management*: In WPA, encryption with TKIP is needed. TKIP uses a new encryption algorithm that is stronger than the WEP algorithm.

- *Michael algorithm*: In 802.11 and WEP data integrity is given by the 32-bit integrity check value (ICV). In WPA, the Michael technique identifies the algorithm which determines an 8-byte message integrity code (MIC) with the help of methods present in wireless devices. This MIC is located between the data portion of an IEEE 802.11 frame and the 4-byte ICV. MIC gets encrypted with frame data and ICV.

- *AES support*: WPA supports Advanced Encryption Standard (AES) as a substitute for WEP encryption. This support is optional and depends upon vendor driver support.

- *Supporting a mixture of WPA and WEP wireless clients*: A wireless AP maintains both WEP and WPA simultaneously to help the gradual transition of WEP-based wireless networks to WPA.

WPA is a stop-gap solution that solves the following issues related to the WEP encryption itself:

- IVs are larger (48 bits instead of 24)

- Shared key is used more rarely

- Used to negotiate and communicate temporal keys

- Temporal keys are used to encrypt packets

- Does not solve issues with the management frames

- Collision avoidance mechanism can still be exploited

- Can be supported by most of the 802.11b hardware

DMZ (Demilitarized Zone)

A *DMZ* acts as a "neutral zone" between a public network and a company's private network. It is a small network that protects the database server of the company from direct access by outside users (Figure 10-8). A DMZ is a safer approach to a firewall and successfully works as a proxy server.

Users of a public network can access only the DMZ host. The DMZ usually contains a company's Web pages, which the public can access. When outside users break the DMZ host security, the Web page of the company may be damaged but the company information remains unexposed.

Message Integrity Code (MIC)

MIC is the portion of the draft standard from the IEEE 802.11i working group. The algorithm that explains the MIC is called the Michael algorithm. The Michael technique identifies the algorithm that determines an 8-byte MIC with the help of methods present in wireless devices. This MIC is located between the data portion of an IEEE 802.11 (Wi-Fi) frame and the 4-byte ICV. MIC gets encrypted with frame data and ICV. MIC works similarly to the older ICV. The ICV protects the packet payload while the MIC protects both payload and header.

WTLS

WTLS (Wireless Transport Layer Security) is based on the TLS v1.0 security layer, which is generally used in the Internet. It is the advanced version of the TLS v1.0. It supports wireless low bandwidth, datagram connection, limited processing power and memory capacity, and cryptography exporting restrictions.

It is the security layer of WAP, which supports:

- Privacy

- Data integrity

- Authentication for WAP services

WTLS is necessary because both the client and server have to be authenticated to maintain a secure wireless transaction. For this, the connection needs to be encrypted. It is specially developed for wireless networks.

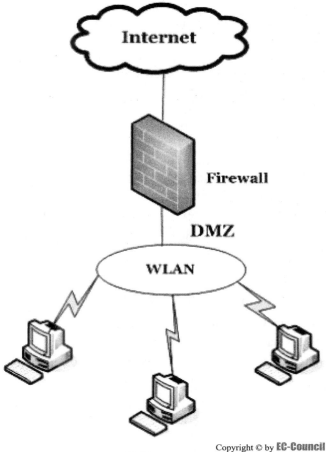

Figure 10-8 DMZ.

Mobile Security Through Certificates

Certificates are provided by third parties for data security on mobile devices. Every certificate must include the entity's distinguished name and the public key. The signing entity's public key is the digital signature on the certificate. This certificate must be distributed (e.g., as part of a software package) and verified (through a published SHA1 or MD5 hash algorithm). The simplest architecture for security through certificates is built with two certificates. One certificate contains the public key of the entity to communicate with. The other certificate contains the readily available public key of the entity with the certified certificate.

There are two types of certificates: root and chained. The owners of commercial entities recognized as trustworthy issue root certificates. The root certificate's originator is called a certificate authority (CA). Chained, or intermediate, certificates are the subordinate or low-level certificates of the same trustworthy entities. These certificates must also be validated and verified. Verifying the signature on data presented by an end entity (EE) is done by checking that the signature actually belongs to that EE and is signed by the EE's CA.

Certificates have multiple formats such as: X.509 certificates, Pretty Good Privacy (PGP) certificates, and Simple Distributed Security Infrastructure (SDSI) certificates.

Certificate Management Through Public Key Infrastructure

A PKI (Public Key Infrastructure) is a set of technologies that provide compatibility between standards that exist and are implemented in the digital world. PKI conducts dealings by appending digital certificates to messages between various parties. It involves the hardware, software, people, policies, and procedures needed to create, manage, store, distribute, and revoke certificates. It makes use of two mathematically related keys (the public key and the private key) that cannot be derived from each other. PKI supports security architecture granting user authentication, data confidentiality, message authentication and integrity, and nonrepudiation. PKI involves two processes: encryption and decryption. Encryption involves converting information into some coded language. Decryption involves conversion of coded language into its original form. It is done by using hashing algorithms.

The following issues must be considered to form an effective PKI:

- Provides privacy between two parties exchanging data and disallows other users
- Ensures authentication to valid users
- Nonrepudiation validates electronic events such as signed contracts and wire transfers
- Access to authenticated users must exist all the time
- Provides scalability for network growth as required
- Provides security to private and public networks

WifiScanner

WifiScanner is a tool that has been designed to discover wireless nodes, i.e., access points and wireless clients.

- It can dump traffic in real time (like Tcpdump) and the user can interactively change the sniffed channel
- It listens alternately to 14 channels and displays information on every collected package
- It works with Cisco cards and Prism cards with Host-Ap driver or wlan-ng driver, Prism54g, Hermes/ Orinoco, Atheros, Centrino
- An IDS system is integrated to detect anomalies such as MAC usurpation[2]

BTScanner

BTScanner is a tool designed specifically to extract as much information as possible from a Bluetooth device without the requirement to pair. A detailed information screen extracts HCI and SDP information, and maintains an open connection to monitor the RSSI and link quality. BTScanner is based on the BlueZ Bluetooth stack, which is included with recent Linux kernels, and the BlueZ toolset. BTScanner also contains a complete listing of the IEEE OUI numbers and class lookup tables. Using the information gathered from these sources, it is possible to make educated guesses as to the host device type.

BTScanner 2.0 is a completely revamped version of the original. With all the features of 1.0, version 2.0 now boasts the ability to perform brute force scans of OUI ranges. Both inquiry and brute force scan types are able to utilize multiple dongles to increase coverage and the chance of finding a device. Additional features include the ability to export the scan results to a text file and improved sorting.

BTScanner 2.1 contains minor bug fixes over 2.0, specifically related to the use of multiple dongles when scanning.

BTScanner for XP is a Bluetooth environment auditing tool for Microsoft Windows XP, implemented using the bluecove libraries (an open-source implementation of the JSR-82 Bluetooth API for Java).[3]

Wireless Network Security Checklist

Following is a checklist to use to ensure a wireless network is as secure as possible:

- Confirm that all the ports which are not in use are closed
  - The ports which are in use can be open
  - "Pessimistic" network view (close all other ports or access)
- Implement the rules in such a way that only authenticated persons can access it
- Ensure that SSIDs are regularly changed
- Make sure that the insurance and authentication standard is developed and implemented
- Make use of strong encryption
  - Use the SHA-1 (Secure Hashing Algorithm) for the encryption

- Start the encryption at the user side and close it at the server that is behind the firewall and outside the demilitarized zone (DMZ)
- Consider WLAN as an unsecured network that must be operated in the DMZ
- Access the confidential network through VPN and two-factor authentication
- Application security can be increased
  - by the use of an enterprise application system
  - by an increase in the use of encryption techniques
- Do not allocate access for ad hoc or peer-to-peer WLANs
- Make use of the 802.11i IEEE security standard
  - Apply access control for each user so that only particular users can access the data
  - Apply strong authentication such as tokens, smartcards, and certificates
  - Apply strong encryption; make use of strong encryption algorithm

Securing the Wireless Network

Follow the suggestions below to secure your network from attacks. The steps contain some common mistakes commited as network settings are configured.

- *Secure your wireless router or access point administration interface*: All the routers and APs must have an administrator password that is required to log on to the device and change the configuration settings.
- *Change default administrator password*: The Web tools are protected from hackers by a login screen (username and password). With a correct name and password, the user may access the device. To protect the password and username, change the setting of the administrator account immediately upon installation.
- *Change of SSID*: Access points and routers use an SSID. If a hacker knows the SSID, they may initiate an attack. Change the SSID immediately upon installation.
- *Do not broadcast your SSID*: WLAN APs and routers automatically broadcast the SSID, but it makes the WLAN open to other systems within that range. Do not broadcast your SSID as it makes your network visible to other systems.
- *Enable WPA encryption instead of WEP*: WPA provides better protection than WEP, and it is easy to use. In WEP, characters are limited to zero through nine and A through F, but in WPA they are not limited.
- *Use MAC filtering for access control*: Access points and routers offer owners an option to key in the MAC addresses of their home equipment that controls the network to allow connections only from those devices.
- *Assign static IP addresses to devices*: Use a static IP address on the router or access point instead of a dynamic IP address.
- *Position the router or access point safely*: The position of the access point or router determines the Wi-Fi signal reach. Put those devices near the center of the home or office instead of near a window.
- *Reduce your WLAN transmitter power*: Reducing the power of WLAN transmission reduces the range of the signal. It also reduces the chances that outside users can access your WLAN.
- *Disable remote administration*: WLAN routers have the capacity to be remotely administered over the Internet. A user can do this with a specific IP address to access the router. If you are not going to use this feature, turn remote administration off.
- *Turn off the network during extended periods of nonuse*: Always shut down or turn off the network when it is not in use to prevent hackers from breaking in.

Chapter Summary

- Business is at high risk from whackers (wireless hackers) who do not require physical entry into a business network to hack, but can easily compromise the network with the help of freely available tools.

- Wireless LANs are susceptible to the same protocol-based attacks that plague wired LANs.

- Wired Equivalent Privacy (WEP) is the encryption algorithm built into the 802.11 (Wi-Fi) standards.

- Passive attacks are common and difficult to detect.

- The SSID is a unique identifier that wireless networking devices use for establishing and maintaining wireless connectivity.

- Beacon frames are part of the IEEE 802.11 wireless network protocol and broadcast the SSID.

- Authentication is accomplished by a station providing the correct SSID or through shared key authentication.

- The MAC address is used by the MAC sublayer of the data-link layer (DLC) of telecommunication protocols.

- A rogue, or unauthorized access point is one that is not authorized for operation by a particular firm or network.

- A stream cipher is a symmetric encryption algorithm.

- A pad collection attack is a semipassive attack. It collects a set of pads and then decrypts any packet for which a pad is present.

- Wi-Fi Protected Access is the first generation of advanced wireless security to provide Wi-Fi users with a high level of assurance that only authorized users can access their wireless networks.

- WTLS is the security layer of the WAP, providing privacy, data integrity and authentication for WAP services.

Review Questions

1. Compare the security scenarios for a wired and wireless network.

2. What different kinds of attack on a wireless network were discussed in this chapter?

3. In what kind of attack does the attacker intercept the identification information of the sending and receiving parties?

    a.   Man-in-the-middle attack

    b.   Denial-of-service attack

    c.   Social-engineering attack

    d.   Dictionary attack

4. Define warwalking and wardriving.

    _____

    _____

    _____

    _____

5. _____ is a high-level WLAN scanner.

    a.   Kismet

    b.   NetStumbler

    c.   Wellenreiter v2

    d.   Airopeek

6. What are the different measures used to secure a wireless network?

    _____

    _____

    _____

    _____

7. What is a demilitarized zone, as it was used in this chapter?

    _____

    _____

    _____

    _____

8. Explain various authentication methods used by wireless networks.

    _____

    _____

    _____

    _____

9. Is there any tool that can be used to compromise the security of a wireless network?

    _____

    _____

    _____

    _____

Hands-On Projects

Please attempt the following exercises to reinforce what you have learned in this chapter. Write down your observations or process notes for later reference.

1. Determine whether SSID and WEP are enabled in the wireless equipment employed in your network.

2. Use the WEPCrack tool and try to crack the WEP keys used in your wireless network.

3. Find out the MAC addresses for each of the nodes in your network.

4. Run Wellenreiter, the wireless network discovery and auditing tool, to ensure security from MAC address spoofing attacks on your wireless network.

5. Perform a penetration test on your wireless network using tools such as NetStumbler, Kismet and AirSnort.

Endnotes

[1]http://airsnort.shmoo.com/ (accessed June 2008).

[2]http://sourceforge.net/ (accessed June 2008).

[3]http://www.pentest.co.uk/ (accessed June 2008).

Index